Critical theory and feeling

MANCHESTER
1824

Manchester University Press

Critical theory and contemporary society

Series editors:

David M. Berry, Professor of Digital Humanities (Media and Film),
University of Sussex

Darrow Schecter, Professor of Critical Theory and Modern European History,
University of Sussex

The *Critical Theory and Contemporary Society* series aims to demonstrate the ongoing relevance of multi-disciplinary research in explaining the causes of pressing social problems today and in indicating the possible paths towards a libertarian transformation of twenty-first century society. It builds upon some of the main ideas of first generation critical theorists, including Horkheimer, Adorno, Benjamin, Marcuse and Fromm, but it does not aim to provide systematic guides to the work of those thinkers. Rather, each volume focuses on ways of thinking about the political dimensions of a particular topic, which include political economy, law, popular culture, globalization, feminism, theology and terrorism. Authors are encouraged to build on the legacy of first generation Frankfurt School theorists and their influences (Kant, Hegel, Kierkegaard, Marx, Nietzsche, Weber and Freud) in a manner that is distinct from, though not necessarily hostile to, the broad lines of second-generation critical theory. The series sets ambitious theoretical standards, aiming to engage and challenge an interdisciplinary readership of students and scholars across political theory, philosophy, sociology, history, media studies and literary studies.

Critical theory and feeling

The affective politics of the early Frankfurt School

SIMON MUSSELL

Manchester University Press

Published by Manchester University Press
Altrincham Street, Manchester M1 7JA, UK
www.manchesteruniversitypress.co.uk

British Library Cataloguing-in-Publication Data is available

ISBN 978 1 5261 0570 7 hardback
ISBN 978 1 5261 5594 8 paperback

First published by Manchester University Press in hardback 2017

This edition published 2021

Typeset by Out of House Publishing

Contents

Acknowledgments

The cover of this book is a lie, for no book has a single author. Over the past decade, I have had the good fortune of sharing ideas with many friends and comrades. Their generosity and engagement have made this book possible. Our interactions – some fleeting and sporadic, others more sustained – have moved me, both affectively and intellectually. In this regard, I am particularly grateful to Darrow Schecter, Doug Haynes, Chris O'Kane, Élise Derroitte, Antonia Hofstaetter, Gordon Finlayson, Federica Gregoratto, Tim Carter, Zoe Sutherland, Christos Hadjioannou, Annabel Haynes, Daniel Steuer, Silvia Panizza, Teodor Mladenov, Arthur Willemse, Danny Hayward, Phil Homburg, Keith Tester, Marc Botha, Jennifer Cooke, Chris Allsobrook, Matthew Feldman, Verena Erlenbusch, and Jana Elsen.

At a time when there is much talk of the intangible and immaterial qualities of the arts and humanities, we must not lose sight of the material conditions that surround and enable any act of writing. For all its abstraction, this book could not have been written without the concrete support of my family and friends. I am forever indebted to them.

Finally, I am especially grateful to Julie Taylor for her love, encouragement, and intellectual stimulation over the years. The book is dedicated to her.

Whatever material has made it into the following pages bears traces of this collective experience. Needless to say, responsibility for the text's inevitable shortcomings lies solely with me.

Introduction: once more, with feeling

Once the last trace of emotion has been eradicated, nothing remains of thought but absolute tautology.

– Theodor W. Adorno[1]

For most of its history, political philosophy has been distrustful of feelings. Its adherents have often cordoned off the mind from the body, thought from feeling, active subjects from passive objects. From the pre-Socratics onward, the bulk of philosophical tradition has been concerned with policing the boundaries between *reason* on the one hand, and *emotion* on the other. In turn, this division gives rise to an axiological hierarchy in which reason is placed over and above emotion. Where reason is respected for being universal, objective, and principled, emotion is rejected for being particular, subjective, and unruly. For many philosophers, the emotions constitute a threat to the procedural march of reason, having the potential to derail the calm process of rational deliberation with their unpredictability and volatility.

Numerous examples from the ancient world can be said to have established a precedent for this rationalist philosophical discourse. Plato famously banished the poets from his ideal republic because they awaken and nourish feelings, induce *pathos*, and impair reason. Aristotle wrote of the importance of *catharsis*, the arousal and subsequent purgation of fear and pity via the aesthetics of tragic drama, which would serve as a useful safety-valve so that such affects would not encroach upon the properly rational life of the *polis*. The Stoics believed that feelings denoted incorrect judgements about the world and one's place in it; emotionality was seen as a false step that the mature and learned individual would soon overcome through acceptance of one's circumstantial limitations. For instance, in *The Enchiridion*, Epictetus offers the following guidance: 'When therefore we are hindered, or disturbed, or grieved, let us never attribute it to others, but to ourselves; that is, to our own principles.

An uninstructed person will lay the fault of his own bad condition upon others. Someone just starting instruction will lay the fault on himself. Some who is perfectly instructed will place blame neither on others nor on himself.'

But perhaps the most revealing moment in philosophy's anti-emotional narrative is to be found in Plato's dramatic account of the moment when Socrates drinks the fatal hemlock:

> Crito had turned away even before I did, when he was unable to restrain his tears. Apollodoros had been crying throughout the entire time, and when he howled with grief and anger at that moment in particular, nobody who was present could help breaking down, except Socrates himself. And he said, 'What a way to behave, you remarkable men! I sent the women away mainly for this reason, so that they would not make such an offensive sound, because I have heard that one must meet one's end in calmed silence. So be quiet and collect yourselves'.

From ancient philosophy, then, one quickly learns that emotions are too vulgar and fickle to be granted entry into the lofty realm of ethical and moral life. Indeed, if on occasion certain emotional states (for instance, 'anger' in Aristotelian philosophy) have been granted a degree of virtue *in potentia*, this is only on condition that reason be brought in to validate and justify such emotions in an appropriately philosophical register.[2] Understood in this way, rationalized or justified feelings may even be pressed into the service of the self, enhancing our 'emotional intelligence', as more recent self-help guides proclaim.[3] But emotion in and of itself, that is to say, feeling without or prior to rational regulation, the capacity to affect and be affected, is seen as philosophically and politically illegitimate.

Additionally, revisiting the scene of Socrates' death provides a vivid reminder that the historical denigration of feeling and affect has often contributed to a gendered division of labour in ways that reaffirm the conditions of women's oppression. In this regard, one can point to the ways in which reason is traditionally figured as masculine-active, while emotion is figured as feminine-passive. Indeed, the word 'passive' has in common with 'passion' the Latin root *passio* meaning 'suffering', which proves crucial to the respective values attached to thinking and feeling. As Sara Ahmed notes:

> To be passive is to be enacted upon, as a negation that is already felt as suffering. The fear of passivity is tied to the fear of emotionality, in which weakness is defined in terms of a tendency to be shaped by others ... The association between passion and passivity is instructive. It works as a reminder of how 'emotion' has been viewed as 'beneath'

the faculties of thought and reason. To be emotional is to have one's judgement affected: it is to be reactive rather than active, dependent rather than autonomous ... Emotions are associated with women, who are represented as 'closer' to nature, ruled by appetite, and less able to transcend the body through thought, will and judgement.[4]

This fear of affect-as-passivity is a theme that runs through the anti-emotional history of politics and philosophy. Indeed, the suspicion inaugurated by the ancients has been inherited and reaffirmed in the modern era. The reassuringly neat textbook version of the Enlightenment, shorn of all conflicting impulses and self-critique, has all but cemented the superiority of Reason over against its myriad others.[5] Immanuel Kant – that most unavoidable, paternal figure within the history of European philosophy's *Bildung*[6] – provides one of the strongest and most influential cases against feeling. In the development of his moral philosophy, Kant seeks a wholly rational and disinterested foundation for action. He sharply distinguishes between universal, objective, rational principles on the one hand, and particular, subjective, capricious sensations ('melting compassion') on the other. Only the former are held to be justifiable grounds for moral conduct. A curmudgeonly Kant advises that the 'ineffectual sharing of one's feelings in order to appear sympathetically in tune with the feelings of others, thus allowing oneself to be affected in a merely passive way, is silly and childish'.[7] Indicative of the historical continuity of philosophy's general vilification of feeling is the fact that Kant's modern philosophy shares much in common with the ancient Stoics' renunciation of affect. Kant cites his forebears approvingly when he writes of the 'principle of *apathy* – namely that the wise man must never be in a state of affect, not even in that of compassion with the misfortune of his best friend, is an entirely correct and sublime moral principle of the Stoic school; for affect makes us (more or less) blind'.[8]

Admittedly, the Kantian position in relation to feeling is somewhat more complicated than my heuristic account can accommodate. There are moments when Kant ventures to include affect in the moral universe by way of a fine-grained distinction between 'sensitivity' [*Empfindsamkeit*] and 'sentimentality' [*Empfindelei*]. But this simply equates the former with power and strength, and the latter with weakness and docility, reiterating the original dualism between the active and passive. Sensitivity, Kant tells us (in atrociously, if unsurprisingly, sexist language), is 'manly'; it represents the capacity one has to allow pleasure or displeasure to enter the mind, which implies an act of volition. By contrast, sentimentality is a weakness, a yielding that allows others to affect us, even against our will.[9] Thus, inasmuch as we might cultivate and control such 'sensitivity', this should only be done to bolster the development of the rational will. If an inclination arises that is in conflict with the moral duty to act, then the rational will must override it; if an affect naturally moves us to an action that duty would require of us in any case, then (and only then) can the affect be permitted. In either case, in practical terms affective content is seen as extraneous to the need to obey the moral law, which for Kant must be rational through and through.[10]

The tradition of all dead rationalist philosophers weighs like a nightmare on the brains of the living. One of the reasons for my wanting to revisit early critical theory is to recall and mobilize certain moves against the anti-emotional core of the Continental philosophical and political tradition, many of which have yet to receive the attention they warrant. By way of an opening salvo in the service of such a project, it is worth turning to *Dialectic of Enlightenment*, in which Theodor Adorno and Max Horkheimer offer a trenchant critique of Kantian rationalism, or 'formalized reason', taking their cue from the work of Marquis de Sade (1740–1814). The authors make their case with reference to Sade's *Juliette*. In that novel, the eponymous character, having been seduced by a woman who swiftly disabuses her of religious faith and morality, undertakes all manner of cruel and inhumane acts utterly without affect or sentiment. She acts purely by cold reason alone. Juliette is in no way 'enthusiastic' or 'fanatical' (the two terms that would become synonymous with revolutionary terror); 'her procedure is enlightened and efficient as she goes about her work of sacrilege'.[11] To take but one example, on the calm discipline required of the would-be criminal, Juliette offers the following advice:

> Work out your plan a few days beforehand; consider all its consequences; be attentive to what might assist you ... what might betray you, and weigh up all these things with the same callousness you would apply if you were certain to be discovered [...] Let your features express calm and equanimity; and try to summon up an extreme degree of callousness ... [I]f you were not certain that no pangs of conscience would attack you ... all your efforts to control your features and gestures would be of no account.[12]

Similarly, Juliette's accomplice, Clairwil, proudly asserts her stoic virtue, her 'serene command over the emotions', while denouncing compassion as womanly and childish (echoing Kant's language above). Clairwil's avowed stoicism – the bourgeois philosophy *par excellence* – allows her 'to do, and to continue to do, everything without any feeling'.[13] Adorno and Horkheimer cite Sade and Nietzsche – the darkest writers of the modern age – because their writings lay bare the unsettling core of *ratio* unencumbered by any social or historical phenomena, untouched by feelings, customs, beliefs, values, and so on. Uprooted from its material and historical basis, reason becomes naturalized, free-floating, and formalized; in other words, mythic. This process of formalization is dangerous, not just because it can all too readily produce a theodicy for the status quo, but also because its weight of obligation resists all particularity, meaning that atrocities can be carried out without the least pang of conscience or compassion.

In addition, there is undoubtedly something ironic in philosophy's long-standing opposition to feeling, insofar as this aversion has often been accompanied by a fervent passion and zeal of its own. One need not have recourse to psychoanalysis to note that such disavowal likely discloses the ghostly presence of that which one most desires to purge. In his 1959 lectures on the *Critique of Pure Reason*, Adorno mischievously refers to the 'emotional thrust' of Kant's work, a provocative description given the Königsberg philosopher's resolute attempts to disqualify feeling from the moral universe. Defending the use of such a seemingly incongruous turn of phrase, Adorno draws his students' attention to the fact that identical theses, when differently expressed and cathected, can convey divergent meanings.[14] It is not the case that affect simply follows on from, or is subjectively appended to, an objectively reasoned argument; rather, an argument's very structures and theses are charged with affective content. From a critical-theoretical perspective, then, far from being merely supplementary to an otherwise dispassionate argumentation, the 'emotional force' is in fact a constitutive part of an argument. For Adorno and Horkheimer, the enlightenment exaltation of Reason turns 'mythical' precisely by imagining itself to be free of all somatic elements, and by severing all affective components of experience from thought. The present project will try to show how a re-reading of early critical theory can help reconnect thinking with its extra-conceptual other.

The project is a timely one. The legacy of pro-rational/anti-emotional discourse is prevalent to this day. Alongside the steady rise of 'militant atheism', which prizes a secular, robust, scientific rationality above all else, there has been a resurgence of interest in traditional methods of emotional management. This is especially evident in the United Kingdom, a country that not only retains but also trades in a nostalgic fascination with its own (un)emotional history, unerring pragmatism, sangfroid, and famed 'stiff upper lip'. Indeed, while the UK government has funded large-scale investigations into the nation's emotional wellbeing (via the 'Happiness Index'), many of its leading business advisors, management consultants, therapists, and academics (not to mention welfare officers) have been rediscovering the tenets of stoicism. 'Stoic Week', an annual event now in its fifth year, is the result of a collaboration between Birkbeck College and the University of Exeter. The experiment brings together a range of academics and psychotherapists with the aim of evaluating the extent to which Stoic philosophy can offer useful and practical guidance on how to live well today. Participants are encouraged to 'live like a Stoic for a week', and are provided with a handbook containing a range of daily activities to carry out and reflect upon. At the end of the week, self-assessments of the participant's wellbeing are completed and compared to those filled out at the start of the week.[15] For an ancient philosophy so steeped in principles, it seems telling that one of the event's organizers, Donald Robertson, a cognitive-behavioural psychotherapist, has previously provided workshops on 'psychological resilience' to managers at Shell Oil, under the title 'How to think like a Roman Emperor'.[16] Presumably, the ancient Stoics' disavowal of material goods, comfort, and plenitude, in favor of cardinal virtues such as justice, wisdom, temperance, and courage, has not fully transferred to all of stoicism's modern-day champions.

But quite apart from this direct conflation of emotional management and business management, more generally it is hardly surprising that an interest in stoicism should return at a time when neoliberalism and its inherent crises have become 'second nature', our latest *habitus*. Both the modern-day Stoic and the neoliberal self are well trained in viewing conflict and adversity as not simply unavoidable, but valuable opportunities for 'growth'. For the modern Stoic, one's experience of hardship is creatively rebranded as a chance for personal and moral development, while for the neoliberal, major crises attest to the market's tendency towards 'creative destruction', which again produces important new prospects, new revenue streams, new investment sites, and so forth.[17] At the individual level too, the neoliberal self is compelled to be endlessly entrepreneurial, seeing itself as an ongoing project. In such a cold climate, joblessness, to take but one example, rather than being the effect of systemic, political-economic developments, variable capital flows and outsourced (as well as surplus) labour, simply reflects a 'learned helplessness',[18] an insufficiently developed work ethic or lack of desire on the part of the individual concerned. The best response to such 'inevitabilities', so the dominant discourses tell us, is to 'keep calm and carry on'. As ever, unbridled feeling, emotion, and affect are seen as obstacles to a more balanced, rational, and reasonable response to suffering and hardship. Today, both neo-stoicism and neoliberalism converge on the same point of hard-nosed idiomatic realism: shit happens.[19]

The point of a critical theory is to interrogate how and why certain types of shit tend to happen more frequently and systematically to certain groups of people. Once it becomes clear that shit does not 'just happen' (in the manner of an ostensibly 'natural' disaster), then the grounds for forever remaining calm in the face of adversity seem rather uneven. This is where an alternative or subterranean history of philosophy can gain traction. It would augur the return of the repressed precisely in the expression of feeling (and 'structures of feeling', to use Raymond Williams's suggestive phrase). It would also reanimate notions of the social and of totality, which are conspicuously absent from prevailing accounts that not only treat political subjects as atomized, rational agents seeking to maximize their self-interest, but also replicate the political-economic framing of neoliberal capital. Of course, theorists and activists on the left, while usually maintaining a better grasp on the broader social conditions that shape experience, have also all too often neglected the vital role of affect. In response to new and unique historical situations, the more traditional, 'organizational' left frequently resorts to well-worn practices of the past – mantras, sloganeering, pamphleteering, marching, meeting (interminably), sit-ins, bombarding people with statistics, information, lengthy reading lists, and so on.

Something important is missing from these accounts. It may be summed up as follows: the transition from *interest* to *knowledge* to *action* is not straightforwardly 'rational'. That is to say, people will not (necessarily) be moved to act differently simply by the acquisition of more or correct knowledge. They must *feel compelled* to act.[20] They must be *affected* in some way. Even an arch-rationalist like Spinoza acknowledges the inexorable part played by the passions in the founding of a political state when he notes that since people 'are led more by passion than by reason, it naturally follows that a people will unite and consent to be guided as if by one mind not at reason's prompting but through some common emotion, such as a common hope, or common fear, or desire to avenge some common injury'.[21] In lieu of an originary affective connection or striving, then, there can be no development of a reasonable political state. Similarly, there can be no defeating an absolute and unreasonable state without the passion and drive to do so. Broadening out the point, we might say that perpetual deferral of action on the grounds that one can always await more precise planning, or more detailed or reasoned analysis, can easily become a recipe for acquiescence or *attentisme*. To break through the rationalist's infinite recourse to reason,[22] it is my claim that contemporary leftist thought needs to better understand and (re)activate passion, desire, feeling, and affect. This does not mean surrendering thought to blind impulse; rather it means recognizing that no political theory or praxis is reasonable through and through.

With this in mind, then, there is surely a need for an effective and affective counter-history of philosophy. What is more, this would certainly have to include the early Frankfurt School as a major part of its remit. This book, then, aims to contribute to just such a counter-history, by retrieving the affective core of critical theory with an eye towards contemporary political concerns and theoretical developments. Critically engaging with some of the recent investigations into affect, I want to draw out and draw upon the *politics of affect*, and the *affect of politics*, in the hope that others might take up the theme in their own research.

Outline of the book

The chapters that follow will aim to revisit early critical theory in the light of emerging theories around affect. Given the breadth and diversity of the work and theorists associated with the Frankfurt School (in itself a rather loose affiliation with porous borders), this book will be suggestive rather than exhaustive, seeking out useful, timely, or speculative interventions that can provoke further research and debate. The chapters will selectively draw out and evaluate certain themes, concepts, and arguments from within the rich archive of critical theory, particularly those of its so-called 'first generation', in order to highlight the latter's hitherto underappreciated concern with the affective, emotional, and sensate aspects of experience.

Chapter 1 sets out the theoretical terrain on which the wider project is based. I begin by revisiting some of the founding tenets of critical theory in the context of the establishment of the Institute for Social Research in the early twentieth century. I then discuss some of the contemporary theories of affect that have emerged in the past couple of decades as part of the so-called 'new materialisms'. Taking on board some of the key findings of this recent work on affect, I also highlight the potential political deficiencies that accompany such accounts, particularly within a growing 'post-critical' context. The chapter closes with suggestions as to how early critical theory – read through an affective lens – might provide the social and political grounding that affect theory often lacks, while at the same time noting how contemporary theories of affect are invaluable in shedding light on the efficacy of the pre- or extra-rational, so often sacrificed on the altar of political philosophy.

Chapter 2 focuses on feelings of melancholy and unhappiness. Historical accounts, both medical and cultural, have traditionally defined and diagnosed such feelings as negative, unhealthy, and undesirable. Despite cultural recognition of the double-sided character of melancholia – as potentially enabling as well as debilitating – the sense in which melancholy has been understood since Freud's seminal essay of 1917 is pejorative. After charting the history of melancholy, the chapter then turns to the work of Walter Benjamin, whose varied engagements with the subject of melancholia prove to be far more mobile and complex than traditional accounts. Benjamin attempts to mine new readings of melancholic experience (and criticism) that show the latter to be profoundly social, political, and productive. This places his work at odds with the prevailing consensus, which characterizes melancholia as a personal psychological failing that is thoroughly stifling, passive, and anti-social. Developing this theme further, the chapter closes with a section on what I term 'conscious unhappiness'. Drawing on the critical theory of Theodor Adorno, this section affirms the importance and connectedness of affective and political refusal. Rather than seeking to avoid or relieve dysphoric feelings by way of psychic adjustment, conscious unhappiness amplifies the unmet needs, giving voice to the suffering that arises from a social world in need of wholesale transformation. As part of its revolutionary critique of capitalist social relations, critical theory refuses to privatize the notion of happiness and in so doing aligns itself with the (negative) truth-content of unhappiness – the bad that cannot be made good.

Chapter 3 looks at how an affective politics underpins critical theory's engagement with the world of objects. The chapter begins by outlining the recent upsurge in theoretical writing on objects/things, especially within the much-touted field of 'object-oriented ontology' or 'speculative realism'. After drawing attention to the major social and political deficiencies of these contemporary approaches to objects, the chapter offers an account of early critical theory that draws out what I take to be a more philosophically viable and socially engaged orientation towards the object world. To make the case, I seek to recover elements of Siegfried Kracauer's materialist film theory, before exploring two complementary concepts from Adorno's work: namely, the preponderance of the object, and mimesis. The chapter considers critical theory's emphasis on a political and affective aesthetics as playing a crucial part in how we conceptualize and experience objects. As a result, a key distinction is drawn between today's avowedly post-critical, non-humanist ontologists on one side, and the critical proto-humanism that motivates the early Frankfurt School on the other.

Chapter 4 explores the affective politics of hope. I begin by surveying the ways in which historical events and their narrativization – both on the right and on the left – have (re)produced certain ideological positions and affective dispositions. The post-Cold War triumphalism of many on the right, accompanied by claims of the 'end of history', created a sense of fearlessness, righteousness, and unfettered optimism. At the same time, much of the left appeared to internalize the position of honourable defeat, licking its political wounds, and bemoaning the insurmountable nature of capital as vehemently as any of the latter's most faithful handmaidens. The end of history is also said to signal the end of utopia, as all speculation as to possible alternatives to capitalism is condemned as unrealistic, idealistic, and unreasonable. I note how political realism has become the dominant paradigm, banishing utopian impulses and diminishing political hopes to the most myopic of visions. After plotting the familiar narrative of decline, and showing how an affective structure (and affecting narrative) can constrain a certain brand of politics while enabling others to flourish, the remainder of the chapter analyses the critical potential of hope as a political affect, especially as it finds expression in the work of Ernst Bloch.

Notes

1 Theodor W. Adorno, *Minima Moralia: Reflections on a Damaged Life*, trans. Edmund Jephcott (London: Verso, 2005), 123.

2 Martha Nussbaum is probably the best-known advocate of such a rationalist view of emotion working today. See, for example, Nussbaum, *Upheavals of Thought: The Intelligence of Emotions* (Cambridge: Cambridge University Press, 2003), and *Political Emotions: Why Love Matters for Justice* (Cambridge, MA: Harvard University Press, 2014). Other arguments for the rational content of emotions can be found in Robert C. Solomon, *True to Our Feelings: What Our Emotions Are Really Telling Us* (Oxford: Oxford University Press, 2007), Patricia Greenspan, *Emotions and Reasons: An Inquiry into Emotional Justification* (New York: Routledge, 1988), and Ronald de Sousa, *The Rationality of Emotion* (Cambridge, MA: MIT Press, 1987).

3 Daniel Goleman, *Emotional Intelligence* (New York: Bantam Books, 1995).

4 Sara Ahmed, *The Cultural Politics of Emotion* (Edinburgh: Edinburgh University Press, 2004), 2–3. See also Silvia Federici, *Caliban and the Witch: Women, the Body and Primitive Accumulation* (New York: Autonomedia, 2004).

5 Alberto Toscano notes the two main responses to 'fanaticism', understood in the Hegelian sense of 'enthusiasm for the abstract': 'Philosophically, the response to fanaticism is broadly divided between thinkers who regard it as the outside of reason, the persistent threat of pathological partisanship or clerical irrationality, and those who instead perceive some unconditional and unyielding abstract passion as intrinsic to a universalizing rationality and an emancipatory politics'; Toscano, *Fanaticism: On the Uses of an Idea* (London: Verso, 2010), xviii.

6 Writing of the ineludible influence of Kant on both defenders and detractors alike, Jacques Derrida notes that 'the authority of Kantian discourse has inscribed its virtues of legitimation to such a depth in our philosophical training, culture, and constitution that we have difficulty performing the imaginary variation that would allow us to "figure" a different one. Better, the "relation to Kant" signals the very idea of training, culture, constitution, and especially "legitimation" '; Derrida, *Who's Afraid of Philosophy? Right to Philosophy 1*, trans. Jan Plug (Stanford: Stanford University Press, 2002), 49.

7 Immanuel Kant, *Anthropology from a Pragmatic Point of View*, ed. Robert B. Lauden (Cambridge: Cambridge University Press, 2006), 132.

8 Kant, *Anthropology*, 152.

9 Here again there are obvious parallels between Kant's views and contemporaneous dismissals of 'sentimentality' in literature and culture more broadly, which often take gendered and sexist forms. Some valiant efforts have been made to construct a Kantian moral theory that is not wholly allergic to emotionality; see, for example, Nancy Sherman's 'The Place of Emotions in Kantian Morality', in *Identity, Character, and Morality: Essays in Moral Psychology*, ed. Owen Flanagan and Amélie Oksenberg Rorty (Cambridge, MA: MIT Press, 1990), 149–70, as well as her book *Making a Necessity of Virtue: Aristotle and Kant on Virtue* (Cambridge: Cambridge University Press, 1997).

10 David Hume is often cited as an important counterpoint to such hard-line rationalism, particularly in his famous statement: 'Reason is, and ought only to be, the slave of the passions.' But Hume ultimately ends up reinstating the exceptionality and priority of philosophical reason over pre- or non-philosophical passions, even while attempting to delineate reason's limitations; for a useful summary, see the following piece: http://plato.stanford.edu/entries/emotions-17th18th/LD8Hume.html.

11 Theodor W. Adorno and Max Horkheimer, *Dialectic of Enlightenment*, trans. John Cumming (London: Verso, 1997), 94.

12 Sade, *Juliette*, Vol. 4, cited in Adorno and Horkheimer, *Dialectic of Enlightenment*, 95.

13 Sade, *Juliette*, Vol. 2, cited in Adorno and Horkheimer, *Dialectic of Enlightenment*, 101.

14 Theodor W. Adorno, *Kant's Critique of Pure Reason*, ed. Rolf Tiedemann (Stanford: Stanford University Press, 2001), 31.

15 Details of the 'Stoic Week' experiment can be found at www.blogs.exeter.ac.uk/stoicismtoday/.

16 Carrie Sheffield, 'Want An Unconquerable Mind? Try Stoic Philosophy', *Forbes* (1 December 2013), www.forbes.com/sites/carriesheffield/2013/12/01/want-an-unconquerable-mind-try-stoic-philosophy/.

17 Philip Mirowski charts the historical development of neoliberalism and its strategic response to the most recent 'crisis' of 2007/8; see Mirowski, *Never Let a Serious Crisis Go to Waste: How Neoliberalism Survived the Financial Meltdown* (London: Verso, 2013). For a more theoretical analysis of neoliberalism, see Christian Laval and Pierre Dardot, *The New Way of the World: On Neoliberal Society* (London: Verso, 2014). In 2013, Lord Young, the UK prime minister's advisor on enterprise at the time, made much of the fact that recessions are good times for businesses to expand their market share, given the downward pressure on wage levels and the availability of cheap labour: www.theguardian.com/business/2013/may/11/young-recession-cheap-labour.

18 The phrase 'learned helplessness' was originally formulated by the psychologist Martin Seligman in 1975; see Martin Seligman, *Helplessness: On Depression, Development, and Death* (San Francisco: W.H. Freeman, 1975). Coincidentally, in July 2011, it was Seligman who encouraged David Cameron to consider wellbeing as a supplementary indicator of national prosperity.

19 Examples abound of these neo-stoic norms in action. I will cite just two of the most notable of recent times. The failure to indict Darren Wilson (the police officer who murdered Mike Brown in Ferguson, Missouri, in August 2014) sparked a series of riots and shutdown actions in cities across the United States. In response, Barack Obama stated: 'I know the events of the past few days have prompted strong passions, but as details unfold I urge everyone … to remember this young man through reflection and understanding.' In a similar vein, in October 2015, David Cameron described how best to respond to the ongoing refugee crisis, drawing particular attention to the widely publicized photograph of Alan Kurdi, a three-year-old boy from Syria who had drowned in the Mediterranean Sea. Cameron said: 'Like most people, I found it almost impossible to get the image of that poor Syrian boy, Aylan *[sic]* Kurdi, out of my mind. We know in our hearts our responsibilities to help those fleeing for their lives. But we know too that we must keep our heads.' The Kiplingian euphemism of keeping one's head, in both cases, rehearses the anti-emotionality that undergirds so much of the dominant cultural, political, and legal frameworks.

20 Towards the end of their controversial chapter on the culture industry, 'Enlightenment as Mass Deception', from the mid-1940s, Adorno and Horkheimer qualify their otherwise unrelenting critique of the 'culture industry' with a telling admission, namely, that the real triumph of advertising is that 'consumers feel compelled to buy and use its products even though they see through them'. In other words, consumers are not straightforwardly 'duped' at the level of cognition and ideology. Rather, they must *feel compelled* to act and consume in particular ways; Adorno and Horkheimer, *Dialectic of Enlightenment*, 167.

21 Spinoza, 'Political Treatise', in *Spinoza: Complete Works*, ed. Michael L. Morgan, trans. Samuel Shirley (Indianapolis: Hackett, 2002), 700.

22 Both here and throughout the book, I do not advocate an 'anti-rationalist' position (such as might be found in the work of Nietzsche). Rather, the aim is to draw attention to the irrationality and unreasonableness of the present uses of reason, the glaring disparity between what is ideally claimed on reason's behalf and what is actually experienced by the majority of human beings. This position takes inspiration from Marx's oft-cited letter to Arnold Ruge of September 1843, in which he notes: 'Reason has always existed, but not always in a rational form.' Similarly, Adorno would later call for philosophy to undertake a 'rational appeal hearing against rationality'; cited in Rolf Wiggershaus, *The Frankfurt School: Its History, Theories, and Political Significance*, trans. Michael Robertson (Cambridge, MA: MIT Press, 1995), 4.

1

Thinking through feeling: critical theory and the affective turn

> The assumption that thought profits from the decay of the emotions, or even that it remains unaffected, is itself an expression of the process of stupefaction.[1]

In this opening chapter, I will begin by offering an overview of the particular form of critical theory on which this book will focus, namely that of the first-generation Frankfurt School, since I believe that there is still much of interest within this tradition of thought for our present time. I will then set out the contemporary theoretical context that informs my re-engagement with the earlier work of the Frankfurt School. In particular, I want to chart the recent 'affective turn' in the arts, humanities, and social sciences, which has proven to be a fertile, if somewhat disorderly, ground for research within the broader field of 'new materialism'. My aim is to draw on some of these theories of affect to prompt new readings of first-generation critical theory, readings that will emphasize the latter's often overlooked concern with *feeling*, in all its senses.

As will become apparent throughout the chapter, whilst I believe there are some important and constructive findings from within the broad ambit of affect theory and new materialism, I do not fully endorse them as adequate models for theorizing social, political, and cultural phenomena. Indeed, the political economy of 'intellectual labour', of which the production and circulation of academic theory is a considerable part, should make one wary of exaggerated claims to theoretical innovation. There are endless institutional and market imperatives to concoct novel methodologies and modes of analysis, which serve to accelerate output and inflate the impact and prestige of the attached individuals and departments. Moreover, in throwing oneself headlong into the most recent theoretical trends, one inevitably risks abandoning what remains valid or simply under-explored within previous approaches. As such, part of this chapter will serve to situate the affective turn and the new materialisms within a wider context of the 'post-critical'.

Of course, there are also risks associated with the present project. For some, the voguish nature of the term 'affect' is sufficient grounds to ignore it and proceed in the belief that it cannot have anything of import to contribute to leftist political discourse. Conversely, for some affect theorists it might appear anachronistic for me to utilize their analyses for the purposes of returning to social theories of the early to mid-twentieth century. But my aim in this book is to show that affect theory and critical theory can be effectively brought into dialogue, especially with a view to bringing to light the potential blind spots and missed opportunities of each. What is more, I believe this is a necessary intervention, because just as the political content of critical theory needs an affective supplement in order to be actualized, so theories of affect need to be mediated by political conviction and engagement, lest they become ahistorical and free-floating, betraying their much-vaunted materialist credentials by retreating to a naive idealism via the backdoor.

Thoughts untimely: critical theory in the twenty-first century

Before making a case for the importance of revisiting critical theory for and in the twenty-first century, we ought to define precisely what variety of 'critical theory' will be revisited here. After all, the very term has come to enjoy currency in an increasingly diverse array of discourses since its original inception in early twentieth-century Frankfurt. Indeed, without additional specification the use of 'critical theory' today can invoke all manner of intellectual movements and scholarly fields. These include: the gender theory of Judith Butler; the critical genealogies of Michel Foucault; the postcolonialism of Edward Said, Homi Bhabha and Gayatri Spivak; the poststructuralism of Gilles Deleuze and Félix Guattari; the queer theory of Eve Kosofsky Sedgwick; the literary and cultural criticism of Lauren Berlant; the affect theory of Brian Massumi; the deconstructionism of Jacques Derrida; the theories of the postmodern of Jean-François Lyotard and Fredric Jameson; the cosmopolitanism of Seyla Benhabib; the cyborg feminism of Donna Haraway; the post-secular rationalism of Jürgen Habermas; the socialist-humanism of Zygmunt Bauman; and the ubiquitous Lacanian-Hegelianism of Slavoj Žižek, to name just some of the most prominent figures and trends. The concerns that now come under the rubric of critical theory continue to traverse disciplinary boundaries: social theory, cultural studies, psychoanalysis, literary theory, queer theory, feminism, politics, philosophy, pedagogy, ecology, geography, and so it goes on. Critical theory is a broad church indeed.

But such varied threads are nevertheless loosely drawn together by their adjectival counterpart – namely, their *critical* standpoint in relation to the given state of affairs. All critical theories (in the plural) exceed mere description and either directly deploy or indirectly imply *normative* arguments. That is to say, a theory that is critical will not just claim that 'this is the case'; it will also make (or imply) the additional claim that 'this *ought not to be* the case'. This normative orientation – albeit in a negative form – is characteristic of both classical and contemporary critical theories. While there exist major disagreements as to what exactly is the case in theory, and how things should be improved in practice, it is this implicit normative charge, the dissatisfaction with what exists, that connects the vast array of theorists listed above to the original formulators of critical theory in the early twentieth century.[2] In all genuinely critical theories, there is an overriding concern with real obstacles to human flourishing and betterment (even if positive conceptions of what counts as such 'betterment' remain subject to ongoing debate). Keeping this in mind, then, let us recall the origins of critical theory, along with some of its central political and epistemological concerns, as well as its social and historical context.[3]

As one of the most influential strands of what Perry Anderson labeled 'Western Marxism', critical theory, in its originary form, is primarily associated with the work of the Frankfurt School. As an umbrella term, the 'Frankfurt School' only came about in retrospect to refer to the Institute for Social Research [*Institut für Sozialforschung*] at Goethe University, Frankfurt. Felix Weil had established the Institute in 1923. Its first director was Carl Grünberg, a historian from the Austro-Marxist tradition, whose tenure followed a more orthodox form of Marxism. The very early work of the Institute aimed at uncovering the economic imperatives, dynamics, and logics that give rise to complex social and superstructural phenomena. Much of this initial research still adhered to a scientific, mechanistic version of historical materialism.[4] From the end of Grünberg's directorship in 1929, the Institute would continue to be broadly guided by Marxist principles (at least, arguably, until the late 1980s), but its output became far more heterodox, self-reflexive, and critical.

In this regard, one can say that critical theory followed Georg Lukács's lead in pursuing Marxism as a dynamic *method*, rather than a static doctrine. Lukács reproached the positivist materialism of Bukharin's 'Theory of Historical Materialism' for its simplistic scientific model (transposed wholesale from the natural to the social sciences), as well as its prioritization of the forces of production and the false universalization of the Bolshevik experience in Russia. At the same time, Lukács also wrote vehemently against the 'decadence' of bourgeois idealism, existentialism, and modernism. The Frankfurt School can be seen to follow a similar trajectory to that of Lukács, insofar as they also sought to transcend the well-worn antitheses of idealism and materialism by way of a thoroughly dialectical method. Indeed, when Max Horkheimer became director of the Institute in 1931, his inaugural speech gestured towards the same kind of dialectical synthesis advocated by Lukács. In the speech, Horkheimer comments on a tendency for social philosophy to proceed dogmatically from a general thesis:

> [O]ne usually takes up in a simplifying manner one of the theories that have arisen historically and then uses it to argue against all others, remaining dogmatically in the realm of the general. It can thus be asserted that economy and Spirit are different expressions of one and the same essence; this would be bad Spinozism. Or, alternatively, one maintains that ideas or 'spiritual' contents break into history and determine the action of human beings. The ideas are primary, while material life, in contrast, is secondary or derivative; world and history are rooted in Spirit. This would be an abstractly and thus badly understood Hegel. Or one believes, contrariwise, that the economy as material being is the only true reality; the psyche of human beings, personality as well as law, art, and philosophy, are to be completely derived from the economy, or mere reflections of the economy. This would be an abstractly and thus badly understood Marx. Such notions naively presuppose an uncritical, obsolete, and highly problematic divorce between Spirit and reality which fails to synthesize them dialectically.[5]

In turn, it is worth recalling that this move towards method is precisely what Marx himself outlined in the afterword to the second German edition of *Capital*, Volume I, in which he states that dialectics, in its rational form (in contrast to the Hegelian, 'mystified' form), 'includes in its positive understanding of what exists a simultaneous understanding of its negation, its necessary decline ... [I]t regards every historically developed form as being in flux of motion, and therefore grasps its transient aspect as well ... [I]t does not let itself be impressed by anything, being in its very essence critical and revolutionary'.[6] This inheritance of Marxism as the dialectical method *par excellence* would become the red thread running through the Institute.

The shifting sands on which the Frankfurt School was founded betoken the fact that there was no actual 'school' as such, in the sense of a shared, agreed-upon set of theoretical positions, nor a physically localized group of people.[7] Those associated with the Institute for Social Research, either officially or more informally, may have shared a common methodological basis, but a range of biographical and historical factors – e.g. different (or no) party and political affiliations, working relationships and practices, experiences of activism, disciplinary backgrounds, areas of expertise, and so on – made for a heterogeneous set of thinkers. Yet rather than being a hindrance to the Institute's cohesion and purpose, as might be expected, it was precisely this intellectual independence and political non-conformity that fostered some of the Institute's most productive and provocative pieces of research.[8] What is more, the collaborative, interdisciplinary character of the Institute did not come about by accident; it was a resolute objective of the Institute's second director, Max Horkheimer, who sought to cultivate a new kind of transdisciplinary theory.

In the programmatic essay 'Traditional and Critical Theory' (1937), Horkheimer sets out his vision for the Institute's innovative brand of *critical* theory in opposition to what he terms 'traditional' theory. According to Horkheimer, the 'traditional idea of theory is based on scientific activity as carried on within the division of labor at a particular stage in the latter's development. It corresponds to the activity of the scholar which takes place alongside all the other activities of a society but in no immediately clear connection with them'.[9] In observing and reporting on empirical facts with no broader consideration of the societal values and impact of their work and its place within the production process, traditional theorists uncritically reproduce what exists, rather than examining it more holistically and analytically. In traditional theory, scientific activity is divided into multiple disciplines that set themselves apart from the wider world and context in which their activities are situated. In the misbegotten belief in science's supposed disinterestedness, social reality is seen as entirely extrinsic to the theorist. Objects of study become separate entities, alien matter to be observed, experimented with, mapped out, described, and so on. In this way, Horkheimer argues, traditional theory mirrors all bourgeois thought insofar as it is 'essentially abstract, and its principle is an individuality which inflatedly believes itself to be the ground of the world or even to be the world without qualification, an individuality separated off from events'.[10]

In light of the limitations of traditional theory, one of the central aims of a *critical* theory must then be to re-establish the connections between the individual and society, subject and object, facts and values, in a way that brings theory to bear on the *totality* of social relations and practices. Doing so will also of necessity draw out the inevitable partiality and value-laden investments of all theoretical work, as well as the latter's role in social (re)production. There is no neutral standpoint whence one might theorize. A critical theory will not seek to explain away, or smooth over, the numerous tensions and contradictions that persist in a given situation; rather, it will attempt to magnify and sharpen these contradictions, exposing their unsustainability, all the better to presage their future abolition. In Horkheimer's words:

> [T]he critical attitude of which we are speaking is wholly distrustful of the rules of conduct with which society as presently constituted provides each of its members. The separation between individual and society in virtue of which the individual accepts as natural the limits prescribed for his [*sic*] activity is relativized in critical theory. The latter considers the overall framework which is conditioned by the blind interaction of individual activities (that is, the existent division of labor and the class distinctions) to be a function which originates in human action and therefore is a possible object of planful decision and rational determination of goals.[11]

Mention of the 'rational determination of goals' here is significant, for it prefigures what would become one of the central themes of critical theory's development, namely, the critique of instrumental reason. The members of the Frankfurt School noted with dismay the rise of an instrumentalized reason whose formalism focused solely on the most efficient means by which to achieve an end, without ever consciously reflecting on the ends themselves. In his work of the 1940s, Horkheimer further develops this critique. In *Eclipse of Reason* (1947), he distinguishes between what he calls 'subjective reason' and 'objective reason'. Subjective reason is used to refer to an instrumental and ultimately irrational form of reason that is founded on notions of self-preservation and calculability. As Horkheimer writes, subjective reason is essentially concerned 'with the adequacy of procedures for purposes more or less taken for granted and supposedly self-explanatory. It attaches little importance to the question whether the purposes as such are reasonable'.[12] In this form, reason is measurable by virtue of its apparent utility, how well it performs a function in an already established situation; in other words, if something serves an extant end, then it must be reasonable. By contrast, objective reason implies a more substantive understanding of reason, one that is couched in truth- and meaning-seeking within a more comprehensive totality. Horkheimer recalls the ancient philosophical origins of reason, noting: 'When the idea of reason was conceived, it was intended to achieve more than the mere regulation of the relation between means and ends: it was regarded as the instrument for understanding the ends, *for determining them*.'[13] For critical theory, only the use of objective reason is capable of questioning the very validity and desirability of a given end. If an end is unreasonable or irrational (insofar as it does not serve any genuine, non-exclusionary social good), then no amount of technical competence in reaching it will be sufficient to make the end in question 'reasonable'.[14] The notion of objective reason, then, intends to break through the narrow limits of a procedural reasonableness that misconstrues rationality as simply a form of atomistic self-preservation (with its economic counterpart in liberal individualism and rational choice theory). The scope of objective reason extends to include the material conditions of social production and reproduction – forms of life based around the sensuous, affective relations and mutual interdependencies of people living in common.

For critical theory, an important element in defining reason's 'reasonableness' is that which is routinely denigrated as the very antithesis of reason: feeling. Recognition of the vital connection between thought and feeling, cognition and affect, plays a central role in the dialectical method as reformulated by the early Frankfurt School. Ernst Bloch describes this technique well when he writes of the 'combined research into objective tendency and subjective intention', which taken together constitute the 'cold' and 'warm' streams of a critical Marxism.[15] In following this method, the Frankfurt School situates itself in opposition to both the excessively doctrinaire approaches of Marxism in its Second and Third International form,[16] and the politically deficient subjectivism represented by phenomenology and existentialism. The task for a critical theory of society, then, is to effectively mediate objectivity and subjectivity, and to reflect this mediation in theory that does justice to both moments in the historical process – the subjective motivations that characterize human praxis and develop social needs and desires, as well as the systemic, objective conditions that act as an enabling context for all social production and interaction. In other words, critical theory aims to theorize the peculiar tensions and contradictions of an exchange society in which, to paraphrase Alfred Sohn-Rethel, the actions are social but the minds are private.

In order to cultivate and maintain a degree of theoretical autonomy, critical theorists have been highly attentive to the many dangers associated with theorizing: for example, rediscovering philosophical 'first principles', positing various instances of 'immediacy', identifying alleged sites of cultural immunization, and so on. Moreover, critical theorists are only too aware of their own role and complicity in the existing state of affairs (perhaps to a fault).[17] While such awareness is crucial for avoiding the pitfalls of dogmatism, at the same time it should not be allowed to inhibit one's engagement and critical positioning. After all, critical theory (in its original opposition to traditional theory) makes clear that the very act of theorizing unavoidably involves taking a position; nobody can claim a pure or non-partisan standpoint. The thinkers who will feature most prominently in the present book – Walter Benjamin, Ernst Bloch, Siegfried Kracauer and Theodor Adorno – were all sufficiently mobile and self-reflexive in their thinking to recognize the various inadequacies, compromises, privileges, and entanglements involved in the production of theory.

Yet they remained steadfast in their conviction that an unjust and unfree social order calls for nothing short of wholesale transformation.

If we are to avoid reducing 'society' to a natural object, subjecting it to the same methodologies and criteria of the natural sciences, then we ought to accept that all theories – critical or otherwise – entail some form of affective addendum. For instance, there are many reasons given for investigating particular modes of (anti-)social behaviour, or for investing in certain forms of energy extraction, or for supporting certain kinds of education. But these are not reducible to their overtly rational content. Rather, they convey a whole host of emotional and visceral attachments to certain forms of living, of certain relations, hopes, expectations, living conditions, and so forth. For such things to take hold in a substantive way, there must be an affective influence or striving, a *cathexis*. One of the aims of the book is to draw out the interrelation between affect and critique, but to do so in a way that reinvigorates, rather than undermines, the latter.

At a time of ongoing crisis, now appears an opportune moment to revive the critical-theoretical approach to society. Let us summarize what that approach entails: a return to dialectical thinking; a heterodox, non-mechanistic form of Marxism as method (not doctrine); a supradisciplinary approach to social research; a thoroughgoing critique of instrumental reason; and a recognition of the inherent affectivity of thought. I do not claim that critical theory since its inception has consistently lived up to the demands that accompany these fundamental ideas. But I do believe that these features represent its best legacy and might furnish us with some useful tools for reviving critical thinking in our increasingly *post*-critical moment. I will have more to say on the idea of the 'post-critical' presently. But first, it will be necessary to explore some of the most influential theoretical developments of recent years, in particular the 'affective turn', which itself forms part of the so-called 'new materialism(s)'.

New materialism and the turn to affect

Here comes the New, it's all new, salute the new, be new like us!
– Bertolt Brecht, *The Darkest Times*

A number of commentators and researchers have identified and contributed to the rise of so-called 'new materialism'. The umbrella term serves to cover a range of recent works within social and political science, art theory, the natural sciences, cultural theory, and literary studies, which have in common a motivation to (re-)engage with matter, materiality, and the physical world. Rejecting what they deem to be an unhelpful aversion to science on the part of the arts and humanities, new materialists seek to utilize the latest findings from diverse scientific fields – such as neuroscience, physics, biology, ecology, geology, and so on – in order to map the complexity of material interactions in human, non-human, and post-human forms.[18]

As with all movements of theoretical inquiry, new materialism emerges in relation to a particular context and in contrast to existing approaches to knowledge and experience. More specifically, new materialism marks a concerted effort to move beyond what its adherents see as inhibiting and outmoded forms of critical and cultural theory: these include older, cruder versions of materialism (in particular, structural Marxism or 'historical materialism'), as well as the linguistic idealism and radical constructivism of the so-called 'cultural turn' of the late 1970s onward. The historical materialism of structural Marxism is dismissed as being economically deterministic, placing too much emphasis on the conditions of social (re)production and human labour. Meanwhile, the 'cultural turn' – as an extension of the earlier 'linguistic turn' inaugurated by philosophers of language[19] – is seen as giving undue weight to the constitutive power of language, signification, and cultural practice.

The new materialists do not deny that the global political economy continues to have a profound material (and detrimental, if not catastrophic) impact on the world and its inhabitants, nor that cultural values and discourse, whilst seemingly 'immaterial', have a significant bearing on social behaviour, interaction, and the reinforcement of dominant attitudes (what many used to call 'hegemony'). But new materialists remain sceptical of the overly 'textual' methodologies characteristic of the cultural turn, since the latter do not readily acknowledge the ontological or physical excess that precedes and resists our routine modes of signification. Constructivism cannot account for the manifold interactions and dynamic vitality of matter that occur beneath or prior to the discursive level. As Diana Coole and Samantha Frost note in their introduction to *New Materialisms: Ontology, Agency, and Politics*:

> While we recognize that radical constructivism has contributed considerable insight into the workings of power over recent years, we are also aware that an allergy to 'the real' that is characteristic of its more linguistic or discursive forms – whereby overtures to material reality are dismissed as an insidious foundationalism – has had the consequence of dissuading critical inquirers from the more empirical kinds of investigation that material processes and structures require.[20]

So a cornerstone of the new materialisms is a revived appreciation and awareness of 'the real', whereby 'the real' can be seen to stand for a new ontology. Returning to reality in this sense means respecting or recovering the sheer *haecceity* (the unique 'this-ness') of a thing or the 'facticity' of matter, in a way that decentres the human subject as chief arbiter and giver of value. Let us leave aside the question of how much of this thinking can be said to be genuinely 'new' or indeed 'materialist'. There will be more to say on this in the next section, which locates these theories within a wider field of 'post-critical' thought. For the moment, it suffices to note that the rise of new materialism has been influential in prompting many to rethink the 'critical' methodologies of the arts and humanities.

One of the most significant strands of research within the field of new materialism has centred on the turn to *affect*. Like the advent of new materialism, the 'affective turn' has developed in part through the rhetorical construction of a hegemonic obstacle, an all-powerful behemoth that only a few visionary critics and theorists are capable of defeating. In the case of affect theory, that enemy is figured less as 'historical materialism' (which hardly registers any interest within the broader confines of the affective turn), and more as the dominant intellectual paradigms of the 'cultural turn', represented through the linguistic and discursive models of criticism that have prevailed in the arts, humanities, and social sciences since the late 1970s (chiefly poststructuralism and deconstructionism). Although the term itself – the 'affective turn' – was coined by Patricia Ticineto Clough in 2007,[21] the most recent renewal of interest into theories of affect can be quite precisely dated to 1995, a year which saw the publication of two articles that would become hugely influential in the shaping of affect theory's subsequent development: (1) 'Shame in the Cybernetic Fold' by Eve Kosofsky Sedgwick and Adam Frank; and (2) 'The Autonomy of Affect' by Brian Massumi.[22] While both articles share a common concern with overturning the inflated claims to subjective intentionality that characterize the cultural turn, making way for a more visceral, pre-cognitive model of experience, their respective inspirations and influences are nevertheless quite distinct. In light of this, it is worth briefly noting the intellectual background to each of these influential strands of affect theory, beginning with Sedgwick and Frank.

Sedgwick and Frank develop a theory of affect that takes its cue from the often overlooked work of American psychologist Silvan S. Tomkins (1911–91). Through the four volumes of *Affect Imagery Consciousness*, Tomkins mounts a case for an alternative (anti-Freudian) psychobiological theory of human behaviour at its most fundamental level.[23] Whereas Freud had posited the *drives* as the most fundamental motivators of action – indeed, so imperious as to require the myriad repressive apparatuses of society and civilization to inhibit them – Tomkins insists that it is in fact *affect* that serves as the primary motivational mechanism. Tomkins defines affect in evolutionary terms as a biologically hard-wired response to external stimuli. Affects constitute the most visceral components of emotional experience. Being innate to and observable in human beings (especially in facial expressions), Tomkins enumerates nine inborn affect groupings, which are highly specifiable and clearly identifiable through their corresponding physiological manifestations. These clusters of basic affects are as follows: Surprise-Startle; Distress-Anguish; Anger-Rage; Enjoyment-Joy; Interest-Excitement; Fear-Terror; Shame-Humiliation; Disgust; and Dissmell.

These fixed sets of affects are present from birth and remain present, to varying degrees, throughout the life process. What distinguishes the affect mechanism from the drive mechanism is the fact that affects are not localized in the same way as drives. Whereas the drive system communicates specific spatiotemporal information, the affect system is more generalized, since affects are not tied to any particular actions, ends or timeframes, and are subject to variable levels of intensity. For instance, a basic drive like hunger subsides after a sufficient amount of food has been consumed, but an affect like anger, interest or shame can be felt for an indeterminate amount of time. Affects may be triggered at any moment. What's more, any affect can take any object, just as any object can amplify or diminish any affect. This makes affects more adaptable and plural than drives, which are generally fixed and singular. According to Tomkins, drives in and of themselves are insufficient motivators for action; they need to be accompanied by affective arousal. Returning to the previous example, if one experiences hunger while also feeling angry, ashamed, excited, or otherwise affected, then the hunger will not register the same degree of urgency as when it is experienced in isolation. For Tomkins, then, affect is the primary motivational system, for without its amplification, nothing matters, whilst with its amplification, anything *can* matter.

For Sedgwick and Frank, the inherent expansiveness of affect makes it an exceptionally generous and useful theoretical model. Furthermore, Sedgwick approves of affect on account of its randomness and autonomy, its capacity to attach to, or be ignited by, any object, often overriding other motivational factors (the satisfaction of drives, social norms, legal demands, and so on) in the process. The unpredictability and utter singularity of affective life thereby revives and reinserts an element of surprise, spontaneity, and subjective freedom into cultural-theoretical accounts that are too often predictable, deterministic, and heteronomous. Since 'emotion', for Tomkins, is understood as affect *plus* the cognitive content of memories associated with that affect's previous amplifications, and since all experience is seen to be suffused with affect, it is clear that the proverbial archive of affective life ought to bear witness to an absolute unrepeatability, an irreducible plurality of individual histories. Indeed, for Sedgwick, that is precisely what theory should do. It should attend to these unique, surprising, autonomous (non-intentional) attachments, as well as take into account affect's potential for contagion and transferral. In so doing, affect theorists can provide a more open and less prohibitive explanation of how the self develops and is transformed in relation to others. What is more, that such a capacious theory of the affects derives from an ostensibly deterministic, psychobiological approach is proof that 'theory' in the arts and humanities ought to openly engage with scientific developments, rather than seek to undermine them through theory's 'paranoid' reading practices.[24] We will return to the last point in the next section, since it is arguable that a major point of attraction for the recent affective turn derives from its proponents' rejection of overly pessimistic, deterministic or negativistic theories of the social. But first, let us briefly outline the other major strand of affect theory, which stems from the work of Brian Massumi.

Massumi develops his theory of affect by way of Spinoza and Gilles Deleuze. For Massumi, affect is to be equated with *intensity*. As intensity, affect permeates bodies in an unmediated way; that is to say, affect moves through bodies at a moment that forever precedes all interpretive gestures and discursive qualifications. In evading the significatory practices and conscious internalizations that accompany 'emotion', affect-as-intensity is unassimilable. On Massumi's account, affect cannot be contained in language, nor can it be captured by our cognitive apparatus, since the latter is restricted by an as yet unbridgeable latency.[25] Discourse is always late to the party, so to speak; it arrives *after* affect. While discursive bodies might *make sense*, they do not *sense*. Affect, by contrast, is 'irreducibly bodily and autonomic'.[26] In other words, we cannot *not* be affected.

Although Massumi shares with Tomkins a foundational or ontological claim to affect's importance, there are crucial differences in their respective understandings of affect and emotion. Whereas Tomkinsian affects are tightly defined, identifiable through bodily movements, and can combine with memories to form specific emotions, Massumi posits a break between affect and emotion, with the former being utterly distinct from, and prior to, the latter. If emotion presupposes a proprietary subject who in some sense owns, defines or lays claim to such an emotion, then affect is marked by conjunction and in-between-ness.[27] Affect-as-intensity moves through and between bodies; it neither resides in, nor is claimable as such, by an identifiable subject. Fleshing out and reinforcing the distinction between emotion and affect, Massumi writes the following:

An emotion is a subjective content, the sociolinguistic fixing of the quality of an experience which is from that point onward defined as personal. Emotion is qualified intensity, the conventional, consensual point of insertion of intensity into semantically and semiotically formed progressions, into narrativizable action-reaction circuits, into function and meaning. It is intensity owned and recognized.[28]

In attempting to map out the pre-conscious contours of affect, Massumi wants to shift theoretical attention away from the epistemological and towards the ontological. This also entails moving from subjective content to objective intensity, and from an analysis of stasis/being to one of process/becoming. This intended shift is reflected in the manner in which affect takes primacy in understanding social relations. While affect is rendered as unmediated sensation in Massumi's account, older concepts such as ideology and hegemony – as structures of knowledge-formation and circulation – are seen as no longer all encompassing. According to Massumi, ideology, though still very much present, 'no longer defines the global mode of functioning of power'; rather, ideology constitutes one mode of power within a larger field of force.[29] Because ideology functions at the level of interpellation and constructed meaning, its subsequent theorization lacks the capacity to account for the immediacy of the affective moment, which by contrast is processual and indeterminate, forever in motion, or between states. In this regard, affect (unlike ideology) is 'resistant to critique'.[30]

This opposition of *ideology–affect* can also be reconfigured as one of *structure–event*. In prioritizing structure and meaning above all else, so Massumi claims, cultural theorists have divested the world of all becoming, freeze-framing the perpetual movement of affect so as to codify and reincorporate it into existing modes of signification (i.e. plotting points, rather than running lines, to paraphrase Deleuze). Here is Massumi on what he takes to be the crucial difference between the predominant structural approaches on the one hand, and the unassimilable intensity of the 'expressive-event' (affect in motion) on the other:

> Much could be gained by integrating the dimension of intensity into cultural theory. The stakes are the new. For structure is the place where nothing ever happens, that explanatory heaven in which all eventual permutations are prefigured in a self-consistent set of invariant generative rules. Nothing is prefigured in the event. It is the collapse of structured distinction into intensity, of rules into paradox.[31]

If the solidity of structure represents entropy and death, then the fluidity of affect is what escapes those structures. The autonomy of affect derives from its serial movement, potential, and openness, all of which perpetually exceed the confines of identifiable subjects, objects, emotions, thoughts, and so on. As the passage of intensity, affect is both pre- and post-personal, impersonal even: 'Impersonal affect is the connecting thread of experience. It is the invisible glue that holds the world together'.[32]

Despite the different valences accorded to affect within the respective theorizations of Sedgwick and Frank (drawing on the work of Tomkins), and Massumi (drawing on the work of Deleuze), both strands maintain an anti- or non-intentionalist position, which posits the autonomy of affect in contrast to critical theories concerned with meaning, cognition, and interpretation. For affect theorists, the prevailing modes of social, cultural and political critique are beholden to systems of signification, discourse, coding/decoding, ideology, and so on, all of which are preceded (and exceeded) by affective phenomena and dispositions. At its best, the turn to affect delineates the limitations and presuppositions of a rationalist ideology critique, and epistemology more generally, by giving renewed attention to the pre- or supra-rational, bodily, material and visceral layers that prefigure experience, those features that register their effects on us before and even beyond our conscious engagement. This represents a timely materialist riposte to the discursive-constructionist excesses of 'high theory'. However, if decoupled from concrete historical contexts and political tasks, the turn to affect runs the risk of romanticizing a supposedly unmediated and uncognizable facet of life, and replacing social critique with matter-of-fact, 'flat' or 'post-critical' description. Indeed, there are signs that some prominent theorists are willingly taking the latter path and in the process hastening the demise of substantive critique.

On the 'post-critical' and the exhaustion of critique

At this juncture, one might wonder what it is that makes the new materialisms and the turn to affect so appealing at this time. What do these theories offer that previous methodologies did not? How do they position themselves in relation to other theoretical approaches? What practices and relations do they amplify or diminish? And how might they prompt a rethinking of what remains unrealized within the contested legacies of critical theory?

Considering the wider intellectual context out of which these movements have grown, we might note that much of the varied work of new materialists and affect theorists alike registers a palpable sense of fatigue with both 'theory' and 'critique'. Indeed, whilst one of the aims of this book is to reconsider the work of early critical theory in light of recent theories of affect, for many today the very idea of a critical theory has become an obstacle to more 'productive' and additive reading practices. In response to this, a new, more affirmative consensus is emerging through the figure of the 'post-critical'. In particular, there has been a noticeable reaction against any theoretical manoeuvres that even hint at determinism (weak or strong), systemic causality, abstraction, totalization, or foreclosure of agency. A number of commentators have sought to propagate this post-critical move in response to the apparent failings and proscriptive nature of critique.

One of the most influential theorists in this emergent climate of post-criticality is Bruno Latour, whose work over the past two decades evinces a growing distrust of prevailing modes of critique. Latour does not use the specific term 'post-critical', but his sardonic, negative descriptions of what he calls 'critical barbarity' quite clearly indicate that we are in post-critical territory. His article of 2004, entitled 'Why Has Critique Run Out of Steam? From Matters of Fact to Matters of Concern', has quickly gained almost canonical status for new materialists. In the article, Latour claims that critique effectively secured its position of superiority on the back of a theoretical sleight of hand, whereby a triumvirate of techniques (namely anti-fetishism, positivism, and realism) are applied independently to different topics so as to guarantee the critic's rightness in each and every instance. Critics' well-worn 'gestures' and techniques are said to reveal secret forces and fetishes at work everywhere, apparently giving undue credence to even the most fantastical of conspiracy theories. But at the same time, Latour argues, critics hold their own fetishistic, discipline-specific beliefs beyond reproach. As he puts it, with the flippancy that has become a hallmark of his recent writing:

> Antifetishists debunk objects they don't believe in by showing the productive and projective forces of people; then, without ever making the connection, they use objects they do believe in to resort to the causalist or mechanist explanation and debunk conscious capacities of people whose behavior they don't approve of ... This is why you can be at once and without even sensing any contradiction (1) an antifetishist for everything you don't believe in – for the most part religion, popular culture, art, politics, and so on; (2) an unrepentant positivist for all the sciences you believe in – sociology, economics, conspiracy theory, genetics, evolutionary psychology, semiotics, just pick your preferred field of study; and (3) a perfectly healthy sturdy realist for what you really cherish – and of course it might be criticism itself, but also painting, bird-watching, Shakespeare, baboons, proteins, and so on.[33]

According to Latour, the de-fetishizing rituals of critique have outlived both their usefulness and their timeliness. This is chiefly because critics rely upon a conception of the world that is hierarchical (not only in its understanding of cause and effect, but also in the superiority of the elite knower over the naive believer, and the real essence beneath the unreal appearance). Moreover, for Latour, the critical gesture is bound to a reductionist and destructive methodology. It is reductionist insofar as the world and all relations within it are explained via a singular overarching cause only accessible to the knowing, transcendent critic. This does a disservice to the radical plurality, emergence, and difference that is immanent to the world. Critique is also destructive to the extent that it attacks, debunks, and breaks down extant beliefs, theories, relations, commitments, and so on, all in the service of revealing a reality behind the veil of appearances. As Latour puts it, critique 'has all the limits of utopia: it relies on the certainty of the world *beyond* this world'.[34] One might add that critique is often described as being parasitic, vampiric even, in that it feeds off its objects, subtracting content from the world rather than adding anything to that world. (As will become clear, these positions are not exclusive to Latour; they find expression in a range of post-critical writings.)

In place of what he rejects as an outmoded 'critical impulse', Latour proposes his 'actor-network theory' (ANT) and 'compositionist' methodology. Where critique occupied a transcendent position in relation to the existing world, compositionism is 'all about *immanence*'.[35] The latter takes shape by way of reassembling the fragments of reality already present or immanent, building relations rather than breaking down or demystifying them. For Latour, the negation necessitated by critique makes it antithetical to compositionism: '*what performs a critique cannot also compose*'.[36] In tandem with this move from critique to compositionism is a similar shift from the 'social' to the 'network' as the key framework with which to analyse phenomena.[37] Where critique deployed modes of speculation, abstraction, and detachment so as to grasp the broader structural and hierarchical features of various objects and relations, compositionism proceeds on a flattened plane of non-hierarchical networks. These networks are the loci of hidden potentialities and a rich heterogeneity, where all manner of 'actants' (Latour's somewhat slippery term for anything that modifies other entities through action) pass through and assemble. In contrast to the allegedly stifling protocols of traditional social theory with its zealous hunts for anonymous systemic forces, ANT is said to restore elements of surprise, spontaneity, emergence, and agency. Where critique was bound up with transcendence, structure, and the social, compositionism builds up from immanence, agency, and the network.

Theoretical moves in a post-critical direction are not exclusive to Latour's work. In a similar register, albeit from a different disciplinary background, Rita Felski has also made the case for moving beyond the naysaying rituals and 'suspicious' protocols of critique. Echoing Latour, Felski describes the supposed hegemonic status of critique as follows:

Critique is widely seen as synonymous with intellectual rigor, theoretical sophistication, and intransigent opposition to the status quo. Drawing a sense of intellectual weightiness from its connections to the canonical tradition of Kant and Marx, it has managed, nonetheless, to retain a cutting-edge sensibility, retooling itself to fit the needs of new fields ranging from postcolonial theory to disability studies. Critique is contagious and charismatic, drawing everything around it into its field of force, marking the boundaries of what counts as serious thought. For many scholars in the humanities, it is not just one good thing but the only conceivable thing. Who would want to be associated with the bad smell of the uncritical?[38]

Like Latour, Felski presents critique as an analytical method couched in a heritage of disenchantment and de-fetishizing, which is then applied to all manner of objects – save the critical method itself. In all of this, critics inadvertently posit and affirm their own belief system (i.e. critique), without ever subjecting that system to a similar level of questioning. As Felski argues, 'critique has its sacred texts, rites of passage, and articles of faith … [T]he faith in critique is no different, in certain respects, from other forms of faith. It involves an attachment to certain precepts and practices that can be experienced with an almost primordial intensity, that is often impervious to counterarguments'.[39] Of course, the structure of this argumentative strategy is a familiar one, for it is precisely the kind of debunking manoeuvre that Felski and Latour ascribe to suspiciously minded critics – namely, *you critics think you're doing X, when actually you're doing Y!* In this regard, it is hard to identify the point at which critique ends and the post-critical begins.

Felski draws out five qualities that have helped to make critique *the* preeminent model of thinking. (1) Critique is *negative*: it diagnoses, dissects, deconstructs, and negates its object. (2) Critique is *secondary*: it comes after its object; it cannot stand alone. (3) Critique is *intellectual*: it disassociates itself from everyday language and practice, instead engaging in high-level abstraction, extrapolation, and complex acts of interpretation. (4) Critique *comes from below*: in commingling with politics, critique stands in opposition to authority and domination, and sides with oppressed and marginalized groups. (5) Critique *does not tolerate rivals*: it is the only game in town, for alternative approaches are simply *un*critical.[40] By virtue of these five characteristics, critique is said to actually close down debate, exclude alternative voices, and reduce texts to contexts. In the process, critique fails to allow for any autonomy or agency on behalf of the non-critic and the texts themselves. One could add that while Felski's complaints pertain primarily to the critique of literary and cultural texts, the broader post-critical move of which she is part extends to all social and political phenomena, as will become clear. Indeed, perhaps the most notable trope of post-critical writing is its antipathy towards any hint of determinism, which is then utilized in turn to underwrite a renewed affirmation of agency.

This salvaging of agency finds expression not only in the work of Latour and Felski, but also in that of new materialists and affect theorists. In their introduction to *New Materialisms*, Coole and Frost are candid about their desire for a new 'ethos'. New materialists, they note, prefer

> a creative affirmation of a new ontology, a project that is in turn consistent with the productive, inventive capacities they ascribe to materiality itself. The prevailing ethos of new materialist ontology is consequently more positive and constructive than critical or negative: it sees its task as creating new concepts and images of nature that affirm matter's immanent vitality.[41]

Again, there are strong nods to Latour, whose compositionism also advocates a more productive, additive, enabling, constructive approach to materiality.[42] Following the same trend, both of the main lines of affect theory, as outlined above, convey a rejuvenated sense of agency, becoming, and spontaneity, all of which serve to thwart the best attempts of the critical-cum-pessimistic theorists to subsume all points of action and reaction into their prefabricated schema. Brian Massumi follows Latour *et al.* in speaking of the world as being 'in a condition of constant qualitative growth', 'the fact that with every move, with every change, there is something new to the world, an added reality'.[43] In fact, when Massumi states that 'when you are busy critiquing you are less busy augmenting',[44] his words could easily be mistaken as those of Latour. And sure enough, Massumi arrives at the same post-critical position shortly after noting the 'limited value' of 'critical thinking'. In light of the shortcomings of critique, he advises fellow and future theorists on how best to productively attend to the processual becoming of reality, and our active entanglement in its unfolding: 'Prolonging the thought-path of movement ... requires that techniques of negative critique be used sparingly. The balance has to shift to *affirmative* methods: techniques which embrace their own inventiveness and are not afraid to own up to the fact that they add (if so meagerly) to reality.'[45]

Although in nearly all other ways, Sedgwick's affect theory remains qualitatively distinct from that of Massumi, she also makes a clarion call for more affirmative or, in her terms, 'reparative' reading methods. A profound dissatisfaction with 'paranoid' theory and its knee-jerk negation prompts Sedgwick to turn a purposely *un*critical (or post-critical) eye to the neglected and often idiosyncratic work of Silvan Tomkins. For Sedgwick, temporarily shelving the critical 'toolbox' (so highly prized by theorists and dutifully disseminated through their graduate programmes and seminars)[46] proved to be a necessary step in opening up new avenues for affective and intellectual practice – ones that go beyond what Paul Ricoeur famously termed the 'hermeneutics of suspicion' with its rituals of textual excavation, exposure, and demystification. What is more, on Sedgwick's account, the preferred techniques of the paranoid (critical) theorist have hardly been that effective anyway. As she writes:

> The paranoid trust in exposure seemingly depends, in addition, on an infinite reservoir of naïveté in those who make up the audience for these unveilings. What is the basis for assuming that it will surprise or disturb, never mind motivate, anyone to learn that a given social manifestation is artificial, self-contradictory, imitative, phantasmatic, or even violent?[47]

Others have taken inspiration from this move towards post-criticality, using slightly modified terms for the practice. Stephen Best and Sharon Marcus have sought to develop a form of 'surface reading'.[48] More recently, they have joined with Heather Love in advocating a new, more complex (even 'critical') kind of 'description'.[49] Similarly, Timothy Bewes has argued for 'generous reading' or what he calls 'reading with the grain'.[50] Graham Harman has tried to apply his object-oriented philosophy to literary criticism.[51] Despite the deliberately heuristic nature of my account here, one can see that reading these initiatives alongside the now canonical articles of Sedgwick, Latour, and Massumi, as well as Felski's voluminous additions to the cause of late, it is clear that the post-critical field is being prepared for the next academic harvest. While there is much to be gained from the development of new materialism and the findings of affect theory, unless these can be decoupled from an increasingly *post*-critical framework, transposing these insights to a wider socio-political field might prove to be problematic. In light of this potential drawback, I am keen to make use of the affective turn while maintaining the aspect of social criticism that lay at the root of critical theory in its originary form.

Critical theory after affect: one shudders to think

There are three senses in which we might consider reading critical theory *after* affect. The first and most obvious sense is the chronological. In recognizing the affective turn as an intellectual and historical intervention (if a somewhat indistinct one), any return to an earlier kind of critical theory must be undertaken in the light of such a development. There is no use in simply rehearsing well-known arguments from the past as if nothing has happened in the interim. The second sense is the stylistic. Revisiting critical theory after affect signals a certain style (*à la mode*), a shift in emphasis away from disinterested commentary (itself characterized by a whole host of unacknowledged affectations and interests) and towards an invigorated, solidary, and affective form of critique. The third and final sense is that of belatedness. The writing of, on, and about critical theory always, of necessity, comes after affect. It labours after the fact. Critical theory is born of a sense that 'something's missing', that the social order as it stands is out of joint and in need of radical reorganization. Recognition of this situation might well be deepened through theoretical investigations into the systemic contradictions of capitalism, but the primary source is more affective. A visceral awareness of and aversion to avoidable suffering and injustice presses down upon the subject, pre-reflexively, and this in turn compels thought. One might think of this proto-cognitive embodiment or shuddering as the materialist kernel of critical theory. *One shudders to think.*

What, then, might critical theory bring to bear on the new theories of affect, and conversely, how might recent work on affect help to sharpen our readings of critical theory? To begin with, a critical-theoretical perspective can shed light on the social, cultural, and historical conditions that surround and inflect certain modes of thought and discourse. Indeed, when bold claims to 'the new' are made, it is important to distinguish between the substantive content of the claim on the one hand, and the performative gesture of the claimant on the other. For some, as noted above, the development of new materialism represents a welcome and much-needed return of the 'real' following the pre-eminence of linguistic, discourse-centric, constructivist theory, which by focusing excessively on 'textuality', language, and culture is said to have too often overlooked or downplayed the vivacity, instability, and generative powers of matter. Yet for other, more sceptical observers, new materialism's very claim to novelty is unearned and exaggerated, acquiring its inflated value only via the wilful exclusion of past and ongoing research (especially in feminist theory, critical race studies, and Marxist political economy) into the regulation of bodies, social reproduction, labour, and biopower.[52] In this book, I want to show how the work of the early Frankfurt School still resonates with our contemporary moment, especially insofar as its theories are read as simultaneously historical-materialist *and* affective. This is not so straightforward a task, given that critique and affect have often been put into opposition.

As shown in the previous section, in bringing together some fruitful avenues of investigation within a range of disciplines, the affective turn has sought to bring materiality and biology back into social, political, and cultural enquiry.[53]

Nigel Thrift welcomes the fact that 'distance from biology is no longer seen as a prime marker of social and cultural theory'.[54] Likewise, Massumi claims that 'the humanities need the sciences ... for their own conceptual health – a lot more than the sciences need the humanities'.[55] But in its haste to redress a prevailing imbalance, one has to wonder whether affect theory has shifted the emphasis too far in the opposite direction – that is to say, going beyond all signification and epistemology, diving headlong into an ontology of affect. The risk here is that in ontologizing affect one merely inverts the existing hierarchy and defends an anti-intentionalist position that is difficult to consistently maintain beyond certain low-level thresholds of enquiry. In addressing the embodied dimension of experience, the turn to affect has arguably been too ready to give up the epistemological gains offered by a critical hermeneutics. Of course, this is certainly no reason to return to an equally constrictive rationalist paradigm, since that has also shown itself to be inadequate to the task of critique. Indeed, in trying to navigate between affect theory and critical theory, it is important to avoid falling into the classical bifurcation between empiricism/materialism on the one hand and rationalism/idealism on the other.[56] While affect theory often risks lapsing into the former (especially in the hands of Massumi and his ilk), critical theory in its linguistified (Habermasian) form falls into the latter. For different reasons, and from different angles, both affect theory and more recent incarnations of critical theory have taken issue with earlier modalities of critique, which are subjected to a pincer movement. For Massumi *et al.*, critical theory is not materialist enough, insofar as it focuses on cultural texts and concepts, and ignores the underlying power of asignifying bodies, intensities, and affect; meanwhile, for Habermas *et al.*, early critical theory is overly materialist, insofar as it overstates the importance of political economy and ideology, and downplays the capacity for communicative action, rational consensus-building, processual intersubjective argument, and so on. In light of the perceived pessimism and negativism of established methods of critique, both positions gesture towards the post-critical.

One can understand the desire – and, perhaps more crucially, the institutional imperative – to constantly develop and experiment with new forms of theory, ones ostensibly more attuned to the complex material and technological networks of the contemporary world. This desire is undoubtedly enhanced by the provocative imagery of a tired, proscriptive, and formulaic brand of critique. But the post-critical move risks throwing out the baby with the bathwater. We might readily accept the claim that certain strands of critical theory have become 'hyper-critical', insofar as they function habitually, unreflexively deploying a static, pseudo-critical vocabulary that bears little or no real relation to their object of study. But this does not mean that we must hurriedly 'move beyond'[57] the very category of critique, affirming a brave new *post*-critical age. Moreover, it is not as if the revelations presented by the likes of Massumi, Latour, and Felski are especially novel. Indeed, practitioners of critical theory *avant la lettre* frequently called foul when they saw critique being reduced to an abstract formula, applied mechanistically and utterly decoupled from its material conditions. For instance, as early as 1845, the young Marx made distinctions between critique guided by the concrete issues at hand and a practical-revolutionary impulse on the one hand, and critique that is merely self-sufficient, speculative, and self-serving on the other. In the sardonically titled *The Holy Family, or Critique of Critical Critique*, Marx and Engels write mockingly of the prominent Young Hegelians of the time and their particular brand of 'critical criticism' [*kritische Kritik*]. Against the caricature circulated by today's eager post-critics, critique is not simply the cold, disinterested application of a set of analytical techniques to an object of study. Critique – at least in its mediated, dialectical form – is socially directed, politically engaged, and methodologically dynamic. It moves and evolves with the conflicts and contradictions that arise in both its object(s) of study and its own theoretical and historical practice. It thinks through objective conditions alongside subjective experience.

It is true, as Felski rightly notes, that the practice of critique does contain a multitude of affective investments, discreet pleasures, sublimations, and various other payoffs. And it is also true that the tradition of 'critical think- ing' – at least as it is presented and passed down through institutions and discourses – seldom mentions this affective component, instead tracing its lineage to an austere, detached, Kantian brand of *Kritik*. But as Felski con- cedes elsewhere, 'to acknowledge the affective dimensions of argument, however, is not necessarily to invalidate its intellectual or analytical compo- nents, but merely to acknowledge the obvious: modes of critical thought are also forms of orientation towards the world, shaped by sensibility, attitude, and affective style'.[58] As such, to draw attention to affective investment need not diminish or prohibit the practice of critique altogether; in fact, it is likely to actually enhance critical practice. What is more, it is difficult to imagine a manner of argumentation that did not have any affective element to it. Indeed, one would have to readily admit that *post*-critical writing also comes with its own panoply of positively charged affective supplements that derive from its very claim to post-criticality: i.e. the freedom from the burden of choosing between competing interpretations; affirming an ever evolving and fecund cultural field; celebrating the inexhaustible agency and ambiguity of texts, objects, and subjects; marvelling at the autopoiesis of theory itself, and so on. In this regard, it is refreshing to find that Massumi at least acknowledges the tendency towards affirmationist vocabulary whenever affect is invoked (if only to then double down on his original gambit): 'When the continuity of affective escape is put into words, it tends to take on positive connotations.

For it is nothing less than the *perception of one's own vitality*, one's sense of aliveness, of changeability (often signified as "freedom").'[59]

None of the above is meant to suggest that there is nothing of value to be gained from a post-critical perspective; indeed, calling on self-identifying 'critical' theorists to rethink and to defend their conception of (and commitment to) critique is no bad thing. But it is important to recognize that affective intrusions and colourations are not the sole preserve of overtly *critical* theories.[60] More to the point, such affects do not necessarily undermine critique – nor should they. In fact, as stated above, it is more likely that the influence of affect can be felt all the more in critical writing, for where else is there a stronger sense of social, political, and historical entanglement? Adequately recognizing and theorizing the affective dimension of all thinking and argumentation, then, becomes a pressing issue for a variety of reasons. First, it sheds light on the inherent limitations (and political deficiencies) of what we might call the ongoing 'philosophization' of critical theory, especially in light of the latter's deference to bloodless rational argumentation and refusal to consider the validity of a visceral solidarity based on eliminating unnecessary suffering. Second, it draws renewed attention to the importance of style and aesthetics. To this end, the turn to affect has usefully recalled the significance of many ancient methods of political communication – e.g. the power of rhetoric, the art of persuasion, the value of different pedagogical methods, and so on – as well as more modern policy- and state-led, social-psychological practices such as 'nudging'. Finally, foregrounding affect in theoretical writing serves to reconnect critique with its originary bodily impulse in the form of the shudder. Shuddering begins as a pre-cognitive response to a stimulus that is then reflected upon and given form and meaning. It is not the aim of theory to eradicate or simply 'represent' that affective instant; rather, critical theory aims at effectively *sublating* affect – beginning from a sense of unmediated feeling, moving through a stage of mediated thought, and aiming towards a final synthesis of mediated feeling. The aim would be to retain the trace of the initial impulse at a higher level of reflection.

Inevitably, such formulations are bound to seem too orderly and Hegelian to some. But I offer them here more as directive ideals than retrospective evaluations. Moreover, they help to give a sense of the broader framework of affect that will shape my re-engagement with early critical theory. Readers will have to decide for themselves whether or not any of the thinkers considered herein successfully attained such a sublation of affect in their writing. My task in the remainder of the book will be to effectively demonstrate how an affective politics has always been vital to critical theory, both in its political motivations and engagement, as well as in its modes of presentation. In short, the aim is to show how and why critique needs affect, just as much as affect needs critique.

Notes

1 Theodor W. Adorno, *Minima Moralia: Reflections on a Damaged Life*, translated by Edmund Jephcott (London: Verso, 2005), 122.

2 There are certain strands of critical theory (for example, the so-called 'anti-social thesis' in queer theory, usually associated with the works of Leo Bersani and Lee Edelman), which aim at a radical critique without recourse to any positive normative orientation or futurity. Indeed, some have claimed that Adorno's work is also of this radically negative nature, insofar as his dialectical thought moves by way of unending negation (for Adorno, the 'negation of the negation' does *not* yield a positive, as it does in Hegel). It is not possible here to review the possible problems attending such attempts at a resolutely negative critical theory. For detailed explorations of Adorno's negativism, see Michael Theunissen, 'Negativität bei Adorno', and Herbert Schnädelbach, 'Dialektik als Vernunftkritik. Zur Konstruktion des Rationalen bei Adorno', both in *Adorno-Konferenz* (Frankfurt: Suhrkamp, 1983), 41–65 and 66–94, respectively. For outlines and criticisms of the anti-social thesis in queer theory, see Leo Bersani, *Homos* (Cambridge, MA: Harvard University Press, 1995), Lee Edelman, *No Future: Queer Theory and the Death Drive* (Durham, NC: Duke University Press, 2004), and the conference debates recorded in 'The Anti-Social Thesis in Queer Theory', *PMLA* 121/3 (May 2006): 819–28. A recent issue of the journal *Differences* explores the possibilities of a queer theory that does not have anti-normativity as its definitive point of departure; see *Differences: A Journal of Feminist Cultural Studies* 26/1 (May 2015).

3 Readers conversant with the general historical background of the Frankfurt School might wish to forego this section.

4 For example, here is part of Grünberg's inaugural speech of 22 June 1924 in which he outlines the materialist conception of history: 'A generation ago, I believed I still ought to raise doubts about the central pillar of scientific socialism, the materialist conception of history. But I have been taught my lesson by developments since that time, and have now given up my doubts … It has long since been shown that the materialist conception of history is not intent on brooding away over eternal categories or on attaining to the "thing-in-itself". Nor does it aim to explore the relation between the mental and the physical world. Real social events, social existence in its never-ending, constantly renewed transformations are the objects of its attention. The ultimate causes of this process of transformation, so far as they can be ascertained, and the laws according to which it develops these are the objects of its inquiries. It is found that the driving pressure of the material interests which are systematically at work in economic life, and their collision one with another, produce a regular progression from lesser to greater perfection'; cited in Rolf Wiggershaus, *The Frankfurt School: Its History, Theories, and Political Significance*, trans. Michael Robertson (Cambridge, MA: MIT Press, 1995), 26.

5 Max Horkheimer, 'The Present Situation of Social Philosophy and the Tasks of an Institute for Social Research', in *Between Philosophy and Social Science: Selected Early Writings*, trans. John Torpey (Cambridge, MA: MIT Press, 1993), 12–13.

6 Karl Marx, 'Postscript to the Second Edition', *Capital: A Critique of Political Economy*, Vol. 1, trans. Ben Fowkes (Harmondsworth: Penguin, 1976), 102.

7 As Jürgen Habermas notes, the 'suggestive fiction of a unitary school should not divert too much energy to self-thematisation in the history of ideas. We would do better to turn to the problems themselves, to see how far one can get with the ruthlessly revisionist exploitation of the stimulative potential of such a diverse tradition of research'; cited in William Outhwaite, *Critical Theory and Contemporary Europe* (London: Continuum, 2012), 6.

8 Listing some of the many researchers affiliated with the early years of the Institute, alongside their respective scholarly fields, showcases the diversity of interests represented there: Max Horkheimer (philosophy, social science), Franz Neumann (political economy), Erich Fromm (psychoanalysis, social psychology), Theodor Adorno (musicology, sociology, philosophy), Siegfried Kracauer (film, sociology, journalism), Friedrich Pollock (political economy), Walter Benjamin (aesthetics, cultural criticism), Herbert Marcuse (philosophy, psychology), Leo Löwenthal (sociology of literature), Otto Kirchheimer (political science), and Henryk Grossmann (political economy). It is telling that most authors associated with the Frankfurt School would not claim individual ownership of their ideas, as if a thought once expressed can be fixed in time and stamped with the authority implied by a recognizable proper noun. If we can justifiably speak of a 'tradition' of critical theory, then an important part of its continual appeal lies in its genuine spirit of collaboration, whereby thought is de-individualized (if not fully communized), something that is hard to comprehend from the jaded standpoint of contemporary academia which is quick to deploy the rhetoric of 'interdisciplinarity' while effectively destroying it through competitive individualism.

9 Max Horkheimer, 'Traditional and Critical Theory', in *Critical Theory: Selected Essays*, trans. Matthew J. O'Connell (New York: Continuum, 2002), 197.

10 Horkheimer, 'Traditional and Critical Theory', 210.

11 Horkheimer, 'Traditional and Critical Theory', 207.

12 Max Horkheimer, *Eclipse of Reason* (London: Continuum, 1974), 3.

13 Horkheimer, *Eclipse of Reason*, 10.

14 Critical theory's most provocative and controversial elaboration on the instrumentalization of reason is to be found in Adorno and Horkheimer's co-authored *Dialectic of Enlightenment* (1944). I discuss this text in Chapter 3, particularly in the section on mimesis.

15 Ernst Bloch, *The Principle of Hope*, Vol. 1, trans. Neville Plaice, Stephen Plaice, and Paul Knight (Cambridge, MA: MIT Press, 1986), 5.

16 Horkheimer explicitly highlights the limitations of orthodox Marxism: 'But it must be added that even the situation of the proletariat is, in this society, no guarantee of correct knowledge'; Horkheimer, 'Traditional and Critical Theory', 213.

17 Indeed, at times critical theory's auto-critique is so thorough as to border on the pathological. This risks making of vulnerability, sacrifice, entanglement, guilt, pessimism, and so on, prescriptive and formalized principles, for which Rebecca Comay's phrase might be an apt shorthand: 'the slave logic of recuperative self-denial'; Rebecca Comay, 'Materialist Mutations of the *Bilderverbot*', in *Sites of Vision: The Discursive Construction of Sight in the History of Philosophy*, ed. David Michael Levin (Cambridge, MA: MIT Press, 1997), 342.

18 For example, see Diana Coole and Samantha Frost (eds), *New Materialisms: Ontology, Agency, and Politics* (Durham, NC: Duke University Press, 2010); Rick Dolphijn and Iris van der Tuin (eds), *New Materialism: Interviews & Cartographies* (Ann Arbor: Open Humanities Press, 2012); Estelle Barrett and Barbara Bolt (eds), *Carnal Knowledge: Towards a 'New Materialism' Through the Arts* (London: I.B. Tauris, 2012).

19 The two terms – 'cultural turn' and 'linguistic turn' – are often used interchangeably to denote the major shift in theoretical focus that occurred from the late 1970s and 1980s towards issues of discourse, signification, interpretation, ideas, meaning, cultural values, etc. Figures associated with this turn include Roland Barthes, Jacques Lacan, Gilles Deleuze and Félix Guattari, Michel Foucault, Jean-François Lyotard, and Jacques Derrida (and more recently Judith Butler and Avital Ronell). Of course, many of these theorists can be considered 'poststructuralist', but the

cultural turn is not confined to poststructuralism. I will use 'cultural turn' to refer to the more recent shift, so as to distinguish it from the 'linguistic turn' (which I take to refer to the earlier developments in analytic philosophy in the first half of the twentieth century, usually associated with Gottlob Frege, Bertrand Russell, and Ludwig Wittgenstein).

20 Coole and Frost, *New Materialisms*, 6.

21 Patricia Ticineto Clough (ed.), *The Affective Turn: Theorizing the Social* (Durham, NC: Duke University Press, 2007).

22 The articles can be found in: Eve Kosofsky Sedgwick and Adam Frank (eds), *Shame and Its Sisters: A Silvan Tomkins Reader* (Durham, NC: Duke University Press, 1995); Brian Massumi, *Parables for the Virtual: Movement, Affect, Sensation* (Durham, NC: Duke University Press, 2002).

23 Silvan S. Tomkins, *Affect Imagery Consciousness*, 4 Vols (New York: Springer, 1962–92).

24 Adam Frank has since tried to make good on the claim that affect theory can be applied to, or read alongside, literary and cultural artefacts; see Frank, *Transferential Poetics: From Poe to Warhol* (New York: Fordham University Press, 2014).

25 A number of writers interested in affect have drawn on the experimental findings of Benjamin Libet, which are said to show a 'missing half-second' between a bodily action and the conscious registering of a decision to undertake such action. This is taken to suggest that consciousness acts more as a belated vetoing system than as a pre-emptive initiator of action. Massumi utilizes Libet's findings in order to accentuate the non-intentional, unassimilable nature of affect, as do others including William Connolly, Antonio Damasio, Nigel Thrift, and Tor Nørretranders. See Connolly, *Neuropolitics: Thinking, Culture, Speed* (Minneapolis: University of Minnesota Press, 2002); Damasio, *Looking for Spinoza: Joy, Sorrow, and the Feeling Brain* (London: Vintage, 2004); Thrift, *Non-Representational Theory: Space, Politics, Affect* (Abingdon: Routledge, 2008); Nørretranders, *The User Illusion: Cutting Consciousness Down to Size* (London: Penguin, 1999). For Libet's original paper, see Benjamin Libet, 'Unconscious Cerebral Initiative and the Role of Conscious Will in Voluntary Action', *Behavioral and Brain Sciences* 8 (December 1985): 529–39. For useful essays on Libet's experiments, see Susan Pockett, William Banks, and Shaun Gallagher (eds), *Does Consciousness Cause Behavior?* (Cambridge, MA: MIT Press, 2006). For criticisms of the ways in which affect theorists have appropriated Libet's work for their own purposes, see Ruth Leys, 'The Turn to Affect: A Critique', *Critical Inquiry* 37/3 (Spring 2011): 434–72. Adam Frank and Elizabeth Wilson offer an excellent response to Leys, at least on behalf of the Tomkinsian affect theorists, in: Frank and Wilson, 'Like-Minded', *Critical Inquiry* 38/4 (Summer 2012): 870–7.

26 Massumi, *Parables for the Virtual*, 28.

27 The Deleuzian heritage of Massumi's notion of affect is perhaps most apparent in this sense of conjunction. See Deleuze's description of the rhizome: 'A rhizome has no beginning or end; it is always in the middle, between things, interbeing, *intermezzo* ... [T]he fabric of the rhizome is the conjunction "and ... and ... and ..."'; Gilles Deleuze and Félix Guattari, *A Thousand Plateaus*, trans. Brian Massumi (London: Continuum, 2004), 27.

28 Massumi, *Parables for the Virtual*, 28.

29 Massumi, *Parables for the Virtual*, 42.

30 Massumi, *Parables for the Virtual*, 28.

31 Massumi, *Parables for the Virtual*, 27.

32 Massumi, *Parables for the Virtual*, 217.

33 Bruno Latour, 'Why Has Critique Run Out of Steam? From Matters of Fact to Matters of Concern', *Critical Inquiry* 30 (Winter 2004): 240–1. It is worth noting that in roundly dismissing the very plausibility of critique in the old style, so to speak, Latour smuggles in his own form of immunization against any potential counter-claims. Since subjecting his argument to 'critique' would involve reaching for the very tools that have been deemed off-limits by his post-critical position, Latour seems to have found a cunning way of reproducing the figure of the always-right critic in the guise of the always-right *post*-critic.

34 Bruno Latour, 'An Attempt at a "Compositionist Manifesto" ', *New Literary History* 41 (2010): 475.

35 Latour, 'An Attempt at a "Compositionist Manifesto" ', 475.

36 Latour, 'An Attempt at a "Compositionist Manifesto" ', 475.

37 In a footnote, Latour restates his earlier rejection of the category of 'the social', claiming: 'It is probably the whole notion of *social* and *society* that is responsible for the weakening of critique'; Latour, 'Why has Critique Run Out of Steam?', 230n.

38 Rita Felski, 'Critique and the Hermeneutics of Suspicion', *M/C Journal* 15/1 (2012). See also: Felski, 'Suspicious Minds', *Poetics Today* 32/2 (2011): 215–34; Felski, 'After Suspicion', *Profession* 8 (2009): 28–35; and Felski, *The Limits of Critique* (Chicago: University of Chicago Press, 2015).

39 Felski, *The Limits of Critique*, 134.

40 Felski, 'Critique and the Hermeneutics of Suspicion'.

41 Coole and Frost, *New Materialisms*, 8.

42 For example, Latour asks: 'What would critique do if it could be associated with *more*, not with *less*, with *multiplication*, not *subtraction*'; Latour, 'Why Has Critique Run Out of Steam?', 248.

43 Massumi, *Parables for the Virtual*, 12.

44 Massumi, *Parables for the Virtual*, 13.

45 Massumi, *Parables for the Virtual*, 12–13.

46 Indeed, the apparently widespread institutionalization and routinization of 'critical thinking', reducing it to a transferable skill, is often seen as blocking its realization. This is certainly a common theme that unites the otherwise disparate concerns of Sedgwick, Massumi, Felski, and Latour summarized above.

47 Eve Kosofsky Sedgwick, *Touching Feeling: Affect, Pedagogy, Performativity* (Durham, NC: Duke University Press, 2002), 141. Interestingly, Marx and Engels lampooned the Young Hegelians' 'critical criticism' on similar grounds, i.e. for artifi-cially constructing a stupid mass against which their speculative critique can always shine, irrespective of the critique's lack of empirical foundation.

48 Stephen Best and Sharon Marcus, 'Surface Reading: An Introduction', *Representations* 108/1 (2009): 1–21.

49 Heather Love, 'Close but not Deep: Literary Ethics and the Descriptive Turn', *New Literary History* 41 (2010): 371–91; Sharon Marcus, Heather Love, and Stephen Best, 'Building a Better Description', *Representations* 135/1 (2016): 1–21. In rela-tion to description, one could also include Franco Moretti's recent work on 'dis-tant reading', which also turns away from humanistic or hermeneutical readings of individual texts, focusing instead on large data sets that combine scientific and social-scientific methodologies to identify systematic patterns in literary texts across time and space. Of course, in some respects, the very 'distance' of Moretti's approach actually affords a certain critical purchase that makes it somewhat more amenable to a historical-materialist tradition; see Franco Moretti, *Distant Reading* (London: Verso, 2013).

50 Timothy Bewes, 'Reading with the Grain: A New World in Literary Criticism', *Differences: A Journal of Feminist Cultural Studies* 21/3 (2010): 1–33.

51 Graham Harman, 'The Well-Wrought Broken Hammer: Object-Oriented Literary Criticism', *New Literary History* 43/2 (2012): 183–203. For a discussion and critique of object-oriented ontology, see Chapter 3.

52 Sara Ahmed provides an interesting critique of a certain kind of feminist new materialism, which she claims 'offers a false and reductive history of feminist engagement with biology, science and materialism'. On the basis of this constructed 'anti-biological' orthodoxy, new materialists can strategically position themselves as intellectual activists 'embarking on a heroic and lonely struggle against the collective prohibitions of past feminisms'; Ahmed, 'Imaginary Prohibitions: Some Preliminary Remarks on the Founding Gestures of the "New Materialism"', *European Journal of Women's Studies* 15/1 (2008): 24, 32.

53 Influential interventions that seek to return materiality and corporeality to feminist thought include Rosi Braidotti's *Nomadic Subjects: Embodiment and Sexual Difference in Contemporary Feminist Thought* (New York: Columbia University Press, 1994) and Elizabeth Grosz's *Volatile Bodies: Towards a Corporeal Feminism* (Bloomington: Indiana University Press, 1994). As noted above, in queer theory, Eve Kosofsky Sedgwick's work challenges the dominance of the 'cultural turn', especially as it is found in poststructuralism and deconstruction.

54 Quoted in Constantina Papoulias and Felicity Callard, 'Biology's Gift: Interrogating the Turn to Affect', *Body and Society* 16/1 (2010): 31.

55 Massumi, *Parables of the Virtual*, 21. Massumi's point here is debatable given that the ways in which the humanities and the sciences, respectively, are supported by and related to existing forms of capital differ substantially.

56 Noting the ways in which the materialism/idealism dichotomy is often deployed in philosophical arguments, Louis Althusser writes: '[I]n the philosophical tradition, the evocation of materialism is the index of an exigency, a sign that idealism has to be rejected – yet without breaking free, without being able to break free, of the speculary pair idealism/materialism; hence it is an index, but, at the same time, a trap, because one does not break free of idealism by simply negating it, stating the opposite of idealism, or "standing it on its head". We must therefore treat the term "materialism" with suspicion: the word does not give us the thing, and, on closer inspection, most materialisms turn out to be inverted idealisms'; Louis Althusser, 'Philosophy and Marxism', in *Philosophy of the Encounter: Later Writings 1978–1987* (London: Verso, 2006), 272.

57 The gesture of 'moving beyond' is particularly fetishized by a professionalized academy eagerly awaiting the next theoretical 'innovation', as if the sustaining of their interest were of greater importance than prefiguring the social transformation that would make their concerns obsolete or 'academic' in the everyday sense. In their desire to swiftly 'move beyond' the tedium or outdatedness of critique, these types recall the 'humanitarians' and 'philanthropists' reproached by Marx and Engels for wanting 'all the advantages of modern social conditions without the struggles and dangers necessarily resulting therefrom'; Karl Marx and Frederick Engels, *The Communist Manifesto* (London: Verso, 2012), 70.

58 Felski, 'Suspicious Minds', 219. In the same article, Felski approvingly cites Alexander Shand's reflections on 'suspicion' (which Felski renders synonymous with the 'critical' mind): 'According to Shand, while the consequences of suspicion for the individual are often beneficial, its implications for communal life can be catastrophic. An elusive emotion that combines elements of fear, anger, and

curiosity, suspicion constitutes an asocial form of affect that sows the seeds of division and conflict. Writing in 1916, Shand expounds on the effects of suspicion as an
emotion that destroys what he calls "harmonious co-operation between classes,"[!]
inspiring restless and revolutionary tendencies across Europe, generating dissatisfaction and mistrust, and serving as a powerful catalyst for political upheaval';
Felski, 'Suspicious Minds', 221. It is perhaps telling that Felski ranks 'harmonious
co-operation between classes' above any 'political upheaval'.

59 Massumi, *Parables for the Virtual*, 36.
60 See Amanda Anderson, *The Way We Argue Now: A Study in the Cultures of Theory*
(Princeton: Princeton University Press, 2005).

2

Feeling blue: melancholic dispositions and conscious unhappiness

Nothing that has ever happened should be regarded as lost for history.[1]

Ahead of the 2015 International Day of Happiness, the United Nations announced its plans to create 'the world's happiest playlist'. Employing the musical compilation skills of a few pop musicians and Peace and Goodwill Ambassadors, the UN hoped to utilize 'the universal language of music to show solidarity with the millions of people around the world suffering from poverty, human rights abuses, humanitarian crises and the effects of environmental degradation and climate change'.[2] This campaign is just the latest in a long line of moves by some of the largest political institutions and public bodies designed to promote a discourse of happiness. At the start of 2012, the Chairman of the European Council, Herman Van Rompuy, sent a letter to all world leaders. In the letter, Rompuy praises the powers of 'positive thinking', and writes of the efficacy of 'positive education, positive parenting, positive journalism and positive politics'. Enclosed with the letter, as a gift to see in the New Year, was a copy of *The World Book of Happiness*, a volume bringing together the findings of one hundred 'researchers of happiness' from around the world. Around the same time, in the United Kingdom, the government augmented its usual set of metrics so as to quantify 'national wellbeing'. Informally referred to as the 'Happiness Index', the project has the support of Lord Layard who recently launched an ambitious *Action for Happiness* campaign,[3] whose objective is to build a 'happier society'.[4]

If happiness is becoming increasingly tied to governance and is being routinely pushed (or at least presented) as a policy priority, this raises some serious questions. What are the social and political implications of this move? When happiness is held to be universally and unequivocally positive, productive, and beneficial for national, economic, and social wellbeing, what then becomes of the unhappy, the melancholic, the non-productive, the uneconomic, the depressed? To what extent does the emotional-economism of the new 'Happiness Industry', as William Davies terms it,[5] marginalize those who fail to meet the productivist demands of today's economy? What might it mean to be inwardly, unostentatiously happy, or, more importantly, visibly *un*happy? Will such actions soon be categorized and criminalized as anti-social behaviour? Such are the covert disciplining and pathologizing forces underpinning these new regimes of wellbeing, in which 'depression' is feared less as a debilitating socio-psychological condition, and more as an economic downturn.

In this chapter, I want to explore how the work of first-generation critical theory can offer some interesting and timely insights into the current political economy of emotion that binds happiness and wellbeing to positivity, productivity, and measurable output. Revisiting the work of Walter Benjamin and Theodor Adorno through a more *affective* lens can sharpen our understanding of what is at stake when the political and the emotional are thought together, as opposed to being divided into their respective social/objective and individual/subjective spheres. In foregrounding the complex and potentially critical aspects of melancholic dispositions and conscious (or wilful) unhappiness, this chapter will further pursue an overarching aim of the book as a whole – namely, to retrieve critical theory from the clutches of a fusty historicism that too readily de-politicizes and de-radicalizes its object of study. Rather than reducing the authors and ideas in question solely to the social and historical circumstances of their appearance, I want to demonstrate that critical theory, as an exemplary form of dialectical theorizing, still has a lot to offer in response to our contemporary situation. Indeed, in its acute appreciation of the varied valences of experience, the possibilities that are either opened up or foreclosed by particular constellations of material and social relations, the inextricable intertwinement of thought and feeling, there remains much to be gleaned from the remains of critical theory's corpus.

I will begin by charting the major historical conceptualizations of melancholia, both in its medical and cultural iterations, since these have played such a significant role in shaping our understanding of (un)happiness. Particular attention will also be given to Sigmund Freud's influential writing on the subject of melancholia. This will make clear how the legacy of this affective history persists to this day, calling for a more critical perspective. To this end, the remainder of the chapter will begin by turning to Benjamin's varied and complex engagements with melancholia, many of which contrast with the traditional readings of melancholia as inherently passive, inward-looking, static, and so forth. Instead, Benjamin reveals a latent activity at the core of the melancholic disposition, which manifests itself in a social expansiveness, an acutely historical consciousness, a partial renunciation of subjective sovereignty, and a keen responsibility towards all that has been lost. Following on from this, the chapter closes with an analysis of Adorno's form of social critique and what I refer to as 'conscious unhappiness', that is, a wilful rejection of any privatized or individualized notion of happiness in favour of a militant and political discontent.

Melancholies: medical and cultural

As Jennifer Radden notes in her compendium of writings on the topic, melancholy has a significant place within the cultural history of Western Europe.[6] Since its earliest invocations in the ancient world, melancholia has undergone multiple iterations and has been subjected to sprawling symptomatologies. These have often resulted in evaluations that are disordered, if not outright contradictory. Melancholia has often been regarded as a debilitating disease that diminishes the afflicted person's engagement with the world and inhibits one's capacity for pleasure. It marks a distempered mind with a propensity for feeling sad, fearful, and gloomy that far exceeds what is warranted by extant circumstances. But at various points in its extensive history, melancholy has also been highly prized and glorified as a unique disposition that activates a creative 'genius' that would be otherwise inaccessible. In Book 30 of the *Problemata* (*c.* 350 BC), a follower of Aristotle famously asks: 'Why is it that all men who have become outstanding in philosophy, statesmanship, poetry or the arts are melancholic, or are infected by the diseases arising from black bile?'

Simultaneously ailment and enabler, it is hardly surprising that melancholy has long been a recurrent interest for writers, thinkers, artists, and medical practitioners alike. While the sheer span and complexity of melancholia's history exceed the confines of this chapter, it will be useful to note some of the most influential beliefs that have accompanied and shaped its conceptual development. This will prove especially helpful in determining the continuing influence of historical notions of mental illness and disease on more recent understandings of emotion and wellbeing. It will also set the stage for an appraisal of the centrality of melancholy within the work of early critical theory (especially that of Benjamin and Adorno), indicating how the latter may provide crucial tools for radical social critique in light of the contemporary 'happiness turn' (as Sara Ahmed has called it).[7]

Much writing on melancholia has been motivated by a search for causal connections. This is evident across centuries – from classical medicine's belief that melancholia was the result of some physical irregularity or humoral disproportion, through to early monastic demonology and Christianity in the Middle Ages, which saw the sin of *acedia* (and later idleness) as the work of the devil, as well as the role of astrology that featured in Renaissance human-ism. Even today, our understanding of depression as being caused by chemi-cal imbalances in the brain and the failure of vital neurotransmitters partakes of this sustained quest for causal foundations. The etymological roots of the term itself, deriving from the Greek words *melas* [black] and *khole* [bile], ges-ture towards its underlying symptomatological purpose. Originally posited by Hippocrates (*c*. 460–*c*. 370 BC) and subsequently refined by others, most nota-bly Galen (AD 129–*c*. 217), court physician to Roman emperor Marcus Aurelius, humoral theories of the body have been central to the development of the Western view of melancholia. The four humours posited by Greek science comprised blood, phlegm, black bile, and yellow bile. In turn each humour car-ried additional associations that attached them to particular qualities (cold, hot, dry, wet), the seasons (spring, summer, autumn, winter), and the Pythagorean elements (earth, fire, air, water). A healthy body was seen to result from a good balance between the four humours, while humoral imbalance was deemed the cause of individual variations in mood, temperament, and physi-cal disorder. Melancholy was thus a *somatic* condition, indicative of an excess or overheating of black bile. This humoral imbalance presented itself in two forms: one short-term, the other long-term. In some individuals melancholy could emerge as an aberration – a temporary condition open to treatment and cure, eventually restoring one's otherwise 'normal' balance and health – while in others a melancholic disposition persisted as a quasi-natural, permanent state, a 'normal abnormality', symptomatic of a chronic humoral imbalance. In this classical medical framework, no treatment or intervention could hope to rebalance the latter type of melancholic, for such individuals were simply of a splenetic temperament, 'born under the sign of Saturn', cosmologically and thus irrevocably configured to be hypersensitive to loss, pain, rejection, fear, sadness, and suffering, even in the absence of any genuine cause for such feelings.

The influence of these classical ideas would be hugely significant. Indeed, the humoral understandings of melancholia originating in Greek science proved to be remarkably robust. The Galenic theories took hold in the post-classical Middle East, finding support in such figures as Ishaq ibn Imran, Haly Abbas, and Avicenna. By contrast, early medieval Christian writings, most notably those of the 'Desert Fathers' (Evagrius, Nilus, Johanis Cassian), shifted the causal bases of melancholic experience from the *natural* realm (as posited by the Greeks) to the *supernatural*. The temptation of *acedia* came to be a predominant concern for the medieval Christian worldview, especially as part of the latter's dualistic conception of humanity, which saw human actions as being influenced by good and bad angels or spirits. *Acedia* – a chronic listlessness and despondency – was seen as the most evil of demons or worldly temptations, for it threatened a commitment to religious life altogether. By adapting the core traits of earlier definitions of melancholy into the Christian notion of *acedia*, the Desert Fathers effectively transformed melancholia into a morally perilous condition that opened the way for demonic influences. Some 150 years later, Pope Gregory I (*c.* 540–604), aiming for a more universal readership, merged the temptations of *acedia* and *tristitia* (dejection) into a single sin, namely, *sloth*. From this point on, the seven cardinal sins were consolidated and would form the basis of medieval Christian morality for the best part of a millennium.

Acedia faded from view with the advent of Renaissance classicism and Protestantism, both of which undermined the authority of the Catholic Church within Europe. The Italian humanist Marsilio Ficino (1433–99) proved to be a key figure in returning the classical theories of melancholia to prominence. Ficino's *Books on Life* of 1482 sought to bring together Christian doctrine and Renaissance humanism, and re-established melancholy's classical associations with worthy intellectual pursuits, great achievements, statesmanship, and creative genius first noted by the Aristotelian school. The importance of astrology was also reflected at this time in the rediscovery of the Platonic view of Saturn as the highest planet, bestowing the gift-curse of melancholic insight and genius upon those born under Saturn's sign (such as Ficino). English writers on melancholy of the sixteenth and seventeenth centuries, such as Timothie Bright (1551–1615) and Robert Burton (1577–1640), also elaborated on the central themes of astrology, creativity, and genius, seeing in the last two features a substantial artistic compensation for people afflicted with melancholy.[8] Indeed, as Lawrence Babb has noted, such accounts of melancholy's association with heightened perception and brilliance of mind were so influential as to make melancholy a 'fashionable disease' in Elizabethan England where affectations of the malady's symptoms became commonplace.[9]

The influence of these conceptualizations of melancholy, many of which had drawn upon and incorporated well-established features of the European cultural imagination, began to wane and fragment between the seventeenth and nineteenth centuries. As the Enlightenment advanced, in tandem with the advent of modern science, the authority of most traditional explanations of melancholy was challenged. More reasoned and rigorous accounts were sought, ones that eschewed any unscientific recourse to the supernatural. Of course, within the arts, European Romanticism revived some of the classical notions of melancholic creativity, elevated suffering, poetic genius, and so forth. But the scientific discourse of modernity was steadily working to categorize, define, and medicalize melancholia more fully. In Philippe Pinel's work on melancholia of the early 1800s, for instance, there is no mention of black bile or humours. Instead, the careful observation of presenting symptoms becomes the key to understanding mental disorder.[10] Clinical observation and symptomatology was further developed in the latter half of the nineteenth century, especially in the work of Emil Kraepelin (1856–1926), which was central to the rise to prominence of clinical psychiatry. Kraepelin's *Textbook of Psychiatry*, appearing in multiple editions, laid the foundations for the nosological procedures of modern psychiatry. The sixth edition of his *Textbook* (1896) proved notable for its reclassification of complex psychiatric symptoms into two distinct classes: *manic-depressive disease* and *dementia praecox* (what is now referred to as 'schizophrenia'). The former category grouped together a wide array of symptoms and conditions (including manic-depressive psychosis and other dynamic states) that primarily affected mood. Such conditions would typically be open to fluctuations in severity, with the patient experiencing some periods of exacerbation, but also others of remission. Prognoses could be reasonably positive in many instances, with even a chance of full recovery for some. By contrast, the latter category, *dementia praecox*, was indicative of an underlying disease causing significant intellectual disorder, cognitive damage, and an inexorable degeneration in the patient's mental health. The prognosis for such chronic conditions was unremittingly poor. Kraepelin's dichotomy essentially served to distinguish between disorders of an *affective* character and those of a *cognitive* character, that is, between conditions that affected one's feelings, mood, and passions, and those that affected one's mental faculties. It is interesting to note that despite the strict scientific basis of Kraepelin's psychiatric textbook, his claims retain something of the ancient theories of melancholia, insofar as they maintain a long-standing tradition of distinguishing between milder, mood based occurrences on the one hand, and more severe, physiologically based experiences on the other.

From mood to pathology: Freud on mourning and melancholy

Sigmund Freud's 'Mourning and Melancholia' ['*Trauer und Melancholie*'], a paper written in 1915 and first published in 1917, marks an important point in the conceptual development and cultural understanding of melancholy. The metapsychological essay is written in an accessible manner that belies its ostensibly provisional character. Indeed, though Freud's subsequent work (especially *The Ego and the Id* of 1923) would significantly complicate the definitional boundaries that mark out and differentiate mourning from melancholia, the account outlined in the essay of 1917 has proven far more influential for its strict demarcation of the two psychic responses to loss.

In the earlier work, Freud attempts to chart the unique and abnormal features of melancholia by comparing and contrasting it to what he calls the 'normal affect of mourning'.[11] In the process of describing some provisional observations about patients presenting with melancholic symptoms, and outlining the causal mechanisms that delineate melancholy from mourning, Freud effectively pathologizes melancholia. He writes:

> The exciting causes due to environmental influences are ... the same for both conditions. Mourning is regularly the reaction to the loss of a loved person, or to the loss of some abstraction which has taken the place of one, such as one's country, liberty, an ideal, and so on. In some people the same influences produce melancholia instead of mourning and we consequently suspect them of a *pathological* disposition.[12]

While both mourning and melancholia are seen to result from the experience of (and psychic response to) loss, the 'work of mourning' is held up as an uncontroversial and healthy process, which once completed allows us to disinvest our libidinal attachment to the lost object, 'move on' from (or incorporate) the loss, and thus begin to establish new object attachments. While the work of mourning is genuinely laborious – inasmuch as it requires a withdrawal from the world and a temporary 'hallucinatory wishful psychosis', which psychically extends the existence of the lost object so that we may gradually sever our libidinal ties to it – and may take some time to complete, the sense of mourning's normalcy and appropriateness derives from the assurance of its completion. Mourning ends. We move on.

By contrast, melancholia involves the prolongation or blocking of the normal process of mourning. According to Freud's account, melancholia signals the failure to mourn a loss, and as such it is a form of pathology.[13] He notes that the 'distinguishing mental features' of melancholia are

> a profoundly painful dejection, cessation of interest in the outside world, loss of the capacity to love, inhibition of all activity, and a lowering of the self-regarding feelings to a degree that finds utterance in self-reproaches and self-revilings, and culminates in a delusional expectation of punishment.[14]

Not all of these features are, strictly speaking, distinctive of melancholia, for all (bar one) are also present in the act of mourning. The one exception, which sets apart melancholia from mourning, is the disturbance of self-regard, which occurs when we begin to mourn and withdraw from the lost object, but fail to complete the work of mourning. Instead of redirecting our libidinal energy towards a new object, we internalize the lost object (or rather the 'shadow of the object') into the ego. This act produces a *splitting* of the ego, whereby 'one part of the ego sets itself over against the other, judges it critically, and, as it were, takes it as its object'.[15] This is why Freud claims that 'in mourning it is the world which has become poor and empty; in melancholia it is the ego itself'.[16]

The process of mourning appears so straightforward, so matter-of-fact, because it responds to a loss that is clear, real, concrete, and specifiable; mourning, as we recall from earlier, is a reaction to the loss of a loved person (or the loss of an 'abstraction' that serves as a displacement of the loved person). In any case, the loss is definable in a substantive sense. Through 'reality-testing', we confirm that the beloved object no longer exists in the world – usually as a result of death, but it may also result from betrayal, disappointment, or abandonment. In Freud's account of the healthy response, this finding prompts us to commence the work of mourning, psychically extending the object's presence in order to *decathect* from it, before eventually letting go of the lost object. This then enables us to form new or substitute attachments.

But in cases of melancholia, the original loss often remains unclear and unidentifiable, not just to the observer, but also to the sufferer. As Freud notes, 'melancholia is in some way related to an object-loss which is withdrawn from consciousness, in contradistinction to mourning, in which there is nothing about the loss that is unconscious'.[17] So, there is no denying that both the mourner and the melancholic experience a *real* loss; it is just that the melancholic can neither identify nor specify precisely *what* has been lost. As Ahmed puts it, 'the object of loss for melancholics is missing; they do not know what they are missing'.[18] Indeed, in cases where a loss is the result of some slight or betrayal, there is likely to be an enduring and profound affective *ambivalence* on the part of the slighted, which can also drastically complicate the processes of decathexis and mourning. Unable to accurately pinpoint the particular object of loss, the melancholic internalizes the unspecifiable loss into its (painfully divided) ego. For Freud, the effects of this internalization for the self are often devastating, making melancholia an utterly undesirable and debilitating condition.

Despite the unquestionable impact of the 'Mourning and Melancholia' paper on the theoretical and cultural understanding of melancholy, many commentators have noted how Freud's later work radically revises his sharp division between the two forms of experience: the healthy work of mourning on the one side, counterposed to the pathological paralysis of melancholia on the other. But signs of ambivalence are already discernible in the original essay of

1917. For instance, Freud appears to rehearse the Renaissance associations of melancholy with unrivalled insight when he claims that the melancholic 'has a keener eye for the truth than other people who are not melancholic', before adding, 'we only wonder why a man has to be ill before he can be accessible to a truth of this kind'.[19] We should note, however, that despite the appearance of this surprisingly bold claim in Freud's essay, the 'truth' in this passage relates to a truth about the individual (patient) in question. It pertains to a form of self-knowledge that only becomes properly accessible through the melancholic's unrelenting (self-)scrutiny. The notion of truth invoked here thus sharply diverges from the more societal, objective, and political understandings of truth mobilized by Adorno's 'melancholy science' or Benjamin's redemptive-melancholic criticism. Of course, as is often the case when any theoretical discourse migrates from its specialist origins and enters into the wider cultural milieu, many of the nuances, tensions, and ambiguities of Freud's provisional thoughts on melancholy set out in the 1917 essay have not been preserved. Instead, the enduring legacy of Freud's work on the topic lies in the pathologization of melancholy as a detrimental condition and an inadequate response to loss. As reductive and restrictive as this characterization is, at least it can serve as a useful foil for more critical work on the subject.

To that end, for the remainder of this chapter, I want to revisit the work of Walter Benjamin and Theodor Adorno, both of whom offer alternative and provocative ways of mobilizing melancholy towards more socially and politically productive ends. Their affective mode of theorizing exhibits what I am calling 'melancholic dispositions', which open us up to critical perspectives not only towards ourselves, but also, more importantly, towards the social world in which we live. In so doing, our conception of melancholy can be transformed from a personal state to a transindividual 'structure of feeling'. My use of the term 'disposition' here is meant to convey two meanings. The first understands disposition in the more everyday sense, that is to say, as a general character, a way of being in (and towards) the world; it marks a temperament, a state of readiness, or tendency. The second figures disposition as the way in which something is placed, particularly in relation to other things. So while the first definition might be seen as internally given, suggesting an individual phenomenon in the form of an apparently spontaneously manifested trait, as unique to each person as a fingerprint, the second might be read as externally given, that is to say, it is more relational and porous, viewing everything in an assembly or ensemble of objects and others. Both senses of disposition apply in the case of melancholy. The latter is simultaneously a subjective disposition – a way of being towards the world – and an objective disposition – a relation of self and others within a particular, often inhibiting configuration.[20]

With this in mind, I am interested in the following questions. What forms of agency can accompany melancholia? How can such a notoriously helpless, passive, and subjective disposition be salvaged for an affective politics of the left? What sorts of attachment and detachment underpin a melancholic critique of society? I will suggest some possible answers to these questions through readings of Benjamin and Adorno. In doing so, my aim is to wrest melancholy from its pathological, personal, and psychological straitjackets, and expand our understanding of melancholic dispositions as complex and potentially critical responses to objectively stifling social conditions.

Walter Benjamin: melancholy critique

Constipation and melancholy have always gone together.[21]

I was born under the sign of Saturn – that star of the slowest revolution, the planet of detours and delays.[22]

The troubled nature of Walter Benjamin's life and the tragic circumstances of his untimely death have become almost legendary. Indeed, they have been so widely documented and reproduced that it is difficult to revisit his eclectic writings without surrendering the force of the ideas contained therein to the weight of personal and historical context. Academically inclined readers from all manner of disciplinary backgrounds, as well as general, non-academic readers, will have at least some familiarity with the myriad misfortunes that befell Walter Benjamin: the fragile health of his youth; his troubled relationships, failed marriage, and unrequited loves; his marginalization as a writer and failure to secure a position within the academy; the financial and emotional hardship of his years in exile after 1933; and, of course, his tragic suicide in September 1940 at Portbou. The painstaking job of piecing together the scattered fragments of Benjamin's life has been undertaken by a range of biographers and historians, whose forensic attention to detail has done a great service to intellectual history.[23] But while such efforts are invaluable in illuminating the conditions in which Benjamin lived and wrote, as well as establishing important connections between his various correspondents and acquaintances, all too often his work is merely mapped on to and understood through the contours of his life, as if the one simply derived from the other. Notwithstanding the fact that certain of Benjamin's literary and cultural interests suggest a degree of continuity between his life and his thought, there remains a pressing need for rediscovering the social and political stakes of his critical theory that breach the traditional borders of historicism. This is especially the case when trying to unpack and reconstruct his varied engagements with melancholia, in which the subjective and the personal are inextricably bound up with the objective and the political.

For all the extensive commentary on the life and work of Walter Benjamin, his enduring interest in melancholia has routinely been explained with reference to his own biography and personal disposition. Many of those who knew him well have noted an underlying melancholic sensibility. For instance, when recalling early encounters with Benjamin, Gershom Scholem remarks that in his youth Benjamin's character was marked by a 'profound sadness'. Theodor Adorno echoes this sentiment when he writes the following of his friend: 'Sadness – which is different from the simple fact of being sad – was his nature.'[24] Elsewhere, Adorno notes that 'in Benjamin the devotion to happiness which has been denied is won only through a regretful sorrow'.[25] According to Susan Sontag, Benjamin was 'what the French call un triste'. She goes on to note how this psychological disposition dictated the author's scholarly interests: 'Benjamin projected himself, his temperament, into all his major subjects, and his temperament determined what he chose to write about.'[26] All of which, to varying degrees, reinforce the idea of a strong convergence between Benjamin's personality and his writing.

Some recent biographers and commentators have started to take note of the limitations of such approaches, particularly in the case of Walter Benjamin. For instance, Eiland and Jennings argue that it is 'misleading to characterize him [Benjamin], as certain influential English-language treatments have done, as a purely saturnine and involuted figure'. The authors go on to note: 'This is not to say that he was not plagued by long bouts of immobilizing depression ... nor is it to forget that his diaries – and his conversations with his closest friends – return often enough to thought of suicide. Yet to treat Walter Benjamin as a hopeless melancholic is to caricature and reduce him.'[27] From this description, there are two phrases that require unpacking: 'immobilizing depression' and 'hopeless melancholic'. It could be that Eiland and Jennings are (inadvertently) reinforcing precisely the negative associations that I am keen to challenge, namely, that depression is necessarily immobilizing, that melancholics are inherently hopeless. At the same time, a more generous reading could set out from the basis that the modifiers are conditional and as such serve to specify a particular and predominant form of depression (one that is 'immobilizing') and a particular type of melancholic (one that is 'hopeless'). This would then leave open the possibility of a non-immobilizing (if not actively mobilizing) state of depression and a not-hopeless (if not hopeful) melancholia. Along similar lines, Esther Leslie claims that 'it is frequently reformist-minded theorists who see reflected in Benjamin their own defeatist melancholy',[28] which prompts one to consider an alternative, non-defeatist and productive melancholy – one that is suffused with political affect and historical awareness. This must be especially pertinent in relation to Benjamin, whose melancholy (while undeniable) can hardly be said to be 'defeatist'. Rather, as Max Pensky observes, Benjamin's perceived 'sadness' is 'more than an arbitrary and hence accidental feature of personality'; instead, it enters into 'a creative, essential, complex relation'.[29]

The melancholic force of both Benjamin's work and his disposition refuse any simplistic modelling of causation. Indeed, one should take care not to overlook the complicated manner in which Benjamin himself, as a proponent and advocate of modernist aesthetics, elides any sharp distinction between the life and the text. His writing is often self-referential, incorporating personal experiences, grievances, and memories, transfiguring them into micrological keys to unlock the larger totality. Indeed, Scholem goes to great lengths in his attempts to decipher the hidden meanings and veiled characters that appear in some of Benjamin's writings (such as 'Agesilaus Santander'). For some commentators, this subtle conflation of the biographical and the textual detracts from the 'validity' of Benjamin's ideas, simply confirming their suspicions that cultural criticism (unlike official, bona fide 'Philosophy') is merely 'a mode of autobiography', as Oscar Wilde famously put it. In her lengthy introduction to *Illuminations*, Hannah Arendt complains that Benjamin succumbed to French influences (i.e. *flânerie*, French literature and criticism), rather than pursuing 'normal[!] German intellectual life' (by which she presumably means traditional academic philosophy).[30] Similarly, Bernd Witte suggests that Benjamin's idiosyncratic interpretations of literary texts suffer from the fact that they are so heavily suffused with covert references to a personal history that can only be known to a handful of readers. In addition, Witte – clearly unfazed by the recognized limitations of 'intentional fallacies' – complains of how such individualized readings and allegorical appropriations disregard the intended meaning of a text: 'So strong is the absorptive power of his [Benjamin's] theological interpretive machine that in the end the critic destroys the original context of the work and arrives at a perspective contradictory to the author's intentions.'[31] But what irks some of the most notable readers of his work is precisely what enables others to discern the social and political motives that underwrite Benjamin's particular brand of melancholy praxis, and his refusal to cordon off the personal from the political, or the subjective from the objective (in less anachronistic terms).

Such a creative and productive appreciation of the untapped critical potential within a melancholic disposition is even evident in the archival images of Walter Benjamin. As Beatrice Hanssen notes, the most well-known photographic portraits of Benjamin, such as those taken by Gisèle Freund and Germaine Krull, depict a brooding, gloomy Benjamin, born under the sign of Saturn, whose languid pose and language of gestures – that is, downward gaze, chin leaning on a clenched fist – seem to quote from an ancient pictorial archive of mourning and melancholia. Bidding the beholder to adopt the pose of an age-old face reader, they invite one to glean Benjamin's temperament, no less than his fate, from the lines that define his mimetic image.[32]

What might we make of this inherited 'imago' of Benjamin? Hanssen goes on to convincingly argue that Benjamin's photographic poses can be seen as knowing, witty, even playful interactions with the elevated history of the sensitive brooder [der Grübler], fêted 'men of melancholy' and isolated scholars (like Ficino and Burton) contemplating abstractions, metaphysics, and the suffering of the world. Of course, the irony in this account is that one of the key characteristics of melancholia – at least in its distinctly *modern* version as outlined by Freud – is profound self-criticism.[33] Thus, there arises an element of self-identification and self-deprecation in Benjamin's poses. Insofar as he both evokes and playfully subverts the predominant cultural signifiers and values that have accumulated around melancholia, he must also mobilize a potential that only avails itself by virtue of a melancholic disposition. The very capacity to simultaneously observe and criticize the figure of the melancholic 'man of genius' is one conferred by the unique experience of melancholia itself. As Pensky notes, the melancholic 'realizes that the sentence of melancholia is, if inescapable, also endowed with a dialectical force. The same powers that torment that subject with sadness, despair, and the *taedium vitae* can, through the self's submission to a discipline, be transformed into the powers of a higher insight'.[34]

This dialectical force can be seen in the vacillations that propel Benjamin's thinking and writing. It is this dialectical tension that makes Benjamin at once a melancholy critic and a critic of melancholy. Since he understands melancholia as a socio-historical condition brought on by objective conditions, it contains both opportunities and risks. Depending on how a melancholic disposition is itself disposed in a social world, that is, how it is related to real struggles and practices, one may experience it in different ways: animating or paralyzing, energizing or enervating, amplifying or diminishing. There can be no short-circuiting the links (seldom actualized) between melancholy in itself and a radically transformative way of seeing, as if the condition itself inevitably procured critical insight. At best, one can register the social and political valences that attach themselves to melancholia, and recognize the potential and interpretive power that lay dormant in melancholic dispositions. With this in mind, we might better understand how and why Benjamin seeks to differentiate between his own active, engaged form of melancholic criticism, and others that are shown to be utterly passive, ineffectual, and ultimately quietistic.

Benjamin's steadfast dismissal of what he identifies as 'left-wing melancholy' [*Linke Melancholie*] is exemplary in this regard. In his 1931 critique of Erich Kästner, Benjamin takes the popular Weimar poet to task for essentially offering up a deadening and stultifying vision of a troubled world that merely facilitates idle and purgative contemplation for a reformist, bourgeois readership or 'left-wing intelligentsia'. This is not to say that Kästner and his ilk are not genuinely affronted by social injustices; it is just that this discontent is allowed only the most ceremonial and tempered form of expression. By relying on a stock of tired tropes, stereotypes, and gestures, Kästner relinquishes all individuality and eccentricity – two of the rare qualities of pre-Expressionist bourgeois aesthetics that offered at least a modicum of political independence and insight. Routine extinguishes any spark of discontent: 'This poet is dissatisfied – indeed, heavy-hearted. But this heaviness of heart derives from routine. For to be in a routine means to have sacrificed one's idiosyncrasies, to have forfeited the gift of being disgusted.'[35] As a result, Kästner's poems do not and cannot convey or provoke a genuine sense of despair, disgust, or horror. Instead, they are merely the aestheticized mechanics of a passive and ironic melancholy emptied of its content, an affectation for the most vocal (and least radical) leftists and self-proclaimed humanists. In a way that recalls the fashionable 'men of feeling' of eighteenth-century England, Kästner's poetics transposes whatever 'revolutionary reflexes' might exist in the bourgeois into the ostentatious simulation of feeling of the would-be reformer: 'What is left is the empty spaces where, in dusty heart-shaped velvet trays, the feelings – nature and love, enthusiasm and humanity – once rested. Now the hollow forms are absentmindedly caressed.'[36] The routinized nature of the poet's observations is simply grist to the fatalist's mill, or the obverse side of the absence of political action. Benjamin's diagnosis for this condition is 'tortured stupidity' – 'the latest of two millennia of metamorphoses of melancholy'.[37]

Benjamin concludes his savage review on a physiological note that evokes and yet supplants the ancient humoral theory of melancholy with a digestive one. Through a gastric analogy, he likens Kästner's complacency and fatalism to that of 'those who are most remote from the process of production and whose obscure courting of the state of the market is comparable to the attitude of a man who yields himself up entirely to the inscrutable accidents of his digestion. The rumbling in these lines certainly has more to do with flatulence than with subversion. Constipation and melancholy have always gone together'.[38]

What becomes clear then is that, for Benjamin, melancholy must be on the side of the 'revolutionary dialectic';[39] it ought not to be transfigured into a 'quasi-classless' common sense that eschews political engagement and simply laments the course of the world before helplessly sighing and moving on. Indeed, the very refusal to accept things and move on is what motivates Benjamin's brand of critique. For Benjamin, melancholy opens up 'onto a new methodology and theory of knowledge', which in turn necessitate the critic's 'immersion in natural and cultural objects'.[40] The melancholic disposition is unparalleled in its openness towards the material of the past, which carries with it the marks and indices of its varied meanings, histories, relations, and memories. It is a disposition that gathers in remembrance the discarded things on which the present is built. But though this practice takes form in the subjective mode of spectatorship and transcription, it is by no means one of ahistorical contemplation or lamentation over *la condition humaine*. As Max Pensky notes, 'Memory, for all its invitation to subjective contemplation, does not itself appear as a matter of subjective decision. Under the weight of memory, the subject is pulled into the tide in which each fragment, overladen with memory, appears as a potential correlate to every other'.[41] Adorno, too, acutely observed this move in Benjamin's melancholy critique, writing: 'To interpret phenomena materialistically meant for him [Benjamin] not so much to elucidate them as products of the social whole but rather to relate them directly, in their isolated singularity, to material tendencies, and social struggles.'[42]

The connection to material tendencies and social struggles is something that distinguishes Benjamin's modern(ist) melancholia from its baroque predecessors. Baroque *Trauer* remains bound up with the Dürerian image of Melancholia as constructive brooder, surrounded by tools (saw, block-plane, nails, whetstone) that lay unused. By contrast, the heady, affective cocktail of the modern melancholic consists of more than just sadness and mindful meditation; its act of 'tooling up' is not simply predicated on the concept of construction. Rather, it attests to fear, anger, and the urge towards wilful destruction in the face of injustice and oppression.[43] Writing of Baudelaire's modern allegorizing, Benjamin notes that 'it bears, in contradistinction to that of the baroque, traces of a wrath which was at such a pitch as to break into this world and to leave its harmonious structures in ruins'.[44] In this sense, the modern melancholic not only resides amid the rubble and refuse of the social world, but also envisages the lustrous commodities of the present as ruins *in potentia*. As such, the creative potential of a melancholic disposition, and its allegorical mode of seeing, of constellating, exceeds the traditional dichotomy of production/destruction. Again, Scholem is most perceptive in noting this

element of his friend's method: 'The noble and positive power of destruction –
too long (in his view) denied due recognition thanks to the one-sided, undia-
lectic and dilettantic apotheosis of "creativity" – now becomes an aspect of
redemption, related to the immanence of the world, acted out in the history
of human labour.'[45] 'To interrupt the course of the world – this is Baudelaire's
deepest wish. The wish of Joshua … From this wish sprang his violence, his
impatience and his anger.'[46] Of course, elsewhere, Benjamin famously writes
of the 'destructive character' that 'knows only one watchword: make room;
only one activity: clearing away'. These acts of path-clearing are not motivated
by any specific vision of the future. Instead, the destructive act simply makes
space: 'The destructive character sees nothing permanent … What exists he
reduces to rubble, not for the sake of the rubble, but for that of the way leading through it.'[47] Such sentiments recall Benjamin's vision of revolution as the
attempt to activate the emergency brake, violently rupturing the historical continuum that is our perpetual state of emergency or permanent catastrophe.
Again, it bespeaks a refusal to allow things to simply go on. But despite the
terminology used to describe 'the destructive character', which might suggest
a psychological type or case, Benjamin's melancholic-destructive reflections
are not directed at a particular 'subject' as such.

It might appear somewhat paradoxical that despite dedicating so much of
his life's work to cultural criticism, the role of critical subjectivity seldom arises
in Benjamin's work.[48] In part, this can be explained by his mobilization of melancholic criticism, which takes a uniquely de-personalized and de-subjectified
form. For Benjamin, the renunciation of an authoritative self acts as the gate-
way to critical illuminations that derive from the constellation of objects, fragments, and ruins, rather than the constitutive power of a transcendental,
acquisitive subject. His attempt to redeem or at least recover the unrealized
potential within a much-denigrated and antiquated theatrical form – namely,
the 'mourning play' [*Trauerspiel*] – is testament to the power of melancholy as
de-subjectified critique. As Hanssen notes, 'What counted most for Benjamin
was that in the pathological state of extreme depersonalization that characterized melancholia, even the most innocuous, simple objects [*Dinge*] could be
transfigured into ciphers of enigmatic wisdom'.[49] Pensky describes this notable feature of Benjamin's thought as:

the critical urge to illuminate a dimension of objective truth not through
an act of supreme, autochthonous creativity, but rather by focusing a
beam of critical energy onto the already existent historical object, so
that his own thought could find in it a structure or dwelling for its own
self-expression.[50]

This 'merging of the critical subject into a moment of an objective process' requires a purposeful subordination of constitutive subjectivity, which is one of the foremost features of a melancholic disposition.[51] Of course, one can note the apparent convergence between Benjamin's personal disposition and choice of critical objects and techniques. Indeed, Adorno does precisely this when he notes Benjamin's 'idiosyncratic distaste for words like "personality". From the very start his thought protested against the false claim that man and the human mind are self-constitutive and that an absolute originates in them'.[52] But one can venture beyond the biographical to uncover the theoretical affinities between Benjamin's suspicion of subjectivity and the ways in which mourning and melancholia involve different relations to the subject.

Throughout the analysis of the *Trauerspiel* book, Benjamin deploys the terms mourning and melancholia 'more of less indiscriminately, failing to adopt Freud's 1917 typology'.[53] In ignoring and collapsing the distinction between these two crucial terms, Benjamin implicitly rejects the idea that melancholy incubates a pathological relationship not only towards loss, but also towards the self. Whereas Freud wants to bolster the subject by way of mourning, which forms a necessary part of one's healthy progression in working through loss, Benjamin advocates the radical dissolution of the self through melancholic attachment, an immersion in, rather than confrontation with, the objective world. Thus, in relation to loss and relationality, Benjamin's melancholy stands in stark opposition to Freud's mourning. While the latter undertakes to move beyond the losses of the past for the sake of psychic hygiene, the former refuses to relinquish a loss that can never be comprehended in its fullness nor incorporated into a single authoritative 'I'. As Jonathan Flatley notes, where Freud was 'concerned to develop a universal theory of melancholy that would enable analysts to help patients arrive at individual cures, Walter Benjamin saw melancholia as a definitely historical problem related to the experience of modernity. In this view melancholia is no longer a personal problem requiring cure or catharsis, but is evidence of the historicity of one's subjectivity, indeed the very substance of that historicity'.[54] For the mourner, as we have seen, loss marks an unavoidable, painful yet crucially *specific* obstruction that can and, indeed, must be overcome. In so doing, the subject is fortified and equipped so as to overcome old losses and activate new libidinal attachments. For the melancholic, by contrast, loss becomes generalized, unspecifiable, and insurmountable. Loss accumulates materially and historically, to the point of bursting the internal borders of an allegedly unique, autonomous, rational subject.

It is worth noting that it is precisely this potential for radical de-subjectivation for which Benjamin praises the aesthetic experiments of the Surrealists, whose practices also sought to suspend the protocols of rational, bourgeois individuality. Indeed, both Benjamin and the Surrealists, by different routes and techniques, seek to reawaken forms of secular mysticism and intoxication [*Rausch*] that give space to that which escapes the comfortable interiority of the encased subject. Benjamin writes: 'Overcoming of rational individuality in intoxication – of the motorial and affective individuality, however, in collective action: this characterizes the whole situation.' The 'overcoming of the private' is 'in point of fact a revolutionary virtue'.[55] Just as Surrealist practice tries to transcribe or convey the unconscious desires and fluid imagery of dream-states by the fusing and juxtaposition of everyday objects, so the melancholic's relentless allegorizing tears objects out of their quotidian context, repositioning them in an alternative constellation, prompting repressed meanings to be revealed. Yet, while such revelations are said to temporarily 'flash up' at a moment of danger, they do not constitute religious epiphanies; on the contrary, they remain thoroughly materialistic, anthropological, creaturely – *profane illuminations*, in Benjamin's own terms.[56] In trying to reconstitute a kind of active engagement and agency, melancholia and Surrealism share a common suspicion over the constitutive powers of the rationalizing subject, and instead explore the somewhat counterintuitive idea that substantive experience [*Erfahrung*] might only be retrievable in moments of spontaneity, where lightning flashes of insight involuntarily protrude from the material. Surrendering the psychic (bourgeois) fantasies of total self-control and self-confinement serves as the precondition for collective action. In their desire to transcend or even destroy the individual ego – to 'win the energies of intoxication for the revolution'[57] – Benjaminian melancholia and Surrealism are at one.[58]

The sort of 'intoxication' that characterizes the melancholic disposition stems from an expansive and heightened sense of loss (dizzying in its capaciousness) coupled with the unquenchable, indeed, wilfully *un*reasonable, need to redeem all that is lost. What is more, this may be compounded by the knowledge that such need will likely remain unfulfilled. Indeed, the tension between redemptive urge and catastrophic conditions adds to the ferment of the melancholic disposition.[59] Yet, while no doubt painful at its most intense moments of psychic stagnation, a melancholic response to accumulated losses – precisely in its meta-subjective vision and scope – can provide the conditions of possibility for genuine experience, and in particular non-intentional experience. Benjamin wagers a great deal on melancholy's anti-intentionality as a way of undermining traditional modes of knowledge acquisition and transmission. As Hanssen notes, 'Under Benjamin's gaze, melancholy revealed itself to be an existentialist *mode,* not simply, then, an overwhelming indeterminate *mood (Stimmung),* but, fundamentally, a technique of disclosure and knowledge that replaced the old rationalistic epistemological model'.[60]

Appreciating the link between melancholia and anti-intentionality also helps us to make sense of Benjamin's infamously dense 'Epistemo-Critical Prologue' to the *Trauerspiels* book. For in that prologue, Benjamin counterposes the intentional nature of knowledge with the non-intentional structure of truth, defending the latter against the former. The non-intentional and indeed metaphysical structure of truth interests him the most because it offers a way of breaking through the narrow confines of experience as understood by Kant and his interlocutors, whereby a sovereign rational subject confronts empirical objects. While this intentional structure may lead to the production and possession of knowledge, it cannot enable truth to reveal itself. For Benjamin, the limited and hierarchical relationship that undergirds the idealist conception of subject and object needs to be collapsed if truth is to manifest itself:

> Truth does not enter into relationships, particularly intentional ones. The object of knowledge, determined as it is by the intention inherent in the concept, is not the truth. Truth is an intentionless state of being, made up of ideas. The proper approach to it is not therefore one of intention and knowledge, but rather a total immersion and absorption in it. Truth is the death of intention.

This complex proposition is part of Benjamin's attempt to deflate the epistemological claims of a critical subjectivity that presumes to know reality by subsuming it under its conceptual categories. By contrast, the melancholic critic is transformed into a conduit for the representation of truth, in a constructive act that Benjamin likens variously to constellations and mosaics. This methodology of minimal imposition seeks to recover the historical content and interrelation of objects, by retaining the unique qualities of each individual thing, whilst at the same time revealing the complex arrangement (or *disposition*) of things that betokens their wider meaning and significance.

Thus, in its Benjaminian, historical-materialist form, melancholy can actually be seen to constitute a kind of labour – a creative/destructive activity that harnesses the retroactive force of the past, alongside a collective weak messianic power, which 'will constantly call into question every victory ... of the rulers'.[61] In some respects, such radical claims on behalf of melancholy critics and *Kritik* appear to be without precedent, but in other respects they can be seen to recall and rework the words of perhaps the most devoted chronicler of melancholic paraphernalia, Robert Burton. For in his seminal encyclopedic work of 1621, *The Anatomy of Melancholy*, Burton proudly states: 'They get their knowledge by books, I mine by melancholizing.' The opening euphemistic pronoun – suggestive of an impropriety committed by other, more everyday readers – chimes with Benjamin's later juxtaposition of the historicist and the historical materialist, whereby the former merely attempts to acquire knowledge in a consumptive manner, while the latter actively intervenes in ongoing material struggles over historical truth.

Moreover, Burton's words prefigure the critical practice that Benjamin would take to be central to the melancholic disposition. Amid the governing medical and cultural understandings of melancholy, there remains something qualitatively distinct about Burton's use of the verb 'melancholize'. Indeed, even to contemporary ears, the phrase can sound jarring. This is primarily because throughout its long cultural history, as we have seen, melancholy has routinely been cast as an inherently passive and helpless condition that one simply falls into. This view tends to associate melancholy with the perils of *acedia* (whereby any occasional flashes of insight that accompany the condition are judged to be merely fortuitous, like the proverbial 'broken watch' that gives the right time twice a day). Interestingly, we might note that Freud rehearses this idea and converts it into modern psychological terms when speaking of the 'work of mourning', which is both processual and progressive, in contrast to the state (and stasis) of melancholy, which is said to inhibit movement and progression. Translated into today's value-laden political language, we can say that the underlying assumption of Freud's schema, which in effect crystallizes the most noted symptoms of melancholia throughout its history, is that the mourner works while the melancholic shirks. It is precisely against such an understanding that we can position Benjamin's thought. In revealing the overlooked critical capacity, activity, and allegorical vision enabled by a melancholic disposition, Benjamin is loyal to Burton's notion of 'melancholizing', suggesting a mode of critical practice and worldly engagement that is at odds with any straightforwardly pathological image of melancholy. It is a view that attempts to reverse our focus from inward-looking paralysis to outward-looking praxis. Such a transformative move is central to what I take to be Benjamin's unique contribution to an emerging critical theory of feeling.[62]

In sum: melancholic loss endures beyond that which has been lost, registering the inherent sociality of all relations past, present, and future. There is a radical, redemptive potential within such an expansive sensitivity towards historical catastrophe and loss. It is borne of a view that understands the past not as fixed, forgotten, dead and buried, but rather as a site of real contestation and confrontation in the present. The melancholic critic not only circles her objects parallactically, but also gives herself over to the ruinous manifold of objects thrown together by historical processes, in an attempt to render if not alter the fate imprinted on them by the victors' historical narrative. In this attempt to obstruct the 'triumphal procession in which the present rulers step over those who are lying prostrate',[63] the melancholy critic labours in the spirit of historical materialism.

Conscious unhappiness and critique

> Above all, people must be made to despair of themselves and of the order of society.[64]

> The thought's position toward happiness would be the negation of all false happiness.[65]

How are we to make sense of the above quotations, which at first glance seem to be mere provocations or exaggerations? After all, who would be *against* happiness – that perennial theme that has so preoccupied human endeavours and culture for millennia? How could one defend and even propagate any form of *un*happiness? What can be gained by dwelling on (and *in*) the negative? These questions will be addressed in the remainder of this chapter, in which I will argue that when social conditions are such that the prevailing models of happiness become so tied to and deformed by the imperatives of capital accumulation, it becomes imperative not only to abjure the forms of happiness on offer, but also to encourage others to do the same. To be sure, this is no mean feat, and it is unlikely that any individual in isolation could successfully reject or subvert every instance of socially prescribed happiness. None of us is completely immune to the social and cultural norms that prevail in our historical present. Moreover, there is little helpful – let alone revolutionary – in rejecting a society and its culture *in toto*.[66] As Marx acknowledges in a well-known note from the *Grundrisse*, 'if we did not find concealed in society as it is the material conditions of production and the corresponding relations of exchange prerequisite for a classless society, then all attempts to explode it would be quixotic'.[67] In any case, the point is not to promote some alternative, quasi-monastic refusal that would take place solely at the individual level; rather the aim is to actively foster a collective disavowal of such introverted and debased notions of happiness, and to socialize (and re-politicize) our affective life.

There is a pressing need for such a critical approach to what one might call the political economy of affect. The past two decades or so have seen a sharp rise in the proliferation of media and discourses around happiness and wellbeing.[68] Where once the ideological terrain of happiness was primarily fought over by the hawks of advertising and the doves of the counter-culture, both of which focused almost exclusively on happiness in relation to 'leisure', that is, in opposition to 'work', happiness has now become a central part of today's political economy. The pursuit of happiness is no longer left to the hours spent outside one's place of work; instead, it has become a crucial part of self-management and professional development. As William Davies has recently argued, we can justifiably speak of a 'happiness industry' having emerged in the so-called 'developed' world as a major element in the consolidation of capitalism in its financialized phase.[69] Such personalizing of the public and professional spheres – incorporating traditionally 'subjective' notions of wellbeing right into the heart of objective socio-economic relations – compels us to consider the implications of the happiness turn. This turn has helped to install happiness as an unimpeachable measure of human freedom and flourishing, to the extent that many governments of the so-called 'developed' world attempt to quantify and augment their national wellbeing, even funding happiness studies to discover how best to produce happy citizens, since, as Lord Layard (the UK's 'happiness tsar') puts it, 'the best society' is 'one where the citizens are happiest'.[70]

Of course, in expending such energies to measure, analyse, and promote happiness, it is inevitable that pre-existing norms and inequalities will be reinforced, since those who are already enjoy privilege and success within the current system are most likely to self-report as being 'happy', meaning that these already dominant groups become models for others to emulate (even if objective conditions make this impossible). Thus, the further normalization of 'happy' relations and family 'units' combines with the demonization of all discontent to marshal the narrow borders of social acceptability.[71] In this way, happiness becomes a social responsibility, like economic productivity. To be happy is 'better' for society (conversely, to be visibly or vocally unhappy is seen as socially undesirable, improper even). Like a benign bacteria, happiness is said to reproduce itself and spread like a virus – your being happy is contagious; it will make others happy, and vice versa. Like capital, happiness *accumulates*. But how and where it is permitted to accumulate is not incidental. In fact, the activities, locations, attitudes, and relationships that are said to best promote happiness are anything but neutral or natural. Templates for the good life are moulded and promoted without end, and are often unwittingly reproduced on account of their visibility and perceived normalcy. While a diversity of means might be on offer, the end is always the same: to be happy in such a way that reproduces the status quo. Leaving aside the basic fact that it is often precisely the proliferation of competing means that perpetually blocks the desired end,[72] a critical-theoretical perspective challenges the very idea of happiness as it is currently constructed. This is why I use the phrase 'conscious unhappiness' in relation to critical theory.

As in the case of melancholic critique, conscious unhappiness is not simply meant to suggest a subjective propensity for sadness, pensive brooding and passivity, or chronic oversensitivity to loss. On the contrary, it stands for an unhappiness that is politically willed and socially conditioned; it exists in recognition of suffering, both historical and ongoing. The very term *conscious unhappiness* purposefully transgresses the established borders between cognition and affect, and reaffirms the necessary moment of cathexis – the somatic or material supplement – in thought.

This refusal to extinguish all feeling from thinking is certainly evident in *Negative Dialectics*, in which Adorno acknowledges the experiential turmoil that accompanies such critical attunement. Yet rather than suggesting a psychological pathology or subjective failing, he is adamant that responsibility for such sorrow and despair lies solely on the side of objective reality, the parlous state of the world:

> Unquestionably, one who submits to the dialectical discipline has to pay dearly in the qualitative variety of experience. Still, in the administered world the impoverishment of experience by dialectics, which outrages healthy opinion, proves appropriate to the monotony of that world. Its agony is the world's agony raised to a concept.[73]

Again, note the deliberate collapsing of affect (the world's agony) into cognition (a concept), and vice versa. What is more, this form of conscious unhappiness can be seen as an integral part of social critique, insofar as it places itself in opposition to the existent. In so doing, it performs what Hegel terms the 'labour of the negative'.[74] Indeed, the spectre of Hegel is never far from view when the notion of a dynamic, productive, and fruitful negativity is introduced. In his *Lectures on the Philosophy of World History*, he draws a stark contrast between the progressive nature of discontent and antagonism within historical events, and the relative insignificance of minor gratifications that go under the general banner of 'happiness':

> It is possible to consider history from the point of view of happiness, but history is not the soil in which happiness grows. The periods of happiness in it are the blank pages of history. There are certainly moments of satisfaction in the history of the world, but this satisfaction is not to be equated with happiness: for the aims which are satisfied transcend all particular interests. All ends of importance in world history must be secured by means of abstract volition and energy.[75]

Marx too – ever the progeny of Hegelian dialectics, if sometimes begrudgingly so – takes up the view that history proceeds by way of its 'bad side'.[76] What exists today is the result of a long sequence of conflicts and struggles. Each social formation, as a unity of opposites, contains multiple contradictions, and these contradictions in turn produce significant historical change. 'No antagonism, no progress.'[77]

On the face of it, this standard Hegelian-Marxist view may appear to glorify discontent. Does it not idealize struggle within a single Manichean narrative of heroic defiance, of darkness and light, of good and evil, of friends and enemies, and so on? Well, if taken as some ideal, teleological model of history, then perhaps so. But if one reads this merely as a description of past events, it seems less bombastic and more reflective. To observe struggle and conflict in the world is to recognize and give expression to a profoundly unfree state of affairs. The latter, in turn, compels a response of some kind: interpretation, intervention, antagonism, resistance. What is more, it provokes varying levels of disquiet and discontent, both individually and collectively. But as was shown to be the case with Benjamin's work on melancholy, this profound unease [*Unbehagen*] can also prove to be genuinely productive and mobilizing, expanding one's socio-political concerns beyond those apparently most personal and immediate. In its negative account of the present malaise, critical theory does not claim that happiness cannot be; merely that, as conditions stand, any experience of happiness can only fail to coincide with its substantive idea. The maximalist, universalist concept of happiness cannot be achieved under conditions that forcibly exploit and oppress huge numbers of people across the globe.

If the forms of happiness available to people follow the logic of the social forms in which they develop, and it is hard to see how this would not be the case, then there can be no way of pursuing or achieving a more social and universal happiness under capitalism. This is because capitalist social forms can only permit and promote relations of mutual disinterest that serve to produce surplus value (profit) for the capitalist class. And since capital must constantly expand or cease to exist, it can have no interest in resting, decelerating, 'de-growing', so as to better serve real human needs (happiness included). This is why the conceptions of happiness most widely circulated and valorized are short-termist, exclusionary, and individualist. Indeed, one would be hard-pressed to find any examples of 'happy' lifestyles that are not covertly designed to advance the production process.

Many alternative or counter-cultural visions of 'the good life' have defined themselves precisely in opposition to such ideals. Lukács presciently referred to this trend as 'romantic anti-capitalism'. But movements in this direction are limited by their very derivation from the norms they seek to transgress. They respond to capital's thorough disenchantment of the world by harking back to 'precapitalist social and cultural values'.[78] In so doing, they mainly offer crude inversions of state-sponsored models of happiness – a process that continues to this day. Thus, against the bustle and pollution of the city, the rural retreat or seaside bolthole; against the homogenization of mass production, the artisanal good; against the consumption of new commodities, recycling and 'upcycling'; against corporate greed, so-called 'fair trade' and the sharing economy, etc. These counter-actions are premised on the idea that capitalism's encroachment into all territories of the life-world must be halted, that there are areas of 'the social' that lie beyond the reach of capital (or which are inherently unsuited to marketization and commodification), and that these areas must be protected at all costs.

But advocates of ethical opt-outs or, more recently, 'gift economies' fail to go far enough politically, inasmuch as these responses are marked precisely by their exceptionality. As individualistic retreats from, or localist adaptations to, the otherwise unaffected dictates of global capital, such actions are unlikely to provide the basis for any meaningful social and political resistance to capitalism (and let us be clear: there is no happiness under capitalism that is not underwritten by unspeakable violence and oppression elsewhere).[79] Despite their best intentions, such movements will remain incapable of bringing about any substantive improvement in the overall sphere of human well-being so long as they remain exclusionary and parochial. Indeed, the level of resources (time, money, knowledge) needed to even contemplate certain 'ethical' actions reinforces rather than challenges the vast inequalities that already exist.

Recognition of this fundamental conflict – between, on the one hand, a universal happiness that ought to be, and, on the other, a particular happiness that holds sway in actuality – can provide the basis for politicized negation, that is, a conscious unhappiness, which stands apart from the dictates of the 'happiness industry', renounces the ersatz pleasures on offer, and stands in solidarity with the suffering of others for as long we remain *this* side (i.e. the wrong side) of revolutionary transformation. This is what a critical theory can offer us amid the perpetual catastrophe that constitutes our contemporary moment.

Of course, developing a critical perspective is not as straightforward as it sounds. To coin a phrase, one is not born 'critical'. The process of socialization tends towards successful adaptation and internalization of existing norms, protocols, and procedures. The default setting for interaction tends to be to go with the flow, to follow the line of least resistance, to accept pre-established definitions and modes of behaviour so as to 'fit in' and keep things moving. As Lauren Berlant writes, our 'epistemological self-attachment is all bound up with literacy in normativity, and their relation constitutes the commonsense measure of trust in the world's ongoingness and our competence at being humans'.[80] The mere threat of being othered or ousted, of being subjected to the numerous pains of separation, classification, and exclusion, of being seen as a 'drag' (on one's family, circle of friends, community, society, the economy), is often sufficient in itself to guarantee a minimal degree of conformity.

This is why the development of a 'critical' perspective is likely to be some-thing of a formidable and laborious, even risky, undertaking.[81] It is unlikely to be a smooth and comfortable process, since it necessarily entails a consider-able amount of re-education. A critical perspective might be best understood as a dual process of learning and unlearning: we learn new ways of relating to and perceiving the extant world at the same time as we unlearn the most entrenched, habitual, and preordained forms of life. In proto-dialectical fash-ion, the polarities of the healthy and the sick can be inverted and subjected to critique. Pathologizing the norm and de-pathologizing the sick becomes an effective way of revealing the furtive violence and disciplinary practices of the apparently 'healthy' and 'happy'. In this way, one can shed light on the many exclusions and exceptions on which such norms rest, undoing the socially sanctioned self and reappraising the values and forces that give rise to the dominant models and symbols of successful adaptation.

This process of re-education or learning/unlearning can be seen as one of the underlying forces of Adorno's critical theory, whose restless negativism (or conscious unhappiness) represents a steadfast disavowal of capitalism and its parodies of happiness. Like Benjamin, Adorno's self-proclaimed 'melancholy science', from which emerge his varied reflections on and from 'damaged life', is at once visceral and thoughtful, affective and cognitive, mournful and hope-ful, constructive and destructive. The complex character of Adorno's critical theory derives in part from the purposively liminal standpoint from which his critique emerges. This marginal position is at once close enough to its object to understand the latter's appeal, and yet sufficiently distanced from it so as to maintain a critical space and tension.[82] Adorno refers to such a position of marginality in a number of places. For instance, he writes of the 'distanced nearness'[83] of the 'dialectical critic of culture', who must 'both participate in culture and not participate'.[84] Meanwhile, elsewhere he notes: 'Repudiation of the present cultural morass presupposes sufficient involvement in it to feel it itching in one's finger-tips, so to speak, but at the same time the strength, drawn from this involvement, to dismiss it.'[85] But his critical theory also takes its lead from the propulsion of the negative, that is to say, the force of the non-identical, that which evades our present thinking and concepts. Hence Adorno's distinctive form of dialectics, which remains *negative* through and through.

On the face of it, all this talk of negativism and marginality does little to alter the prevailing image of Adorno as an extremely pessimistic thinker.[86] Critics of his work have long since argued that it is unduly totalizing, that his vision of the social world is irredeemably bleak and allows no room for analytical nuance, let alone political intervention. As a result of this militant negativism, so the argument runs, Adorno fails to recognize the divergent and potentially oppositional encounters that occur within mainstream culture and politics. In this vein, detractors often conjure up the figure of a cultural mandarin to characterize Adorno as being both elitist and anti-democratic, forever exalting the 'difficult', esoteric, and 'high' culture of aesthetic modernism, while deriding all pre-digested, 'low' popular culture.[87] These criticisms will be familiar enough to many readers. Such debates have been commonplace both within and beyond the confines of universities for some time. It is worth rehearsing them here if only to note the ways in which these criticisms of Adorno's work, especially those aimed at his 'culture industry thesis', end up mirroring the (neo)liberal individualism that has become so hegemonic since the political-economic shift to a 'consumer society' (or, if you prefer, 'post-industrialism', 'post-Fordism', etc.). The common charges against Adorno are usually couched in an egalitarian claim to inclusivity, pluralism, anti-elitism, and so on. But this invariably morphs into a passive defence of *what is* over against *what might be*, or even *what could have been but was not*. In a more mischievous manner, one could even argue that such positions stem from a failure to relinquish existing ideas about happiness, pleasure, and enjoyment – ideas that are deeply embedded in and heavily distorted by the dominant forms of social life, or what could otherwise be called the totality of capital.

If one of the bastardized tropes of postmodernism, at least insofar as it has filtered into mainstream consciousness, can be seen as an attempt to elevate commodified culture on the basis of its unending diversity and receptive pliability, then this runs the risk of boomeranging into a pacifying relativism that effectively closes down any substantive debate over the content and formal qualities of particular objects, the conditions of cultural production, curation, reception, and so forth. Correspondingly, values become simply a matter of individual 'taste', and as such are placed outside of the demands of social legitimation and political contestation.[88] Robert Hullot-Kentor has aptly described this state of affairs in relation to aesthetic judgement:

> Though we insist on having our preferences and consider the freedom to like and dislike inherent in democracy, these preferences are limited to the judgment itself. Whatever we find to like in an art gallery, we assume someone else might, with equal justification, dislike. Conversely, what someone else likes, we might just as well, and with equal justification, dislike. In the morality of our everyday aesthetics, what is important to us is that we have our likes and dislikes, and at any moment be ready to call a truce over the objective claim of a distinction in value.[89]

For critical theory, then, the judgements entailed in cultural expressions and experiences cannot be condensed into an apolitical aesthetics based on personal inclination and subjective taste. This is because aesthetics – even at its most abstract and esoteric – is suffused with social import. Adorno's rejection of relativism in aesthetics is bound up with (one could almost say that it stems from) the concept of happiness. Indeed, on Adorno's account, it is art alone that sustains what Stendhal called the 'promise of happiness' (*promesse du bonheur*), although a paradox immediately flows from this – namely, that art can only make good on this promissory note by consistently breaching it:

> Stendhal's dictum of art as the *promesse du bonheur* implies that art does its part for existence by accentuating what in it prefigures utopia. But this utopic element is constantly decreasing, while existence increasingly becomes merely self-equivalent. For this reason art is ever less able to make itself like existence. Because all happiness found in the status quo is an ersatz and false, art must break its promise in order to stay true to it.[90]

This passage echoes a similar one in *Negative Dialectics*: 'From the start, whatever happiness is intermittently tolerated or granted by the existing entirety bears the marks of its own particularity. To this day, all happiness is a pledge of what has not yet been, and the belief in its imminence obstructs its becoming.'[91] Behind this radical undermining of extant forms of happiness is a deliberate provocation. As in Benjamin, this can be read as a provocation aimed squarely at the mythology surrounding the liberal (bourgeois) subject.

As we have seen, the claims made on behalf of happiness carry with them a combination of economic, moral, and normative imperatives. The prevalence of a 'positive psychology' that presumes happiness to be attainable through self-directed behavioural modification, and the commodities and practices with which happiness becomes associated, has the effect of divesting experience of its social and historical content. All that remains is narcissistic self-help whose stark message is the following: you will live a better and more fulfilling life if you start out by cultivating a happier personality and a more positive disposition. Recalling Van Rompuy's letter to all world leaders with which this chapter began, positivity is believed to be a good – not only in the sense of a virtuous personal trait, but also as a commodity in itself with a high market value. By contrast, Adorno is unwilling to privatize the notion of happiness, making it simply reducible to the manifold tastes and predilections of individuals who have been set apart from one another like atoms within a system of universal antagonism: 'the fixation of one's own need and one's own longing mars the idea of a happiness that will not arise until the category of the individual ceases to be self-seclusive'.[92] He continues by claiming that a genuine happiness 'would be nothing short of deliverance from particularity as a general principle irreconcilable with individual human happiness here and now'.[93]

This move recalls the potential for radical de-subjectification that Benjamin locates in melancholia. Indeed, Adorno too, in working to dethrone the subject from its constitutive majesty, socializes the very idea of (un)happiness. He holds fast to the vital connection between aesthetics and happiness precisely because aesthetic experience 'breaks through the spell of obstinate self-preservation; it is the model of a stage of consciousness in which the I no longer has its happiness in its interests or, ultimately, in its reproduction'.[94] As such, there is a latent political power within what might appear at first to be a melancholic renunciation or shattering of the self. Breaking the spell of self-preservation, refusing to preserve the self as constituted by a capitalist social formation, might then be read as the desire that would rather destroy that which holds sway in reality than endure the ignominy of adapting oneself to such a deformed reality. To this end, every neurotic thought or feeling, rather than being catalogued and pathologized, is instead telescopically viewed through the social whole. Thus, even in the most ostensibly personal and autobiographical moments of critical reflection – such as those contained in the dense aphorisms collected in *Minima Moralia* – Adorno turns to the micrological detail as a dialectical method of revealing the constellation of social forces that unavoidably shape each individual life.

This critique is also notable for how it feeds off Adorno's misgivings over the protocols of behavioural psychology and the latter's renunciation of wider social and political phenomena. This is not to say that he advocates the dichotomous thinking that would posit the social on the one hand, and psychology on the other. Such a position would be insufficiently dialectical, and, moreover, would seem to theoretically smooth over practical antagonisms by holding each realm in a mutually independent, that is, unmediated condition. In taking into account the simultaneity of the micrological and the macrological, Adorno's critical theory steers a path between the Scylla of naive subjectivism and the Charybdis of abstract sociologism. For Adorno, the separation of society and psyche 'perpetuates conceptually the split between the living subject and the objectivity that governs the subjects and yet derives from them'.[95] The final part of this claim is crucial for it reinserts the dialectical moment into the critique of psychological explanation, safeguarding against any cursory dismissal of psychic life while at the same time placing the psychological within the sphere of social life.

Adorno readily acknowledges the value of psychological concepts to social and political thought, as when he writes: 'Without psychology, in which the objective constraints are continually internalized anew, it would be impossible to understand how people passively accept a state of unchanging destructive irrationality.'[96] (Such an understanding of how internalization of capital's 'destructive irrationality' persists is of significant import for any critique of ideology.) However, in the very same paragraph, Adorno goes on to note that such psychological motivations cannot be strictly read as *causes*. Rather, such psychological effects merely result from and in response to 'objective obstacles'.[97] Indeed, the very first line of the cited passage states: 'The objective theory of society, in as much as society is an autonomous totality confronting living individuals, has priority over psychology.'[98] Thus, while Adorno unquestionably takes influence from Freud and gives much of his scholarly attention to psychoanalytical concepts – most notably repression, ego-weakness, narcissism, and internalization – the Frankfurt theorist can be said to ultimately relegate psychological approaches, at least at the level of analysing thoroughly *social* phenomena. For Adorno, the latter should be prioritized in theory, for they hold sway in reality.

The refocusing and broadening of this critical perspective seeks to locate the failings of existing society at the macro level, and reignite interest in the earlier and more far-reaching psychoanalytic aim of bringing unconscious forces to light. According to Adorno, this original aim of treatment has been neglected or rather supplanted by the theoretical models proposed by social psychologists (in his time, these included Erich Fromm and Karen Horney). In the process, the more radical premises of Freudian psychoanalysis – which hold out no inherent promise for resolution, but rather emphasize greater self-knowledge as to the foundations of psychic suffering, the repressive features of the civilizing process, the unruly energies of libido, and so on – are revised in a more openly 'progressive' light, so that the primary function of social psychology becomes successful (re)integration of individuals (back) into society.

In today's context, this integrationist model remains pervasive and is especially noticeable in the fact that cognitive behavioural therapy (CBT) and modifications thereof (for example, in the more popularized manner of 'mindfulness') have become the therapeutic norm within mental health provision. Since it is 'cost-effective', short-term, and easily administered (often being delivered via the internet or take-home CD-ROM), with techniques that are held to be universally applicable and subject to crude methods of empirical verification, CBT is highly attractive to governments and companies alike whose primary aim is to maximize economic productivity at all costs. Unsurprisingly, such treatments give inadequate attention to social and environmental causes.

Treatment is seen to be positive and effective when the individual is able to adapt to and be optimally productive in their current environment. Not a moment's pause is given to the hugely detrimental effects of the organization of social production and consumption under capitalism. The point is simply to rehabilitate any aberrant individuals and leave aside all socio-political considerations.[99]

This rather uncritical position, which lends psychological insight a purely functionalist bent, is anathema to Adorno's brand of critical theory as enumerated in multiple instances. In a note from the writing of *Dialectic of Enlightenment*, he writes: 'Where psychology has to be called in to explain human beings they are already disordered ... To resort to psychology in order to understand one's fellow man is an effrontery.'[100] In 'Education After Auschwitz', he argues that the 'recurrence or nonrecurrence of fascism in its decisive aspect is not a question of psychology, but of society'.[101] In the essay 'Sociology and Psychology', he writes: 'All varieties of psychologism that simply take the individual as their point of departure are ideological.'[102] In a critique of sociologist Karl Mannheim, Adorno notes how, in the activities carried out under the banner of the 'sociology of knowledge', the 'growth of antagonisms is elegantly described as "the disproportionate development of human capacities", as though it were a question of personalities and not of the anonymous machinery which does away with the individual'.[103] Most forthrightly of all, a cantankerous Adorno (prefiguring much of Woody Allen's oeuvre) flatly states: 'therapists are frauds'.[104]

At this juncture, the true scope of Adorno's conscious unhappiness (as social critique) becomes clear. One needs to retain the theoretical preponderance of the totality, and work to uncover the objective social forces that demand the problematic responses which psychoanalysis tries to diagnose and treat. At the affective core of early critical theory, the pursuit of happiness is not seen as a matter of individual indulgence, pleasure, or freedom; rather, it is only pursuable as a collective desire for emancipation. If the route towards the latter proves aporetic, or necessitates a militant unhappiness against false reconciliation, then that in itself should at least provide a modicum of solace to those fighting for a better life for all. The point at which critical thought stays faithful to its potential for emancipation is when it refuses to offer easy comforts or compromises, and instead aims to bring extant unhappiness to full consciousness of itself. In so doing, it remains possible to refute the (by now) default Fukuyaman position, whereby liberal-democratic capitalism and its myopic individualism is seen as the summit of human achievement. One of critical theory's lasting virtues is that it not only gives voice to a strong sense of unhappiness and discontent, but also consciously marshals this feeling so as to energize and politicize its readers.

Notes

1 Walter Benjamin, 'Theses on the Philosophy of History', in *Illuminations*, ed. Hannah Arendt, trans. Harry Zohn (Suffolk: Fontana, 1973), 257.

2 www.telegraph.co.uk/news/newstopics/howaboutthat/11473418/Songs-to-make-you-happy-compiled-by-the-United-Nations.html.

3 www.actionforhappiness.org.

4 In doing so, the UK is attempting to follow in the footsteps of Bhutan, which has an official Gross National Happiness (GNH) index, whose principles otherwise stand in stark contrast to those of the UK, based as they are on equitable social development, cultural preservation, conservation of the environment, and the promotion of good governance. Indeed, it is hard to imagine how a government committed to brutal austerity economics can at the same time promote a happier citizenry.

5 William Davies, *The Happiness Industry: How the Government and Big Business Sold Us Well-Being* (London: Verso, 2015).

6 The majority of this section on the history of melancholy broadly follows the trajectory outlined by Jennifer Radden. See Radden, *The Nature of Melancholy: From Aristotle to Freud* (Oxford: Oxford University Press, 2000), and *Moody Minds Distempered: Essays on Melancholy and Depression* (Oxford: Oxford University Press, 2009). For a more recent account that corroborates Radden's findings, see Clark Lawlor, *From Melancholia to Prozac: A History of Depression* (Oxford: Oxford University Press, 2012).

7 See Ahmed, *The Promise of Happiness* (Durham, NC: Duke University Press, 2010).

8 Radden, *The Nature of Melancholy*, 15.

9 See Lawrence Babb, *The Elizabethan Malady: A Study of Melancholia in English Literature from 1580 to 1642* (East Lansing: Michigan State University Press, 1965).

10 Radden, *The Nature of Melancholy*, 10.

11 Sigmund Freud, 'Mourning and Melancholia', in *The Standard Edition of the Complete Psychological Works of Sigmund Freud*, Vol. 14, ed. James Strachey (London: The Hogarth Press, 1963), 243.

12 Freud, 'Mourning and Melancholia', 243.

13 As Jonathan Flatley points out, Freud's pathologization of melancholia significantly diverges from the prominent physiological theories of the time (particularly Kraepelin's). In positing the failure to mourn a loss as the root cause of melancholia, Freud shifts the basis of melancholic experience from the biological and natural realm to the psychic realm. In this way, his intervention transforms melancholia into a particular kind of psychic object relation; Jonathan Flatley, *Affective Mapping: Melancholia and the Politics of Modernism* (Cambridge, MA: Harvard University Press, 2008), 42. This apparent shift proved a vital catalyst in the subsequent development of the 'Object Relations' school of psychoanalysis (especially as elaborated by the likes of Ronald Fairbairn, Melanie Klein, and Donald Winnicott).

14 Freud, 'Mourning and Melancholia', 244.

15 Freud, 'Mourning and Melancholia', 247. This suggestion of the splitting of the ego is a major theoretical development in Freud's work. It anticipates his later, more refined concepts of the *ego-ideal* [*Ich-Ideal*] and, ultimately, the *superego* [*Über-Ich*].

16 Freud, 'Mourning and Melancholia', 245.

17 Freud, 'Mourning and Melancholia', 245.

18 Ahmed, *The Promise of Happiness*, 140.

19 Freud, 'Mourning and Melancholia', 246.

20 In describing his seminal conception of *habitus*, Pierre Bourdieu says that it consists of 'durable, transposable *dispositions*, structured structures predisposed to function as structuring structures, that is, as principles of the generation and structuring of practices and representations which can be objectively "regulated" and "regular" without in any way being the product of obedience to rules, objectively adapted to their goals without presupposing a conscious aiming at ends or an express mastery of the operations necessary to attain them'; Pierre Bourdieu, *Outline of a Theory of Practice*, trans. Richard Nice (Cambridge: Cambridge University Press, 1977), 72. The notion of habitus, then, encompasses the predominant ways in which we can act, perceive, and interpret the world. It is the social written into the body; it is society embodied.

21 Walter Benjamin, 'Left-Wing Melancholy', in *Walter Benjamin: Selected Writings, 1931–1934,* Vol. 2, Part 2, ed. Howard Eiland, Michael W. Jennings, and Gary Smith (Cambridge, MA: Belknap Press, 2005), 427.

22 Walter Benjamin, 'Agesilaus Santander', cited in Gershom Scholem, 'Walter Benjamin and His Angel', in *On Jews and Judaism in Crisis*, ed. Werner J. Dannhauser (New York: Schocken Books, 1976), 207.

23 Biographical treatments include: Howard Eiland and Michael W. Jennings, *Walter Benjamin: A Critical Life* (Cambridge, MA: Belknap Press, 2014); Esther Leslie, *Walter Benjamin: Critical Lives* (London: Reaktion Books, 2007); Momme Brodersen, *Walter Benjamin: A Biography* (London: Verso, 1996); Gershom Scholem, *Walter Benjamin: The Story of a Friendship* (New York: Review Books, 1981); Bernd Witte, *Walter Benjamin: An Intellectual Biography*, trans. James Rolleston (Detroit: Wayne University Press, 1991); Erdmut Wizisla, *Walter Benjamin and Bertolt Brecht: The Story of a Friendship* (London: Libris, 2009).

24 Theodor W. Adorno, 'Introduction to Benjamin's *Schriften*', in *On Walter Benjamin: Critical Essays and Recollections*, ed. Gary Smith (Cambridge, MA: MIT Press, 1988), 15.

25 Theodor W. Adorno, *Prisms*, trans. Samuel and Sherry Weber (Cambridge, MA: MIT Press, 1983), 229.

26 Susan Sontag, 'Introduction', in *One-Way Street and Other Writings*, by Walter Benjamin (London: New Left Books, 1979), 8.

27 Eiland and Jennings, *Walter Benjamin*, 5.

28 Esther Leslie, *Walter Benjamin: Overpowering Conformism* (London: Pluto, 2000), vii.

29 Max Pensky, *Melancholy Dialectics: Walter Benjamin and the Play of Mourning* (Amherst: University of Massachusetts Press, 1993), 18.

30 Arendt, 'Introduction', in *Illuminations*, by Walter Benjamin, 22.

31 Witte, *Walter Benjamin*, 62.

32 Beatrice Hanssen, 'Portrait of Melancholy (Benjamin, Warburg, Panofsky)', *MLN* 114 (1999): 992.

33 Historically, self-loathing or self-reproach has only a tenuous association with melancholia. It is only with the advent of Freud's seminal essay of 1917 that such features become significant to the pathology of the melancholic. They still remain central to contemporary diagnoses of melancholia and depression. Radden, *Moody Minds Distempered*, 161.

34 Pensky, *Melancholy Dialectics*, 175–6.

35 Benjamin, 'Left-Wing Melancholy', 424.

36 Benjamin, 'Left-Wing Melancholy', 425.

37 Benjamin, 'Left-Wing Melancholy', 426.

38 Benjamin, 'Left-Wing Melancholy', 426.

39 Benjamin, 'Left-Wing Melancholy', 424.

40 Hanssen, 'Portrait of Melancholy', 1002. Interestingly, Benjamin's melancholic method appears to stand in contrast to the progressivist philosophies of modernity. Recall the centrality of the purposeful overcoming of the past engendered in the modern philosophies of Hegel, Kierkegaard, Marx, Nietzsche, and Freud. For Benjamin, by contrast, the melancholic represents a cultural-historical hoarder for whom no item or fragment is deemed so insignificant that it escapes the social conditions of both its origins and its observation.

41 Pensky, *Melancholy Dialectics*, 164. This steadfast act of melancholic retrieval has attracted renewed interest in the calls for 'militant mourning' evidenced in more recent theory (e.g. Derrida, Butler), as a refusal to 'move on' and in the process sacrifice the vanquished (and the memory thereof) for the expedience of the status quo. It is truly regrettable that many political actors and states still refuse to consider, let alone admit, any complicity for past events. An example that springs to mind is David Cameron's comments following Jamaica's claims to reparations for the UK's historical involvement in slavery. In response to the claims, Cameron remarked: 'That the Caribbean has emerged from the long shadow it [slavery] cast is testament to the resilience and spirit of its people. I acknowledge that these wounds run very deep indeed. But I do hope that, as friends who have gone through so much together since those darkest of times, we can move on from this painful legacy and continue to build for the future.' www.theguardian.com/world/2015/sep/30/jamaica-should-move-on-from-painful-legacy-of-slavery-says-cameron.

42 Adorno, *Prisms*, 235.

43 Pensky, *Melancholy Dialectics*, 171–2.

44 Walter Benjamin, 'Central Park', *New German Critique* 34 (Winter 1985): 42.

45 Gershom Scholem, *On Jews and Judaism in Crisis: Selected Essays*, ed. Werner J. Dannhauser (New York: Schocken Books, 1976), 194–5.

46 Benjamin, 'Central Park', 39.

47 Walter Benjamin, 'The Destructive Character', in *Reflections*, ed. Peter Demetz, trans. Edmund Jephcott (New York: Schocken Books, 2007), 301–3. Irving Wohlfarth has analysed this aphoristic and provocative text of 1931 in Wohlfarth, 'No Man's Land: On Walter Benjamin's "The Destructive Character"', *Diacritics* 8/2 (1978): 47–65.

48 Pensky, *Melancholy Dialectics*, 61.

49 Hanssen, 'Portrait of Melancholy', 1003.

50 Pensky, *Melancholy Dialectics*, 62.

51 This methodological touchstone is something that Benjamin's work shares with the likes of Bloch, Lukács, and Adorno, all of whom sought in various ways to challenge the neo-Kantian philosophies of autonomous subjectivity. The latter, expressed in the works of Hermann Cohen, Paul Natorp, Ernst Cassirer, Heinrich Rickert, and F.A. Lange among others, were hugely influential throughout the second half of the nineteenth century and into the early twentieth century. For a critique of neo-Kantianism, see Gillian Rose, *Hegel Contra Sociology* (London: Athlone Press, 1985), though Rose is also critical of what she takes to be neo-Kantian vestiges lurking in the thought of Lukács and Adorno.

52 Adorno, *Prisms*, 234.

53 Hanssen, 'Portrait of Melancholy', 1003. It is worth remembering that Freud would later struggle to maintain a clear delineation between melancholia and mourning, admitting a degree of symptomatological overlap.

54 Flatley, *Affective Mapping*, 2–3.

55 Benjamin, cited in Pensky, *Melancholy Dialectics*, 189.

56 This sense of the creaturely, fleshly nature of melancholic insight, that neverthe-less reaches supraindividual heights, recalls older cosmological readings of Saturn, which, as Benjamin notes by way of citing Jacopo della Lana, 'by virtue of its qual-ity as an earthly, cold, and dry planet, gives birth to totally material men … but, in absolute contrast, by virtue of its position as the highest of the planets it gives birth to the most extremely spiritual *religiosi contemplativi*, one who turns his back on all earthly life'; Walter Benjamin, *The Origin of German Tragic Drama*, trans. John Osborne (London: Verso, 2003), 150.

57 'To win the energies of intoxication for the revolution – this is the project about which Surrealism circles in all its books and enterprises'; Walter Benjamin, 'Surrealism: The Last Snapshot of the European Intelligentsia', in *Reflections*, ed. Peter Demetz, trans. Edmund Jephcott (New York: Schocken Books, 2007), 189.

58 For more on Benjamin's relation to Surrealism, see: Pensky, *Melancholy Dialectics*, 184–210; and Richard Wolin, 'Benjamin, Adorno, Surrealism', in *The Semblance of Subjectivity*, ed. Tom Huhn and Lambert Zuidervaart (Cambridge, MA: MIT Press, 1997), 93–122.

59 Pensky comments on the unresolved contradiction: 'For Benjamin's frozen dialectic, no less than for Hegel's dialectic of absolute motion, contradiction fuels speculation but inflicts pain. Melancholy insights into the images of reconciliation threaten that mythologizing moment in which the source of pain is transmuted from concrete historical conditions to "existence" as such. Happiness, the moment of missing contradiction, is both as intimate and as utterly alien to the melancholy mind as the permanently withheld antithesis'; Pensky, *Melancholy Dialectics*, 17.

60 Hanssen, 'Portrait of Melancholy', 1003.

61 Benjamin, 'Theses on the Philosophy of History', 257.

62 My main concern in this section has been to purposively appropriate and reconfig-ure a form of critique that positively claims melancholia as an entry point to such theory and practice. For much of its history, even if it was seen to offer occasional flashes of insight, melancholia has been a designation (or diagnosis) conferred upon certain individuals by authorities as a way of pre-emptively immunizing the social order against criticism. Sara Ahmed comments on this trend: 'But if we judge oth-ers to be melancholic, do we know what they are missing? Or does melancholia become a judgment against others by the very idea that they are missing some-thing when they speak of their loss? Rather than assuming others are melancholic because they have failed to let go of an object that has been lost, I want to consider melancholia as a way of reading or diagnosing others as having "lost something" … To diagnose melancholia would become a way of declaring that their love objects are dead. Others would be judged as melancholic because they have failed to give up on objects that we have declared dead *on their behalf*.' Ahmed, *The Promise of Happiness*, 140–1.

63 Benjamin, 'Theses on the Philosophy of History', 258.

64 This line is from *Le Grand Jeu*, a Surrealist text of 1928, edited by Gilbert-Lecomte, Daumal, Vaillant, and Sima; cited in Maurice Nadeau, *Histoire du surrealisme* (Paris: Editions du Seuil, 1964), 123–4.

65 Theodor W. Adorno, *Negative Dialectics*, trans. E.B. Ashton (New York: Continuum, 1973), 353.

66 Recall Adorno's important yet often overlooked comment: 'to act radically in accord-ance with this principle [i.e. construing culture as pure ideology] would be to

extirpate, with the false, all that was true also, all that, however impotently, strives to escape the confines of universal practice … To identify culture with lies is more fateful than ever, now that the former is really becoming totally absorbed by the latter, and eagerly invites such identification in order to compromise every opposing thought'; Adorno, *Minima Moralia: Reflections on a Damaged Life*, trans. Edmund Jephcott (London: Verso, 2005), 44.

67 Karl Marx, *Grundrisse: Foundations of Political Economy*, trans. Martin Nicolaus (New York: Vintage, 1973), 159.

68 Sara Ahmed provides an indicative litany of texts that have contributed to this turn to happiness; see Ahmed, *The Promise of Happiness*, 3–7.

69 Davies, *The Happiness Industry*.

70 Richard Layard, *Happiness: Lessons from a New Science* (London: Penguin, 2006), 5–6.

71 This demonization of discontent is also expressed in the mainstream media through a stifling politics of 'respectability', which merely serves as a cover for reinforcing established norms. For example, radical feminists and queer critics of both heteronormativity and homonormativity are often depicted as 'killjoys', while many Black Lives Matter activists are depicted as angry, uncivil, and as such unconducive to liberal 'debate' and a threat to 'free speech'. For more on the figures of the 'feminist killjoy', the 'angry black woman', and the 'unhappy queer', see Ahmed, *The Promise of Happiness*.

72 This might go some way towards explaining the fact that despite reported increases in overall quality of life and income, the evidence suggests that most people in Western societies are reportedly no happier now as compared to fifty years ago; Layard, *Happiness*, 3.

73 Adorno, *Negative Dialectics*, 6.

74 G.W.F. Hegel, *Phenomenology of Spirit*, trans. A.V. Miller (Oxford: Oxford University Press, 1977), 10.

75 G.W.F. Hegel, *Lectures on the Philosophy of World History*, trans. H.B. Nisbet (Cambridge: Cambridge University Press, 1975), 78–9.

76 Karl Marx, 'The Poverty of Philosophy', in *Karl Marx: Selected Writings*, ed. David McLellan (Oxford: Oxford University Press, 2000), 227.

77 Marx, 'The Poverty of Philosophy', 213. For an interesting account of Hegelian thought in this regard, see Robyn Marasco, *The Highway of Despair: Critical Theory After Hegel* (New York: Columbia University Press, 2015).

78 Michael Löwy, 'Naphta or Settembrini? Lukács and Romantic Anticapitalism', in *George Lukács: Theory, Culture, and Politics*, ed. Judith Marcus and Zoltán Tarr (New Brunswick: Transaction, 1989), 189. Löwy offers an intricate account of the complex development of Lukács's own work in relation to the concept of romantic anti-capitalism.

79 As Marx vividly puts it, capital comes into the world 'dripping from head to toe, from every pore, with blood and dirt'; Marx, *Capital: A Critique of Political Economy*, Vol. 1, trans. Ben Fowkes (Harmondsworth: Penguin, 1976), 925–6.

80 Lauren Berlant, *Cruel Optimism* (Durham, NC: Duke University Press, 2011), 52.

81 The idea that the process of becoming critical is neither simple nor painless is not accounted for within recent calls for 'post-critical' thinking. This is perhaps unsurprising given that the latter start out from the dubious claim that 'we' (by which they mean primarily university-educated denizens of the capitalist core) are all critical now, as if a critical methodology has become hegemonic to the point of suffocation. See Chapter 1 for more on the 'post-critical' and its limitations.

82 In this regard, there might be something to be said, after all, for the concept of the *guilty pleasure*. Insofar as it registers a complexity of feeling and self-consciousness that gestures beyond the experience or act of consumption, the guilty pleasure sustains if not discloses the inadequacies of certain forms of social and cultural practice. The simultaneous feeling of guilt and pleasure means that each serves to undo and sublate the other. As two sides of a potentially productive dialectic, guilt and pleasure contaminate one another, prompting recognition of their underlying associations and unresolved contradictions.

83 Adorno, *Minima Moralia*, 90. Contrast this to the 'false nearness' that arises from people's enforced proximity; Adorno, *Minima Moralia*, 173.

84 Adorno, *Prisms*, 33.

85 Adorno, *Minima Moralia*, 29.

86 The following descriptions are just some examples of this dominant view: 'a deepening pessimism' (Martin Jay, *The Dialectical Imagination: A History of the Frankfurt School and the Institute of Social Research, 1923–1950* (London: Heinemann, 1973), 107); 'tragic pessimism' (Paul Connerton, *The Tragedy of Enlightenment: An Essay on the Frankfurt School* (Cambridge: Cambridge University Press, 1980), 119); 'bleak pessimism' (Tom Bottomore, *The Frankfurt School and Its Critics* (London: Routledge, 2002), 37); 'implacable pessimism' (Steven Vogel, *Against Nature: The Concept of Nature in Critical Theory* (New York: SUNY, 1996), 101); 'starkly pessimistic' (Oliver Bennett, *Cultural Pessimism: Narratives of Decline in the Postmodern World* (Edinburgh: Edinburgh University Press, 2001), 3); 'Adorno's gloom' (Ben Agger, *The Discourse of Domination: From the Frankfurt School to Postmodernism* (Evanston: Northwestern University Press, 1992), 12); 'so gloomy and pessimistic' (Ingolfur Blühdorn, *Post-Ecologist Politics: Social Theory and the Abdication of the Ecologist Paradigm* (London: Routledge, 2000), 80). In all instances, these descriptions precede a critique of Adorno's pessimism as unwarranted, problematic, and unhelpful to socio-political practice. Gillian Rose has cogently argued that negative dialectics is 'not a pessimistic science', since it 'rejects any dichotomy such as optimistic/pessimistic'; Gillian Rose, *The Melancholy Science: An Introduction to the Thought of Theodor W. Adorno* (New York: Columbia University Press, 1978), ix.

87 Critics taking this line of attack include Jim Collins and Douglas Kellner. It is also worth noting that early methodological outlines for research activity at the CCCS in Birmingham were to a large extent designed in direct opposition to the perceived totalizations and proverbial dead-ends of the Frankfurt School's cultural theory, even if the Centre's intellectual engagement with critical theory is minimal. To my knowledge, only one paper examining the relevance of critical theory to culture was ever produced under the banner of the CCCS. The paper from 1974, authored by Phil Slater and entitled 'The Aesthetic Theory of the Frankfurt School', contains a cursory dismissal of Adorno, reasserting the by now commonplace claim that the latter's overly deterministic view of the manipulated masses at the whim of an omnipotent culture industry signals the irrelevance of his critical theory. Needless to say, the current chapter aims to overturn this verdict and bring to light the political and affective valences in critical theory (and indeed in the work of its detractors).

88 The definitive critical-sociological account of taste, which shows the latter to be anything but innocent or unpredictable, is still Pierre Bourdieu's *Distinction: A Social Critique of the Judgement of Taste*, trans. Richard Nice (Abingdon: Routledge, 2010).

89 Robert Hullot-Kentor, 'Right Listening and a New Type of Human Being', in *The Cambridge Companion to Adorno*, ed. Tom Huhn (Cambridge: Cambridge University Press, 2004), 182. Adorno decries 'shoulder-shrugging aesthetic relativism' as 'reified consciousness'; Theodor W. Adorno, *Aesthetic Theory*, trans. Robert Hullot-Kentor (London: Continuum, 2004), 362.

90 Adorno, *Aesthetic Theory*, 393.

91 Adorno, *Negative Dialectics*, 352.

92 Adorno, *Negative Dialectics*, 352.

93 Adorno, *Negative Dialectics*, 353.

94 Adorno, *Aesthetic Theory*, 439.

95 Theodor W. Adorno, 'Sociology and Psychology' (Part 1), *New Left Review* 1/46 (1967): 69.

96 Theodor W. Adorno, 'Marginalia to Theory and Praxis', in *Critical Models: Interventions and Catchwords*, ed. and trans. Henry W. Pickford (New York: Columbia University Press, 1998), 271.

97 Adorno, 'Marginalia to Theory and Praxis', 271. Alfred Sohn-Rethel makes a similar claim when showing how action in exchange is social, while the mind is private: 'The principles which concern us here belong to the form of interrelation of commodity exchange, not to the psychology of the individuals involved. It is rather this form that moulds the psychological mechanisms of the people whose lives it rules – mechanisms which they then conceive of as inborn, human nature'; Alfred Sohn-Rethel, *Intellectual and Manual Labour: A Critique of Epistemology* (Basingstoke: Macmillan, 1978), 42.

98 Adorno, 'Marginalia to Theory and Praxis', 270.

99 Ernst Bloch notes that at the time of the Great Depression, a Viennese psychoanalytic centre displayed a sign above its door, which read: 'Economic and social questions cannot be treated here'; Ernst Bloch, *The Principle of Hope*, Vol. 1, trans. Neville Plaice, Stephen Plaice, and Paul Knight (Cambridge, MA: MIT Press, 1995), 66.

100 Theodor W. Adorno and Max Horkheimer, *Dialectic of Enlightenment*, trans. John Cumming (London: Verso, 1997), 246.

101 Theodor W. Adorno, 'Education After Auschwitz', in *Critical Models: Interventions and Catchwords*, ed. and trans. Henry W. Pickford (New York: Columbia University Press, 1998), 194.

102 Adorno, 'Sociology and Psychology' (Part 1), 77.

103 Adorno, *Prisms*, 35. It is interesting to note a parallel here in relation to how, amid the fallout from the financial crisis of 2008, certain individuals were exposed and depicted as 'evil', aberrations, high stakes criminals, greedy speculators, and so forth. But is not the more salient point that an *entire system* failed, showing itself to be not only unstable and corruptible, but also unsustainable? It is simplistic to characterize individuals (such as Bernie Madoff) as eccentric or excessive, for this forestalls deeper *systemic* analysis of the political-economic conditions that produce cyclical crises. Projecting collective discontent onto a small number of individuals who merely represent the falsity of a total system is a sure way of re-establishing 'normality' with minimal disruption. Adorno makes a similar criticism in relation to the depiction of film villains: 'Even if [brutal businessmen] were thereby revealed as monstrous characters, their monstrousness would still be sanctioned as a quality of individual human beings in a way that would tend to obscure the monstrousness of the system whose servile functionaries they are'; Theodor W. Adorno, 'The Schema of Mass Culture', in *The Culture Industry: Selected Essays*

on Mass Culture, ed. J.M. Bernstein, trans. N. Walker (London: Routledge, 2001), 66. The 2015 film, *The Big Short*, also falls short in this regard, insofar as it focuses on the actions of individual banks, traders, and ratings agencies, overlooking the inherent contradictions that make finance capital prone to crisis and, in terms of value, a zero-sum game.

104 Adorno, 'Sociology and Psychology' (Part 1), 78. Incidentally, there is a rather Adornian moment in *Annie Hall*, when the titular character admonishes Alvy Singer for his inability to enjoy life, to which Alvy replies: 'I can't enjoy anything unless everybody is. If one guy is starving someplace, that puts a crimp in my evening.'

3

A feeling for things: objects, affects, mimesis

And things, what is the correct attitude to adopt towards things?
– Samuel Beckett, *The Unnameable*

Recent years have seen an explosion of scholarly interest in *things*. From the 'new materialisms' to 'object-oriented ontology', from 'thing theory' to 'actor-network theory', much of contemporary thought is turning its attention to the world of objects. What are the reasons for this shift? One of the principal motivations behind the turn to objects is a reaction against the 'cultural turn' and its subject-centred, discursive, 'critical' modes of textual interpretation and constructivism. These dominant models of thinking are said to overlook the myriad ways in which non-human matter is in itself irreducibly complex, productive, vibrant, dynamic, and so on. Another reason for the proliferation of object-oriented approaches is the growing awareness of ecological threats associated with the changing climate, whose grave implications seem to dwarf the significance and figure of the human being. Indeed, such a rejection of anthropocentric perspectives and methodologies is common to most object-led theory. For the range of thinkers from various backgrounds and disciplines who have contributed to this rethinking of the object world, no longer is the object to be understood simply in contradistinction, or epistemological service, to a human subject. Rather, against the prohibitions set out by Kant, the aim of many of today's prominent thought-dispensers is precisely to think an object in- and for-itself.

This last ambition undergirds the ideas loosely collected under the banner of 'object-oriented ontology' (OOO), also known as 'speculative realism' (SR). In this chapter, I want to show how the contemporary (re)turn to objects initially serves as a useful corrective to social or political theories that fail to properly engage with the object world (this includes forms of traditional Marxism that often presume 'reification' to be a perennial evil, rather than a particular social relation). I take this as an opportunity for a timely reconstruction of early critical theory's own engagements with the object world via aesthetics and mimesis. This is most evident in Siegfried Kracauer's materialist film theory, as well as in Adorno's theories of mimetic comportment and the preponderance of the object. Drawing out the affective qualities of critical theory's relation to objects in this way not only challenges the Marxist orthodoxy that subordinates issues around objects and aesthetics; it will also serve as a rejoinder to today's self-appointed envoys for the object world. My aim is to demonstrate that despite the considerable hype surrounding its leading proponents, OOO/SR suffers from a severe political and historical deficit, rendering it a practice of passive description rather than active interpretation (let alone intervention). The work of early critical theory is shown to avoid the shortcomings evident in OOO by effectively mediating subjectivity and objectivity through aesthetics.

In order to properly situate and re-evaluate critical theory's engagement with objects, it is necessary to understand the dual dangers that accompany any theorization of objects. The first is that of excessive subjugation – evident in traditional, subject-centric political theory (including forms of orthodox Marxism). The second is that of uncritical veneration – the unbridled enthusiasm for new ontologies falls into this category. I will offer brief outlines of the two trends before more extensively examining the qualities that make critical theory a more timely and viable approach to the object world. My argument will be that despite its usual characterization as being fiercely opposed to reification in all its forms, early critical theory actually works to destabilize the categories of subject and object, especially through a rigorous defence of political aesthetics. The accents that attend critical theory's conception of reification are diverse and mobile, shifting as they go from the social (mostly pejorative) formulations to the aesthetic (mostly positive) ones.

The critique of reification and the subjugation of objects

As with other writers in the tradition of what came to be known as 'Western Marxism', the Frankfurt School has routinely been associated with a strong critique of reification. Although deriving principally from the work of Lukács (and his appropriation of certain sociological precepts from Max Weber and Georg Simmel), the critique of reification is commonplace within Marxist thought and political theory more generally. Peter Stallybrass remarks on why the critique of reification has enjoyed such ubiquity over time: 'It has become cliché to say that we should not treat people like things. But it is a cliché that misses the point. What have we done to things to have such contempt for them?'[1]

The axiomatic conceptual distinction between *people* and *things*, invariably subordinating the latter to the former, is a pervasive trope that finds its way into a whole host of political discourses, and Marxism is no exception. For political theorists in general, the conceptual split between people and things supports a conception of politics centred solely on *subjects* and *subjecthood*. To the extent that political theory engages with material conditions, it tends to do so by way of adjudicating between those conditions that are enabling and those that are constraining for human agents. Political recognition, then, is couched – even *enshrined* – in the moral, rational, and juridical discourses of subjecthood. The strict demarcation between active human subjects and passive non-human objects serves to subsume the world of things to the world of people. In this understanding, objects only achieve political or legal recognition as 'property'.[2]

But more pertinent to our immediate concerns, in what we might call the traditional Marxist critique of reification, one also finds the subjugation of objects being reinforced. Although often developed in contrast to the dominant classical liberal traditions, Marxist theory has had an inconsistent relationship to the world of objects. This inconsistency can be traced to its textual roots.

In the *Economic and Philosophical Manuscripts of 1844*, the young Marx criticizes private property, which has, as he puts it, 'made us so stupid and one-sided that an object is only ours when we have it, when it exists for us as capital or when we directly possess, eat, drink, wear, inhabit it, etc., in short, when we *use* it'. He continues: 'all the physical and intellectual senses have been replaced by the simple estrangement of all these senses – the sense of *having*'.[3] But this early (humanistic) critique of private property and possessive object relations evolves into a more generalized, systemic, critique of reification, revealing an antipathy towards thingness itself. As Felski summarizes:

> [W]hile Marxists and cultural materialists retained a recalcitrant grip on the thingness of things, their stance was often one of guarded suspicion, if not outright condemnation. Invoking the language of reification and commodity fetishism, they drove home the theme that things were not to be trusted, that our relation to objects was irreparably damaged by structures of alienation and estrangement.[4]

Thus, while positing a theory of necessarily total commodification brings to light the ways in which every thing is produced (and commodified) in order to be exchanged, and only accrues value in relation to another commodity, the danger is that such a totalization in theory merely reproduces and even inadvertently validates the interchangeability of all things in practice. It ends up merely describing an unbreachable social process in which 'the autonomization of commodity circulation' continues 'behind the backs and over the heads' of individuals.[5] As Marx notes in Volume I of *Capital*, in the process of the valorization of value 'it is still a matter of complete indifference what particular object serves this purpose'.[6] Following the necessary abstraction of Marx's analysis of capital in its 'ideal average', there is often a theoretical duplication of the practical subjugation of the object qua commodity. It is as if our manifold relations with and towards objects are utterly determined by capital's quasi-autonomous movement. Such a totalizing perspective blocks access to the complex interrelations between people and things, which hold the potential (albeit largely unrealized at present) to go beyond their superficial acts of exchange and valorization. As Michael Heinrich notes:

> In a commodity-producing society, people (all of them!) are under the control of things, and the decisive relations of domination are not personal but 'objective' (*sachlich*). This impersonal, objective domination ... does not exist because things themselves possess characteristics that generate such domination, or because social activity necessitates this mediation through things, but only because *people relate to things in a particular way – as commodities.*[7]

As the catch-all diagnostic tool of choice for many Marxists, the critique of reification itself risks becoming reified. The indifference to particularity – that presumably constitutes one of the main targets of the original Marxist critique, i.e. that exchangeability traduces the unique use value of a thing – is thereby incorporated into the critique itself, as the inescapable and omnipotent 'value-form' brings about a blind destiny for all objects under its spell – which, of course, includes every person too.

But as the unspoken part of Heinrich's gloss implies, our associations with things are not so entirely reducible to the overarching narrative of the commodity-form. The particular relation towards things qua commodities is neither natural nor immutable. Rather, our interactions take place within multiple aesthetic, political, and affective registers. In light of this plurality of subject–object encounters and interpenetrations, I will aim to revise the predominant understanding of critical theory as being straightforwardly against reification, instead making good on the claim that Kracauer and Adorno offer valuable resources towards the following ends: (1) avoiding reproducing a simplistic, one-sided critique of reification; (2) making reparations for the subjugation of objects (without merely venerating the latter); and (3) subverting the subjective-idealist hierarchy in the hope of making way for subject/object relations that challenge the confines of the commodity form via aesthetics.

A cautionary note before proceeding is in order here. For in undertaking this task, it will be important to distinguish a critical-theoretical engagement with objects from more recent attempts to rethink the object world, in particular those most often grouped under the headings of 'object-oriented ontology' and 'speculative realism' (hereafter OOO/SR). While the proponents of OOO/SR also purport to advocate the preponderance of objects, their work adopts a vehemently non- or anti-human stance that refuses all relation and social mediation. OOO/SR results in an ahistorical and anti-political perspective, which is reflected in its wondrous prose that looks on in awe at the sheer plurality of stuff. By contrast, the early critical theory of the Frankfurt School does not outright reject the subject, consciousness, praxis, aesthetics, and so on; rather, it seeks ways of attuning subjective thinking to material conditions, recalling the affective and historically inflected bases of conceptual thought. It is born out of the conflicts, struggles, and contradictions of life lived under the baleful totality of capitalism. While critical theory extends its scope to account for objects and objectness, it remains firmly rooted in concrete social conditions.

More post-critical fantasies: object-oriented ontology (or how *not* to think about objects)

As noted at the outset, over the last decade or so, objects have become a central concern for many writers. Trying to philosophically get to grips with the world of objects has become a ubiquitous pastime. In reconsidering some of the ideas from the archive of early critical theory in light of our contemporary moment, one has to acknowledge (if only to lament) the recent rise of OOO or SR. The reasons for my somewhat begrudging tone will become clearer as we proceed. For now, suffice it to say, I find little to suggest that OOO/SR goes much beyond a post-critical fantasy, which gleefully jettisons all relationality and criticality for the sake of concocting a 'new', non-human philosophy. But before considering some of the biggest shortcomings of OOO/SR, it is worth briefly charting the movement's meteoric rise, as well as its principal arguments.

The term 'speculative realism' was coined by Ray Brassier following a seminar at Goldsmiths College, London, in 2007.[8] The leading figures in the rise of OOO/SR are Graham Harman and Quentin Meillassoux, but other contributors whose work is often cited in relation to the movement include Ian Bogost, Levi Bryant, Ian Hamilton Grant, and Timothy Morton. Bruno Latour's 'actor-network theory' is also frequently invoked in relation to OOO/SR's 'flat ontology'. Although the writers associated with OOO/SR have a range of overarching interests and approaches, they do share some core features in common. To begin with, most subscribe to some form of *realism* – namely, the notion that there is a mind-independent reality, a world that exists apart from human perception and experience. The crucial difference is that rather than cordoning off this realm of existence as utterly inaccessible and therefore of no significance for philosophy, OOO/SR is willing to think and speculate about reality in-itself.

Why is this so revolutionary (at least philosophically speaking, which is to say not at all)? Well, according to the overly tidy narrative of OOO/SR, continental philosophy since Kant has been trapped (often wilfully) in a staunchly anti-realist position. Ian Bogost describes the problem as follows:

> We've been living in a tiny prison of our own devising, one in which all that concerns us are the fleshy beings that are our kindred and the stuffs with which we stuff ourselves. Culture, cuisine, experience, expression, politics, polemic: all existence is drawn through the sieve of humanity, the rich world of things discarded like chaff so thoroughly, so immediately, so efficiently that we don't even notice.[9]

The claim is that such epistemological anthropocentrism has had far-reaching implications for how philosophers philosophize. Meillassoux provides the diagnostic term for this predominant philosophical method: *correlationism*. In *After Finitude*, Meillassoux describes correlationism as 'the idea according to which we only ever have access to the correlation between thinking and being, and never to either term considered apart from the other'.[10] The anti-realist line of thought – correlationism – is traced back to Kant's critical philosophy, which sequestered speculation as that which unwisely tries to venture beyond the limits of reason and the conditions of possible knowledge.[11] Kant famously posited a 'block' between *noumena* (things as they are in themselves, i.e. independent of experience) and *phenomena* (things as they appear to us, i.e. given through sensible experience and concepts). Pre-critical philosophy had presumed that concepts (attempt to) conform to their objects as best as possible, whereas, for Kant, objects conform to our concepts of them. We cannot know of any reality other than via the a priori categories and forms of intuition that constitute the universal conditions for knowledge. Given that no direct access to things in themselves is possible, 'we confine ourselves instead to the manifest properties of the world as it appears. The object is stripped of all independent power and considered only insofar as it flares into human view'.[12]

The editors of *The Speculative Turn* further delineate the anti-realist trend in post-Kantian thought in the following passage:

> This general anti-realist trend has manifested itself in continental philosophy in a number of ways, but especially through preoccupation with such issues as death and finitude, an aversion to science, a focus on language, culture, and subjectivity to the detriment of material factors, an anthropocentric stance towards nature, a relinquishing of the search for absolutes, and an acquiescence to the specific conditions of our historical thrownness.[13]

In ways that echo the post-critical sentiments underlying other recent scholarly turns (as outlined in Chapter 1), the editors make an implicit connection between the so-called cultural turn and relativism. This allows them to market OOO/SR as an effective antidote, a buccaneering new movement[14] that bravely restores honour to thinking, by returning to the real: 'By contrast with the repetitive continental focus on texts, discourse, social practices, and human finitude, the new breed of thinker is turning once more toward reality itself.'[15] Or in Bogost's words: 'to proceed as a philosopher today demands the rejection of correlationism'.[16]

One of the main features of this new anti-correlationist thinking is what Levi Bryant calls *flat ontology*. This is the view that all things have the same ontological status; objects equally exist on a single, horizontal plane of being. There is no overarching entity – be it language, human being, culture, God, etc. – to which other entities are subordinated, or from which they derive their content. Flat ontology simply points to a basic binary: either something *is* or it is not. Put differently, in adhering to the fundamental principle of non-contradiction, no object can be said to both exist and not exist simultaneously. So much for flat ontology. What is interesting is that the very flatness of this ontological view inflects the formal characteristics of much OOO/SR writing. For example, one of the latter's unmistakable (and often tiresome) traits is the *list*. Usually traced back to the work of Bruno Latour, much of the OOO/SR prose is replete with litanies of miscellaneous objects. The list is deployed in various registers – often indulging in the playfulness that can accompany incongruities, while at other times bearing the solemnity of a liturgical recitation. But above all, as a supposedly egalitarian mode of representation, the list is meant to perform an anti-hermeneutic function. It serves to visually and linguistically convey the common being of all things, while at the same time retaining and celebrating the particularity of each individual item amid the irreducible 'pluriverse' of things. For the flat ontologist, the humble comma becomes the proverbial magnet that draws together all manner of diverse material in the service of what Latour terms the 'parliament of things', or what Bryant calls the 'democracy of objects'.[17]

One might well accept the first basic claim of flat ontology: namely, that all things equally exist. But to say that all things equally exist does not mean that all things exist on an equal footing. Even the flat ontologists themselves do not make this additional leap. However, once this point is conceded, it becomes obvious that objects have wildly different levels of impact and effect on other objects. In other words, *mediation* quickly returns to the scene. This is one of the major limitations of a flat ontology. For the moment one ventures beyond the principal (and relatively non-controversial) claim that all objects share the same ontological status, it becomes extremely difficult to consistently maintain a non- or anti-human perspective. For instance, to say that the 'Donald Trump' or the 'atom bomb' have the same ontological status as the 'unicorn' or the 'circle' does little to suggest how these particular objects relate to anything else in the 'real world', least of all that peculiar object with the name 'human being'. Indeed, for Harman, objects perpetually 'withdraw' from all relation. They retain an unknowable aspect that no amount of careful observation and parallaxis can ever illuminate (Bennett calls this the 'recalcitrance' of things).[18] Similarly, Timothy Morton writes: '[p]ositive assertions about objects fail because objects have a shadowy dark side, a mysterious interiority'; they remain inherently 'uncanny'.[19]

But to reformulate the previous point, from such an ardently 'non-human' perspective, how might one advocate, say, intervening against the Zika virus, or defending the principle of *habeas corpus*? Do these simply signal yet more humanistic hubris and anthropocentric arrogance? Herein lies the profound limitation of OOO/SR. To listen to its proponents, one cannot help but find their approach to objects utterly devoid of social, political, historical, and cultural content. Indeed, OOO/SR is often held up precisely as an antidote to the reductive practices of philosophical hermeneutics with its preoccupation with texts and meaning. In turning away from this excessive criticality and mining for meaning, Harman exalts the quiet poetic dignity of objects that is only faintly detectable to the sincere, non-critical eavesdropper:

> Existence on the interior of an object is defined by sincerity and involvement, not transcendence and critique ... Instead of asserting one's own unique critical liberation in the world and trying to burn down traditional or reactionary temples, the key is to listen closely to the faint radio signals emitted by objects – so as one night, alone, to hear what was never heard before.[20]

He further elaborates on such wisdom as follows:

> Wisdom means the ability to be surprised because only this ability shows sufficient integrity to listen to the voice of the world instead of our own prejudice about the world, a goal that eludes even the wisest of humans a good deal of the time. While the critical intellect surveys the land from its lofty tower, punishing gaffes and discrepancies wherever it finds them, only inventive thinking is able to be surprised, because only such thinking stays in close contact with the contours of the world, listening closely and in silence to its mysterious intermittent signals.[21]

In this call for post-critical 'inventive thinking', one might detect a degree of performative contradiction. For we might wonder: on whose behalf is Harman actually writing, and for what reason? Or to put it otherwise: to whom is this call addressed? It cannot be directed towards any and all entities, since that would be patently absurd. Harman's ant colony or desolate temple are hardly capable of heeding such a call (although his 'Asian swindlers' might be more open to persuasion). In effect, then, the call of OOO/SR must be made by philosophers, via the medium of language, *on behalf of* objects. Likewise, when Bogost concedes that 'we need not discount human beings to adopt an object-oriented position',[22] I think one ought to go further: we *cannot* discount human beings *and* at the same time adopt an object-oriented position. Such would require an inexpressible, quasi-telepathic, non-human mode of philosophizing – a contradiction in terms given that philosophy is a discipline and mode of conceptual thinking only practicable by human beings.

Given the many problems and inconsistencies involved in propagating OOO/SR, one might wonder what animates the recent clamour around objects and ontology, and the coeval turn to the non-human. Jordana Rosenberg clarifies the necessary task of reading the new ontologies with critical eyes, when he writes: 'we must reckon with the ways in which, in their current iterations, ontologies so frequently and aggressively drive toward the occlusion of the dynamics of social mediation. We need to ask why the lust for dehistoricization, for demediation, for a temporality outside of history, is flourishing now, and in this way'.[23] Of course, theorists of all stripes have often sought various forms of philosophical or cultural compensation for the real damage and deformation wrought by the grotesque forces that structure life under capitalism. These searches are as unending and mobile as capitalist expansion itself, with pockets of resistance, if not mere solace, having been located amid a whole host of productive excesses. In this regard, much theory assumes a neo-Romantic bent in its assorted attempts to delineate a range of phenomena believed to somehow elude the reach of capital or surpass the limits of (all-too-)human cognition. One can think here of contemporary ecological discourse, which maps out unbreachable 'natural' limitations to capital's endless enlargement, inevitable catastrophes of the near future, crises of resource management and energy provisions, the biodiversity of a post-human ecosystem, and so on.[24] There is no doubt that the latest developments in ecological thinking have certainly provided grist to the OOO/SR mill.

This is especially evident in the particular notions of *scale* that populate recent thinking around objects. Even if seldom acknowledged as such, the scale of thought has become a pivotal site of contestation. For example, critical theory (particularly in its Marxist forms) has found itself subject to a two-sided offensive. From the first side, it is denounced as too abstract, subsuming all particularity and spontaneity out of existence in the service of its deterministic structures and 'totality'. This is, of course, a legacy of poststructuralist criticism, which challenged the 'grand narratives' of modern theorizing. But it has found renewed life in the guise of Latourian actor-network theory and flat ontology, which recalibrate theory's gaze to a horizontal, non-hierarchical plane. Meanwhile, from the other side, critical theory is seen as too narrow and anthropocentric, binding its theoretical vision and critique to the myopic standpoint of human activity and social relations. As Christopher Nealon notes, 'To think dialectically, it seems, is not to think hugely enough, or infinitely enough'.[25] From the first position, then, the scale of critique is too big, too global, too speculative; while from the second position, it is too small, too local, not speculative enough.

The latter perspective is central to the work of Morton and Harman. In contrast to the parochialism of existing social, political, and ecological thought, Morton's ecologically-minded brand of OOO/SR advocates 'Thinking Big' as a way of overcoming anthropocentrism and cultivating and embracing an overflowing sense of infinity. To expand on this, he introduces the concept of the 'mesh', which is meant to encompass the infinite interconnectedness of all living and non-living things, but without positing any central hub of orientation. In Morton's words, 'Since everything is interconnected, there is no definite background and therefore no definite foreground ... Each point of the mesh is both the center and edge of a system of points, so there is no absolute center or edge'.[26] Harman's writing also reflects this appeal to the infinite, when, for example, he describes the 'taste for cosmological vastness', which 'reaches us from Buddhist scripture and the roar of the sea and the probes launched toward Saturn', before the by now familiar plaint: 'but the philosophy of human access [i.e. correlationism] persuades us to forget these astonishing spaces, or to leave them to other university departments'.[27]

While the turning towards the infinite might open up a space for anti-hermeneutic cataloguing, dethroning the exalted figure of *Homo sapiens* in the process, it surely does little to instill any sense of the active human engagement whose absence – if realized – would render the very practice of philosophy impossible. Object-oriented ontology too often seems to conflate a 'philosophy of the non-human' and a 'non-human philosophy'. Where the former makes sense, and has a veritable tradition behind it (including thinkers like Dons Scotus and Meister Eckhart),[28] the latter merely lapses into contradiction. What is more, the homogeneity of the ontological field, as construed via OOO/SR, erases the historical-material contexts and effects of philosophy itself, rendering it an abstracted and apolitical practice.

It is in response to these deficiencies that we might do well to return to the first-generation of critical theory, which shows that the attending to objects can take more dialectically and politically imbued forms. Critical theory's method is born of the active mediation between the philosophical, the aesthetic, and the political. If the 'new' materialisms and speculative realisms of today purchase their notoriety at the cost of emptying objects (and subjects) of all social, historical, and political significance, then it would seem necessary to revive an older, more critical materialism. In contrast to the more recent turns towards the object, critical theory remains irreducible to a naive realism on the one hand, or an inflated idealism on the other. It neither celebrates the post-humanist fantasy of spiritless matter, nor embraces the idea of a fully constitutive bourgeois subjectivity. Instead, critical theory dedicates itself to the paradoxical effort to express the inexpressible, that which exceeds the respective borders of 'subject' and 'object', to illuminate the subject *in* the object, and vice versa. A collapsing of these previously rigid ontological and epistemological boundaries need not be anti-political. Indeed, the early work of the Frankfurt School – political through and through – is notable for its attempts to theorize objects and to cultivate a feeling for things. The remainder of this chapter will show how the thought of Kracauer and Adorno contributes to this timely task.

Siegfried Kracauer and the 'thicket of material life'

The cinematographic gaze becomes an innate faculty.[29]

Siegfried Kracauer's work retains a relatively marginal position within studies of critical theory. He is cited relatively infrequently. Moreover, where his work has received attention – most notably, in film theory – it has been widely (if unfairly) disparaged. In engaging with some of his writing here, I hope to revive interest in his critical aesthetics. In addition, I will try to shed some new light on what I take to be some important materialist turns in Kracauer's thought. Recovering these elements of his theoretical work will allow us to situate Kracauer's work in a productive constellation with that of his good friend Adorno. Taken together, they demonstrate how early critical theory gives an active voice and an affective power to the object world and challenges the alleged superiority of constitutive subjectivity, yet without imagining or anticipating the complete annihilation of the subject.

In *From Caligari to Hitler* (1947) – his first foray into constructing a substantive film theory – Kracauer analyses the cinema as an institution whose historical function was largely to 'paralyze social life, reifying it into ornamental patterns, and evacuating the possibility for individual judgment or critical thought'.[30] Such a view of cinema as being primarily and institutionally conservative was also Adorno's default position at the time.[31] But in Kracauer's second English-language book, *Theory of Film* (1960), the reifying process of filmic representation is given a more open-ended and even positive spin. There, cinematic reification appears as a force capable of realizing the submerged liberatory potential of a technological medium within an abstract, alienated, modern age. Such emancipatory potential, however, is not simply an ontological property of the medium itself. Rather, film's 'turn to materiality' has to be realized through particular stylistic choices and techniques – such as editing and framing. In breaking from the established formal conventions that ossify and codify social relations into readable and predictable narratives, Kracauer defends a more materialist film technique that eschews the comforting formulas of subjective individualism – for example, the recourse to psychological motivation, linear plot development and closure, shot–countershot routines, and so on. Taking up a line of thought introduced by Walter Benjamin, Kracauer turns a cinematic eye towards objects as not so much empty and lifeless husks, but more as material fragments that are both independent of human intentions and yet loaded with collective history and congealed labour. Film is championed as a unique medium through which to register the particular dialectic of autonomy and (inter)dependence within objects, since the camera is capable of non-intrusively recording the material before its lens, whilst at the same time being totally dependent upon human operation to achieve this end. Film captures the world of things, albeit always partially, and then transfers its image to the spectator with an illusory immediacy. But the sense of immediacy is itself instantly withdrawn by virtue of its technological mode of transmission. This oscillation between immediacy and withdrawnness continues, rendering the material world both closer and yet remaining distant. The epistemological upshot of this filmic aesthetic is that objects are shown to be coexistent with human praxis, thought and feeling, their relative physical autonomy notwithstanding.

For Kracauer, one of the most notable aspects of film's turn to materiality lies in the way it radically alters and deflates the role of the actor. No longer occupying a privileged space of heightened prominence and foregrounding, an actor becomes merely a 'thing among things'.[32] Of course, the adverb 'merely' furtively reintroduces the hierarchy of people over things, and implies that a degree of indignity or degradation is *inherent* in any form of objectification.[33] But for Kracauer, refiguring the actor as cinematic *material* – a thing among things – can serve to deform if not negate the traditional value accorded to personality, identity, even celebrity (that is to say, all the highly commodified features of acting 'talent'). The camera's objectifying or reifying gaze goes beyond photographic indexicality, and instead renders familiar surfaces – the outer skin of things – strange, unique, and opaque. No longer simply 'recording' or 'capturing' material, imposing symbolic meanings onto things, or incorporating objects into hegemonic allegories and narratives, film is capable of framing material contingency, expanding its field of vision to include those previously overlooked, imperceptible, or unremarkable parts of the physical world. But in doing so the cinematic apparatus does not just alter the modes of *filming* material; it also produces more mimetic forms of *viewing* material. And therein one finds the unique contribution of Kracauer's materialist film theory to a critical-theoretical approach to objects and affects. The productive convergence of human consciousness and machinic receptivity enables a dual movement of heightened objectivity and deflated subjectivity, without however completely relinquishing the subject.

According to Kracauer, our traditional habits of seeing – based on seeking out signifiers, imputing intention and causality, identifying with characters, and so on – are in need of radical transformation. In cinema's decentring mode of reception, its mimetic and mobile forms of assimilation that unsettle the boundaries between subject and object (spectator and spectacle), Kracauer perceives a sharp critique of sovereign subjectivity, self-identity, and interiority.[34] Just as the cinematic apparatus (ideally) assimilates to its manifold material with minimal subjective imposition, so the viewer assimilates to the filmic object in an act of self-effacement. In giving ourselves over to the object, the individual ego is disarmed, if not dissolved, allowing for the possibility of a material 'continuum' to take shape. Such a continuum would encourage more fluid relations between spectator and spectacle, and would aim at breaching the all-too-rigid borders of 'subject' and 'object'. Though again, the point is not to eradicate such distinctions altogether – this would take us along the fruitless byways of a flat ontology. The subject may be an object too (and a vulnerable one at that), but its critical consciousness makes it qualitatively distinct from other objects.

Kracauer attempts to flesh out those aspects of the cinematic gaze that make it uniquely capable of materializing and redeeming physical reality through the filmic spectator. To the extent that film 'addresses' its viewer, it does so at a 'corporeal-material' level, seizing the human being 'with skin and hair' [*mit Haut und Haar*]. As Kracauer puts it, 'The material elements that present themselves in film directly stimulate the material layers of the human being: his [*sic*] nerves, his senses, his entire physiological substance'.[35] The cinematic image, then, is *doubly* invested with materiality – at first in its revealing (and revelling in) the world of *physical objects*, and then once more in its *visceral* spectatorial address. Only after film has affected us at the *sensuous* level are we able to engage with it intellectually. And even then, Kracauer wants to uphold and respect the object's otherness, its indeterminacy, its stubborn resistance to nominalism and conceptual closure. In this way, film dialectically plays out the simultaneous figuring and disfiguring of materiality, the interpenetration of distance and proximity. The close-up on a face,[36] for instance, uncovers infinitesimal detail through its hyper-familiarity and physical closeness, but it also renders the face's contours strange and uncanny, distancing us in the process. Fleshy delineations morph into surreal and dynamic landscapes, as a kind of benign scopophilia takes effect, whereby we – as viewers – assimilate to the objects depicted (or rather to the multiple layers of materiality disclosed). As material is cinematically framed and observed, relations between human and non-human, cognition and affect, are not only brought into sharp relief, but are also unsettled and reordered. Agency is redistributed to account for the mutual interplay between subjects and objects. Such is the transformative potential of a materialist aesthetics of film.

But unlike our contemporary advocates of withdrawn, non-relational objects, Kracauer's film theory does not venerate the physical world for its own sake. As one sees in the groundbreaking work of Dziga Vertov, Kracauer utilizes the unique potential of the cinematic apparatus as an extension of human vision, a form of hyper-subjectivity that brings the material world to view in a new light. His is not a naive-realist theory for post-subjective objectness – as if an unattended camera left to run for eternity, without ever recording or transmitting anything (indeed, with no viewer to address), could translate into a viable model of materialism. Rather, Kracauer's film theory is for a subject/object intensified and mediated by mechanical and material means. The mediating role played by aesthetics is of vital importance for understanding early critical theory's engagement with objects and affects. It is aesthetics that gives the lie to both an incorporeal idealist conception of the subject on the one hand, and a vulgar materialist view of the object on the other. This position is developed and more thoroughly explored in Adorno's work, which fleshes out the implications of prioritizing the object in philosophical, aesthetic, and political terms.

Adorno and the preponderance of the object

> If the subject is no longer able to speak directly, then at least it should
> … speak through things, through their alienated and mutilated form.[37]

> The means employed in negative dialectics for the penetration of its
> hardened objects is possibility – the possibility of which their reality has
> cheated the objects and which is nonetheless visible in each one.[38]

Kracauer's film theory would seem to have an obvious philosophical counterpart in Adorno's notion of the 'preponderance of the object' [*Vorrang des
Objekts*]. But the connection is not so straightforward; it is complicated by
Adorno's own take on Kracauer's work, which is not wholly affirmative. Thus,
to make good on the connection between the two thinkers, we need to first
address the critical comments made by Adorno. It is worth quoting him at
length here, so as to convey some of the peculiar tone of what is meant as a
birthday 'tribute' to his close friend and former mentor:

> In Kracauer the fixation on childhood, as a fixation on play, takes the
> form of a fixation on the benignness of things; presumably the primacy
> of the optical in him is not something inborn but rather the result of this
> relationship to the world of objects. One looks in vain in the storehouse
> of Kracauer's intellectual motifs for indignation about reification. To a
> consciousness that suspects it has been abandoned by human beings,
> objects are superior. In them thought makes reparations for what human
> beings have done to the living. The state of innocence would be the con-
> dition of needy objects, shabby, despised objects alienated from their
> purposes. For Kracauer they alone embody something that would be
> other than the universal functional complex, and his idea of philosophy
> would be to lure their indiscernible life from them.[39]

In this complaint, Adorno smuggles in a hierarchy that registers 'indignation
about reification' (presumably referring to his own work) as the mature critical
position, in opposition to Kracauer's 'primacy of the optical', which Adorno presumes to result from an infantile and playful[40] relationship to objects. In supposedly abandoning the fallen world of people, Kracauer turns to the innocent
world of things as recompense for inescapable alienation. Adorno admonishes
him for this move towards 'needy objects, shabby, despised objects alienated
from their purposes'.

But this critique – quite condescending in its tone – fails to note that in
Kracauer's attention to the world of objects lies an attempt to expand the

sphere of influence beyond bona fide 'subjects' and to include the entire 'thicket of material life' (of which subjects remain a part). Kracauer places human beings neither above nor below, but *alongside* such needy objects. Indeed, one might go so far as to say that human subjects are also precisely these needy, shabby objects alienated from their purposes. In making this move, however, Kracauer is not claiming to subjectivate or dematerialize objects; rather, his aim is to materialize subjects precisely as unique objects. This position is not, then, a naive inversion of the subject–object hierarchy – a slapstick [*Groteske*] philosophy whereby objects transmogrify into conspiratorial agents with humans suffering as a result. Instead, it attests to the dialectical intertwinement and co-constitution of human and non-human – to the point at which such boundaries become more porous, expansive, and open-ended.

In light of this, we can say that not only are Adorno's concerns over Kracauer's work misplaced, they are also disingenuous. For in Adorno's own thesis of the 'preponderance of the object' – a crucial concept in both his philosophy and aesthetics, as we will see – a similar motive is at work, namely, the defence of a critical materialism attuned to the object world that mediates subjective experience and knowledge. What we find in both theorists is not so much a project of *de*-reification as one of distinguishing between different uses and forms of reification. Tellingly, in a letter to Walter Benjamin from 1940, Adorno advises that 'there is absolutely no question for us of merely repeating Hegel's verdict upon reification here, but rather of formulating a proper critique of reification ... [i.e.] of formulating a distinction between good and bad reification'.[41] Although Adorno's tentative suggestion is never explicitly taken up and developed in the rest of his work, there are ways of making good on the apparent ambiguity of 'reification' in critical theory. For instance, I think it is possible to extrapolate an understanding of what might constitute 'good' reification from Adorno's defence of autonomous art and mimesis (a concept examined in detail in the next section). For now, it suffices to merely note the significance of Adorno – whose general account of reification is most often taken over wholesale from Lukács – even hinting at the possibility of breaking away from a wholly pejorative account of reification. Indeed, to ensure that the critique of reification does not itself become reified, Adorno shifts his use of the concept from the social to the aesthetic (and back again). This is the dialectic of reification as it features in early critical theory, and it allows both Kracauer and Adorno to re-engage the world of things anew, via aesthetics. The next section will explore in greater detail the capacities that allow the combination of artistic practice and mimesis to work through various forms of reification. In the meantime, let us turn to a well-known ending.

'Finale' ('*Zum Ende*' in the original), the closing aphorism of *Minima Moralia*, provides an initial indication of what Adorno would later theorize more concretely in *Negative Dialectics*, namely the preponderance of the object. While this passage is widely cited, the focus is ordinarily placed on its gnomic invocation of messianic redemption, the light projecting back to us from the future, and the implications of this for social criticism in the here and now. But in shifting our emphasis, we find that there is more than messianism at stake in the following:

> Perspectives must be fashioned that displace and estrange the world, reveal it to be ... as indigent and distorted as it will appear one day in the messianic light. To gain such perspectives without velleity or violence, *entirely from felt contact with its objects* – this alone is the task of thought.[42]

Entirely from felt contact with its objects. What might this demand mean for the practice of thinking, given that to think is always to exceed 'mere' feeling? Well, as is often the case in Adorno, he offers clearer glimpses of this idea when commenting on the work of others. This haptic trope reappears in fuller form when he describes Benjamin's work:

> [B]ecause the subjective intention is seen to be extinguished in the object, Benjamin's thought is not content with intentions. The thoughts press close to its object, seek to touch it, smell it, taste it and so thereby transform itself. Through this secondary sensuousness, they hope to penetrate down to the veins of gold which no classificatory procedure can reach, and at the same time avoid succumbing to the contingency of blind intuition.[43]

Adorno makes use of this same technique in his own thinking of objective priority. As in Kracauer's film theory, Adorno works to deflate the transcendental ego of idealism (the omnipotent 'bourgeois I') and unsettle the notion of an ahistorical and disembodied reason. In doing so, his aim is to inaugurate what we might call a *heterodox materialism* – by which I mean a mode of thinking that tries to mimetically assimilate to its objects. This mode of thinking actively takes on a reparative role for the damage done to things by conceptualization: 'While doing violence to the object of its syntheses, our thinking heeds a potential that waits in the object, and it [thought] unconsciously obeys the idea of making amends to the pieces for what it has done.'[44] What thought has done is to exclude the multifarious possibilities, singularities and moments within things, in favour of expedient taxonomy and fungibility. By contrast, to 'yield to the object means to do justice to the object's qualitative moments'.[45] By passing to the object's preponderance, 'dialectics is rendered materialistic'.[46]

This materialist mode of thinking is in no way dogmatic or mechanistic though; it does not suggest that only 'matter' matters. Instead, Adorno advocates a critically attuned, historical, and non-reductive materialism that proceeds through a dual recognition: first, of how objects retain an element of independence vis-à-vis thought; and second, of how thinking is always historically and materially affected. The first point invokes the (anti-conceptual) concept of the 'non-identical', namely, that in the object which exceeds conceptual determination.[47] The second point highlights the inescapable objectivity of the historical subject, the affective contamination and embodiment of all thought. Both points are crucial to Adorno's subject–object dialectic, which in turn is at the heart of what I am calling his heterodox materialism.

In elaborating on this idea of heterodox materialism, it is important to note that it in no way simplistically venerates or affirms a brute objectness that predates (and will post-date) human beings. Despite the best efforts of the new materialists and speculative realists (who, in their weariness of epistemological debates over subject–object relations, can only resuscitate their interest in the world by fully ontologizing it), Adorno's materialism is not anti- or post-subjective. Indeed, in good Hegelian-Marxist fashion, he expressly warns against the falseness of positing an immediacy given from nature devoid of all subjective content: 'A nature … which hardens oppressively and gloomily in itself and shuns the light of illuminating and warming consciousness, ought justly to be mistrusted … What is unchangeable in nature can take care of itself. Our task is to change it.'[48] As such, Adorno's critical theory is less antihumanist than *proto*-humanist; that is to say, it does not seek to go beyond the subject so much as foreshadow or imagine its arrival – an arrival that can only be made possible by wholesale social transformation.

Critical theory's 'preponderance of the object' is not to be understood, then, as a timeless poetic groping for some heightened being-in-the-world; rather it is born of a historical-materialist stance that is dictated by the pressing need to give expression to suffering and to eradicate oppressive social relations. These relations are reproduced (at least in part) by prevalent forms of identitarian thinking, through which subjects and objects alike are subsumed under concepts and praxes that extinguish qualitative difference and enforce quantitative equivalence. In response to the affectless instrumentality and taxonomy fostered by identity thinking, early critical theory makes much of the concept of *mimesis*. A qualified defence of mimetic comportment underpins its attempts to break out of the spell of identity thinking, reasserting the importance of affectivity for thought in the process.

Mimesis

> To represent the mimesis it supplanted, the concept has no other way than to adopt something mimetic in its own conduct.[49]

Amid the vast and varied terrain of Adorno's critical theory, the concept of mimesis is a mercurial one. It is put to multiple uses, often with minimal definition. Indeed, as Jameson notes, mimesis is often evoked as if its meaning were already established.[50] This definitional elusiveness might help explain why mimesis has often been overlooked or disparaged, even by other representatives of the Frankfurt School (Habermas especially, as will be examined in more detail below). But I want to show that it is possible to illuminate the most compelling angles of mimesis from within Adorno's work, and in so doing re-establish the inseverable link between conceptual thought and affective (mimetic) relations to objects.

The most prolonged engagement with mimesis is to be found in *Dialectic of Enlightenment*, wherein Adorno and Horkheimer adopt a macro-historical and social-anthropological approach to the topic, tracing the relation between mimesis and processes of civilization and enlightenment. Their interest is in not only the archaic or pre-civilized forms of mimetic behaviour, but also the persistence (or repression) of these earlier forms within contemporary capitalist society. The authors argue that in its archaic form, mimesis can be seen as a form of adaptation to the natural world in order to escape the threats posed by brute nature. This kind of mimetic behaviour is much like mimicry in plants and non-human animals. Indeed, in the early phases of the civilizing process, one could say that mimesis of this kind is prior to the development of rational consciousness and subjectivity. Archaic mimesis entails a concession to the superiority of nature by way of replicating its ossification, its bare existence, its deadness. In its encounters with the harsh realities and unpredictable movements of nature, the developing self has to imitate nature's rigidity in order to survive.

> When men try to become like nature they harden themselves against it. Protection as fear is a form of mimicry. The reflexes of stiffening and numbness in humans are archaic schemata of the urge to survive: by adaptation to death, life pays the toll of its continued existence.[51]

Just as the chameleon adapts to its local environment to avoid easy detection by predators, so the early human being mimics its natural surroundings, sinking itself back into inanimate nature, enacting a form of instinctive regression that Freud claims to be inherent in every organic being.[52] These socio-anthropological interpretations neatly draw attention to the pre-rational status of archaic mimesis, while at the same time suggesting the emergent properties of selfhood. It is clearly inadequate to merely replicate inanimate nature in the hope of avoiding the terror and threats posed by the natural world – much like if one were to 'play dead' when confronted with an incoming tornado.[53] In this sense, mere mimicry of dead nature is irrational, or, rather, *pre*-rational. Yet, inasmuch as the archaic form of mimetic behaviour is, in some degree, *intended*, it already points towards the instigation of selfhood via the gradual differentiation between subject and nature. Archaic mimesis thereby contains an embryonic element of rationality within it. Adorno and Horkheimer argue that this kernel of rationality in archaic mimesis undergoes major development within what they term the *magical* phase of mimesis, to which we shall now turn.

In its magical form, magicians and shamans would interact with nature in ways that signalled a distinctive shift from the one-way subordination of human being to nature characteristic of the earliest (archaic) forms of mimesis. In the magical phase, mimesis undergoes 'organized control' whereby repeated rituals, sacrificial practices, and so forth, are rationally instigated and enacted with the idea of adapting and bending (if not entirely controlling) nature towards the particular interests of humanity. Thus, we witness a social and organizational shift from brute nature dominating the human in the archaic phase, to human beings (attempting to) manipulate and tame nature in the magical phase and beyond.

The development of magical mimetic activity is concurrent with that of self-empowerment. As a result of this shift, a steady yet definite movement towards a rational, instrumental control of nature is set in motion. As rationality accrues greater value for human beings in attempts to secure their own survival, and through increasingly effective domination of mere nature, mimetic impulses come to be seen as regressive, irrational, even animalistic, that is to say, pre-human. Mimesis in the post-magical, industrial phase thereby becomes prohibited, repressed, tabooed.

> Civilization has replaced the organic adaptation to others and mimetic behaviour proper, by organized control of mimesis, in the magical phase; and, finally, by rational practice, by work, in the historical phase. Uncontrolled mimesis is outlawed ... In the bourgeois mode of production, the indelible mimetic heritage of all practical experience is consigned to oblivion.[54]

In order to feel secure in its existence and to offset its inherent physical weakness, humanity in its industrializing and post-magical stage of development employs its cunning and rationality to control nature with ever-increasing intensity and precision. With such rational development within the progress of civilization, mimetic behaviour is seen as either pre-rational or irrational, and in any event wholly irrelevant to modern social life, the latter representing an unequivocally forward step upon the path of progress and civilization. Yet Adorno and Horkheimer argue (with more than a nod in the direction of Nietzsche and Freud) that the price to be paid for such self-constitution and empowerment is disproportionately high. For them, the mimetic faculty should not be discarded as simply an outmoded pre-historical relic. Rather, mimesis is inextricably and dialectically bound up with rationality. As much as the self is never fully rational and transcendent of its mimetic origins, so it is not reducible to its vital, pre-rational, natural core. In trying to eradicate or repress mimesis altogether, the rational subject (ironically) regresses to the archaic form of mimetic practice whereby the self becomes ossified, rigidified, inanimate. In other words, the much-vaunted autonomous subject becomes but a mere object. In order to survive, the self imitates death.

> Only consciously contrived adaptation to nature brings nature under the control of the physically weaker. The *ratio* which supplants mimesis is not simply its counterpart. It is itself mimesis: mimesis unto death. The subjective spirit which cancels the animation of nature can master a despiritualized nature only by imitating its rigidity and despiritualizing itself in turn.[55]

Here we have, then, the Odyssean model of self-renunciation writ large. The cunning of reason and contrivance, in serving to secure the subject's existence when confronted with unbearable risk, doubles back on the self, debasing that which it desperately tries to rescue. The toll for our unprecedented levels of security, brought about through increasing rationalization, is paid for with the surrender of all hopes of happiness drawn from mimetic relations with one's world. Inasmuch as mimesis can provide an alternative conception of subject–object interaction, as well as a nagging recognition of extant unhappiness and discontent [*Unbehagen*], it is an indispensable concept for critical theory.

In his later works, Adorno's deployment of mimesis becomes more complex and diverse, taking on a variety of (related) forms in a manner not dissimilar to that of the non-identical. Mimesis becomes another, what we might call, *dialectical* concept, that is to say, a sort of *anti*-concept. If ideology lies in 'the implicit identity of concept and thing',[56] then one must try to resist the urge to impose upon an object a single, self-identical, conceptual straitjacket. Already we have seen how the notion of mimesis has developed from an archaic form, through its magical phase to the rational-industrial phase, and it should come as no surprise that the content of Adorno's *Aesthetic Theory* serves to shatter any univocal definition one might offer for understanding mimesis. Of course, such mobility of usage serves as a performative exemplar of precisely the kind of expansive and open thinking that resists reductive and taxonomical methods. In this sense, one is encouraged to embrace some degree of conceptual ambiguity in the fight against conceptual reification and the instrumentalization of reason. But before exploring Adorno's later uses of mimesis, it is worth reflecting on the likely reasons for its notable absence from the predominant critical-theoretical discourse of 'communicative rationality'.

The work of Jürgen Habermas, more than most, has exerted a profound influence on the trajectory of the development of critical theory in general, and the reception and interpretation of Adorno's work in particular. Despite giving the impression that the aims and concerns of first-generation critical theorists still motivate his own work, Habermas's significant move away from earlier incarnations of critical theory brings with it some major changes and compromises in the radical perspectives and possibilities within the rich intellectual legacy of the earlier Frankfurt School. Habermas holds to what he sees as the still nascent rational potential in modernity and enlightenment, and as a result steers theory more towards pragmatism than radicalism.[57] In what amounts to a wholesale dismissal of mimesis, Habermas has produced a range of influential criticisms of Adornian critical theory, calling for and subsequently successfully instituting a fundamental paradigm shift from the 'philosophy of consciousness' – i.e. philosophy centred on transcendental subjects representing and tarrying with objects – to 'linguistic philosophy' – i.e. philosophy focused on developing intersubjective communication aiming at mutual understanding and consensus.[58] In the first volume of his seminal *Theory of Communicative Action*, and indeed elsewhere, Habermas gives short shrift to the notion of mimesis, arguing it to be an utterly unhelpful category for critical theory since it can be understood as nothing more than an unspecifiable pre-rational, pre-cognitive 'impulse', the 'sheer opposite of reason'.[59] These comments draw upon and supplement his deep unease with Adorno and Horkheimer's *Dialectic of Enlightenment*.[60]

As he makes unequivocally clear in the fifth lecture in *The Philosophical Discourse of Modernity*, Habermas believes that his philosophical predecessors, in what he refers to as their 'blackest book',[61] lapse into Nietzschean irrationality and 'performative contradiction'.[62] Habermas makes this claim on the basis that without retaining some valid element of reason that can provide a normative grounding for their critique, the authors cannot justify their own position, thereby irrevocably undermining the force and validity of the critique of enlightenment and reason. As a result of this self-refutation and reductive understanding of reason, Adorno and Horkheimer can only follow the inappro-priate paths taken by the likes of Sade and Nietzsche in merely affirming pre-rational or irrational moments as alternatives to an ever-increasing infiltration of instrumental rationality into all forms of modern cultural and social life. The mimetic faculty is viewed by Habermas as just such a pre-rational/irrational moment, inasmuch as it is mere impulse, the 'other' of reason, an entirely ineffable intuition incapable of signifying or communicating any substantive content:

> The critique of instrumental reason, which remains bound to the condi-tions of the philosophy of the subject, denounces as a defect something that it cannot explain in its defectiveness because it lacks a concep-tual framework sufficiently flexible to capture the integrity of what is destroyed through instrumental reason. To be sure, Horkheimer and Adorno have a name for it: *mimesis*.[63]

On Habermas's reading, then, Adorno and Horkheimer regress to a kind of pre-cognitive mysticism, whereby mimesis stands as a placeholder for some-thing about which they can speak 'only as they would about a piece of uncom-prehended nature'.[64] Furthermore, in a simplification that has been replicated by other commentators,[65] Habermas renders Adorno's account of mimesis tantamount to *imitation*. Indeed, the former even uses the two terms inter-changeably. Thus, we read of how 'imitation designates a relation between persons in which the one accommodates to the other, identifies with the other, empathizes with the other'.[66] While imitation may be indicative of *some* aspects of mimesis – one can think back to its archaic form and the mimicry of nature in this respect – it is not particularly helpful to reduce mimetic behav-iour to mere imitation. In doing so, Habermas fails to give sufficient attention to the variable contexts, uses, and meanings to which Adorno puts mimesis, and instead merely serves to bolster his own project of communicative action by subordinating or forthrightly dismissing that which cannot neatly come under the desired new theoretical paradigm.

One of the prominent criticisms of Adorno proposed by Habermas relates to the ways in which the former is apparently still trapped within an obso-lete philosophical tradition in the form of the *philosophy of consciousness*. Habermas argues that, for all his considerable theoretical efforts and deft dia-lectical contortionism, Adorno ultimately fails to move beyond the subject-centric epistemological underpinnings of the philosophy of consciousness, which since Descartes has concerned itself (almost exclusively) with relations between a *knowing subject*, on one side, and a *known object*, on the other. The subject–object dichotomy, according to Habermas, is unintentionally reinforced in Adorno's critical theory through the latter's flitting back and forth between an instrumental or identitarian form of thinking, on the one hand, and an enigmatic, irreducible, non-conceptual mimetic impulse, on the other. This position is then said to prevent the negative dialectician from uncovering the intersubjective potential within his own theory and instead merely flogs a philosophical 'dead horse', so to speak.[67]

One should examine Habermas's claims closely here, for it is not clear that Adorno can justly be lumped together with 'philosophers of consciousness'. It is true that in opening up at random a text by Adorno there is a high probability of encountering innumerable references to 'subject' and 'object'. This is hardly surprising given that his terminology is steeped in the heritage of German Idealism. However, his understanding of and persistent engagement with the subject–object dialectic is not necessarily indicative of a straightforward defence or reinstatement of the philosophy of the subject. Quite the contrary in fact, inasmuch as Adorno is unrelenting in his attacks on phenomenological theories such as Husserl's and existentialism, broadly construed, for their attempts to seek originary epistemological foundations in the subject. In this regard, both Habermas *and* Adorno before him exhibit a concern with undermining the philosophy of consciousness for its propensity to posit an isolated, transcendental, sovereign, and meaning-giving subject. Of course, the conclusions to be drawn from their respective critiques diverge considerably, but it is important to acknowledge the largely shared bases of their critical projects. In need of greater clarity in Habermas's reading, then, are the following two areas of Adorno's thought: (1) the subject–object dialectic; and (2) the relation between mimesis, rationality, and aesthetics.

On the subject–object dialectic, rather than asserting the cognitive and conceptual powers of a transcendental subject, *pace* Habermas, Adorno is wont to draw attention to the 'preponderance of the object' (as outlined in the previous section). This priority of the object marks out the critical materialism of Adorno's thinking. Conversely, in Habermas's communicative project, objects and affects practically dissolve into thin air, with the emphasis being solely on communicative interaction between subjects (intersubjectivity). The communicative turn could be said to have catalysed a distinct move away from subject–object relations to subject–subject relations. As a result of this shift, for Habermas, there is no longer any need to invoke a mysterious reconciliatory interrelation with some 'other' that is beyond the reaches of domination or reification, for in communicative acts we are always already interacting with another subject, that is, a subject with a voice, communicative capabilities, and so forth, who is neither unknowable nor ineffable. Through communicative actions we strive towards being understood and hope to arrive at a rational consensus. The relative lack of tension within Habermas's understanding of communicative practice is indicative of a more general overemphasis on iden-tical meaning and mutual understanding in linguistic usage, which, in forming the basis of a theory of communicative action, largely ignores the discrepan-cies and alternatives of various communicative forms, some of which may have significant ethical, affective, and political import.

For Adorno, it seems clear that trying to put to rest the long-standing philo-sophical struggle and debate over the complex relations between subject and object by unquestioningly positing the *subject* as superior – as is the case for idealists and, indeed, for Habermas – is both problematic and undesirable. Adorno's point is not that the subjective element in thinking be expelled (if such a thing were even possible – and recent attempts by 'speculative realists' seem to further demonstrate the impossibility of such an undertaking). Rather, Adorno is cognizant of the restrictions imposed upon thought when subject-ivity is hypostatized. As noted above, the preponderance of the object is the materialist foundation of Adorno's critical theory, but it also points the way towards a greater reflexivity in subjective consciousness, which is to say that in order to fully realize itself, the subject must reconnect with and give itself over to the object. In so doing, the subject does not fall into the traps associ-ated with hypostatizing itself qua subject, while the object remains freer from domination within such a relation. Adorno's paradoxical yet provocative per-spective on this new form of subject–object dialectic is made most explicit in thinking through the complex connections between mimesis and aesthetics.

In Adorno's work, philosophical concerns are inseparable from those of aesthetics. That is not to say that the two are interchangeable; indeed, Adorno doggedly guards the disciplinary uniqueness of philosophy and aesthetics, respectively.[68] But artworks call forth philosophical interpretation, just as philosophical thought in its formal presentation cannot but express a certain aesthetic character. While philosophy can usefully posit the object's prepon-derance, it is through art that we come closest to actually affirming the priority of the object. In encountering a work of art, the subject gives itself over to the object, allowing the vestiges of *mimesis* to be reignited and redirected. In so doing, we detect the limited cartography of constitutive subjectivity, while leaving the object free – or at least as free as is possible – from domination. The subject does not remain a static accumulator of knowledge, but instead is transformed in the process of its objective mediation. The aporetic attempt in art to voice the mute expressivity of the object world forms a counter-image to visions of the subject as omnipotent and all-knowing. It also stands in oppo-sition to the ceaseless imperialism of the signifier. On Adorno's account, the remains of mimetic possibility, or rather the possibility of mimetic relations between subject and object, are to be found in aesthetics. As he writes, the 'survival of mimesis, the nonconceptual affinity of the subjectively produced with its unposited other, defines art as a form of knowledge and to that extent as "rational" '.[69]

Thus, in contrast to the Habermasian rejection of mimesis as being pre-rational or irrational and thereby of no use to knowledge, interests, communication, and consensus, Adorno believes artworks to contain elements of rationality within them and therefore the potential for world-disclosing or even world-changing experiences and knowledge. As Shierry Weber Nicholsen has argued, in the realm of aesthetics Adorno considers mimesis to be both 'the activity of assimilating the self to the other' and 'the affinity of the creation, the work of art, with objectivity'.[70] This is how the play of interactions between subject and object are internalized and then contained within the art object, without either one being hypostatized or elevated to a level of epistemological or ontological purity. In the act of creating a work of art, of course, the subject (or group of subjects) involved cannot but manipulate, dominate, and identify, to a certain extent, the objective material at their disposal. Adorno openly acknowledges as much when he writes of how, to the extent that all partial elements immanent to the work are subordinated to the unity of the whole, construction is 'the extension of subjective domination'.[71] Yet, he swiftly adds: 'Construction tears the elements of reality out of their primary context and transforms them to the point where they are once again capable of forming a unity.'[72] The countless ways in which such material can be arranged, and subsequently experienced again by individuals, is seen in our postmodern context as lending art its openness and enigmatic, puzzling or even 'playful' character. But, for Adorno, the artwork is not reducible to playful pastiche (e.g. *kitsch*). Rather, genuine works of art are both *mimetic* and *rational*:

> Rationality in the artwork is the unity-founding, organizing element, not unrelated to the rationality that governs externally, but it [rationality in the artwork] does not reflect its [externally governing rationality's] categorizing order.[73]

While the element of subjective domination extends into the creation of the work of art, the objective result (the artwork itself) becomes an autonomous and unified object in its own right, with an 'enigmaticalness'[74] that stands opposed to the categorizing tendencies of the social world in general and instrumental reason in particular. In its objective state, the work of art cannot but remain incomplete yet inexhaustible just as the non-identical cannot be represented directly (given that were it to be identified or conceptualized as such it would cease to be non-identical). For these reasons, Adorno takes interest not only in the objective artwork but also in the subjective activity relating to it, that is, both in aesthetic *production* and *reception*.[75] Through its internalization of mimetic behaviour, as well as what Adorno terms its 'immanent lawfulness',[76] art stands as a conveyor of insight, reflection, communication, and truth amid a social world whose prevalent forms of objective rationalization and reification perpetually reduce the subjective horizons of experience, knowledge, and imagination. As a form of social critique that is both rational yet not reducible to a single repeatable 'message' or eternal meaning, aesthetic objects engage a dialectic of reason and mimesis – intertwined from the very start – and as such act as more than a mere 'substitute for the traditional subject-object relationship',[77] instead destabilizing the basis upon which the epistemological demarcation between subject and object is founded.

Where Habermas sees weakness in mimetic-aesthetic activity vis-à-vis its lack of explicit validity claims – in other words, the very fact that art does not seem to be 'saying' or positing something tangible, rational, immediately communicable, and so forth – Adorno finds in this very openness, opacity and communicative irreducibility, the fundamental basis of art's truth-content [*Wahrheitsgehalt*]. This is not to say that art has no capacity of communicability, or that it lapses into sheer irrationality. Rather, art is 'rationality that criticizes rationality without withdrawing from it; art is not something prerational or irrational'.[78] The mimetic language of art is merely of a different kind to that of philosophy. Yet, while the two forms are distinct in many ways – for example, art's lack of conceptuality contrasted with philosophy's conceptual language – they are neither wholly separate nor incompatible. Indeed, art and philosophy dialectically interweave and consistently call forth one another. Such issues are of importance for our purposes here, for they already hint at the deficiencies inherent in any approach that presupposes a clean break between thought and feeling.

As with Kracauer's ideal spectator, Adorno's advocacy of mimetic comportment disarms the private bourgeois 'I' and promotes an openness to the experience of what is alien and alienated, the non-identical. What seems at first to be an intensely personal experience in attempting to decipher, classify, or read the (aesthetic) object, gradually dissolves into the object's 'enigmaticalness' and congealed historical content. In materially outliving and resisting all subjective claims to finality placed upon it, the object extrapolates that which is irreducible, the stubborn surfeit of its qualities. This liquidizing of individual subjectivity calls forth an expanded sense of collectivity – above and beyond a merely inter-subjective public sphere, and more towards an inter-objective sphere in which subjects and objects, people and things, are reciprocally comprised, no longer reduced to pure fungibility and functionality.

Of course, in our current state, art is but society's bad conscience: its utopia is 'draped in black'.[79] Art can only intimate such a radically transformed order by alienating and constellating its material from the existing world. Art's ostensibly exceptional status is precarious and paradoxical: 'Only as things do artworks become the antithesis of the reified monstrosity.'[80] And yet, if 'it is essential to artworks that they be things, it is no less essential that they negate their own status as things … The totally objectivated artwork would congeal into a mere thing'.[81] The artwork therefore works to perform the dialectic we have been sketching out here. It operates within the positively charged nexus of personhood and thinghood, subjectivity and objectivity. In this dynamic, the subject *merges with* the object, just as the object *emerges as* part-subject. This shift not only forestalls the possible idolatry of subjectless objects (a risk not heeded in the political ecology of Jane Bennett, or in the ontological realism of Levi Bryant); it also dethrones the atomized, constitutive, bourgeois subject. This dialectic marks out early critical theory as being particularly attuned to the materiality, contested historicity, and utopian possibility sedimented in the object world, especially as it is given unique form and expression through aesthetics. Such awareness is replete with political implications and intent. It charges our inter-subjective (and inter-objective) relations with meaning, history, responsibility, and affective intensity. It moves us beyond wide-eyed wonder at the recalcitrance of matter, and engages us in active forms of struggle. In stark contrast to the post-critical reveries that predominate today, a heightened recognition of material preponderance is not meant to absolve human subjectivity of its historical entanglement and critical self-consciousness. Nor is it meant to reduce the human organism to mere matter, a nature-bound objectivity that is wholly susceptible to physical processes. The complex entanglement of human beings, capital, and objects demands theories and practices that are *more*, not less, critical. The early critical theory of Kracauer and Adorno calls for us to appreciate the mutual dependency and co-constitution of people and things, of subjects and objects; to allow for what is irrevocably material to bleed into our thinking and practice, and transform them in the process; to finally acknowledge the things in our hands as equals. No history without materialism, no materialism without history.

Notes

1 Peter Stallybrass, 'Marx's Coat', in *Border Fetishisms: Material Objects in Unstable Spaces*, ed. Patricia Spyer (New York: Routledge, 1998), 183–207.
2 Think here of how even an artwork (an 'absolute commodity', in Adorno's terms) like a Rothko painting only receives legal protection on condition that it 'belong' to someone or some identifiable body (e.g. the artist, the museum, the 'people', etc.).
3 Karl Marx, *Economic and Philosophical Manuscripts of 1844*, retrieved from: www.marxists.org/archive/marx/works/1844/epm/3rd.htm.

4 Rita Felski, 'Object Relations', *Contemporary Women's Writing* 1/1–2 (2007): 185–91.

5 Ernst Bloch, 'Alienation, Estrangement', *Literary Essays*, trans. Andrew Joron (Stanford: Stanford University Press, 1998), 242.

6 Karl Marx, *Capital: A Critique of Political Economy*, Vol. 1, trans. Ben Fowkes (Harmondsworth: Penguin, 1976), 311.

7 Michael Heinrich, *An Introduction to the Three Volumes of Karl Marx's Capital*, trans. Alexander Locascio (New York: Monthly Review Press, 2012), 75.

8 Brassier has since vehemently distanced himself from the 'movement', and has made clear his hostility towards it. In an interview of 2011, Brassier said: 'The "speculative realist movement" exists only in the imaginations of a group of bloggers promoting an agenda for which I have no sympathy whatsoever: actor-network theory spiced with pan-psychist metaphysics and morsels of process philosophy. I don't believe the Internet is an appropriate medium for serious philosophical debate; nor do I believe it is acceptable to try to concoct a philosophical movement online by using blogs to exploit the misguided enthusiasm of impressionable graduate students. I agree with Deleuze's remark that ultimately the most basic task of philosophy is to impede stupidity, so I see little philosophical merit in a "movement" whose most signal achievement thus far is to have generated an online orgy of stupidity.' See: 'Ray Brassier interviewed by Marcin Rychter: I am a nihilist because I still believe in truth', *Kronos* (2011), available at: www.kronos.org.pl/index.php?23151,896.

9 Ian Bogost, *Alien Phenomenology, or What It's Like to Be a Thing* (Minneapolis: University of Minnesota Press, 2012), 3.

10 Quentin Meillassoux, *After Finitude: An Essay on the Necessity of Contingency*, trans. Ray Brassier (New York: Continuum, 2008), 5.

11 Lee Braver charts the legacy of Kantian anti-realism in thinkers such as Hegel, Heidegger, and Derrida; see Lee Braver, *A Thing of This World: A History of Continental Anti-Realism* (Evanston: Northwestern University Press, 2007).

12 Graham Harman, *Guerrilla Metaphysics: Phenomenology and the Carpentry of Things* (Chicago: Open Court, 2005), 16.

13 Levi R. Bryant, Nick Srnicek, and Graham Harman (eds), 'Towards a Speculative Philosophy', in *The Speculative Turn: Continental Materialism and Realism* (Melbourne: re.press, 2011), 4.

14 Such hyperbole is part and parcel of the speculative turn. For example, in the space of a single page, Bogost not only compares the advent of SR to the Big Bang in cosmological theory, supposedly inaugurating 'a condition of new opportunities that demonstrate the quaintness of philosophies of access', but also refers to 'the four horsemen of anticorrelationism'; Bogost, *Alien Phenomenology*, 5.

15 Bryant *et al.*, 'Towards a Speculative Philosophy', 3.

16 Bogost, *Alien Phenomenology*, 5.

17 I am loathed to reproduce the lists here, but some examples from the major figures of the OOO/SR movement will suffice. '[C]oral reefs, sorghum fields, paragliders, ant colonies, binary stars, sea voyages, Asian swindlers, and desolate temples'; Harman, *Guerrilla Metaphysics*, 3. '[Q]uarks, Harry Potter, keynote speeches, single-malt scotch, Land Rovers, lychee fruit, love affairs, dereferenced pointers, Mike "The Situation" Sorrentino, bozons, horticulturists, Mozambique, *Super Mario Bros.*'; Bogost, *Alien Phenomenology*, 12. '[S]unspots, thalwegs, antibodies, carbon spectra; fish, trimmed hedges, desert scenery; "le petit pan de mur jaune," mountain landscapes in India ink, a forest of transepts; lions that the night turns into men, mother goddesses in ivory, totems of ebony'; Bruno Latour, *The Pasteurization of France*, trans. Alan Sheridan and John Law (Cambridge, MA: Harvard University

Press, 1993), 205. On his website, Bogost has created a 'Latour Litanizer', which creates lists of items randomly taken from the content of Wikipedia: see http://bogost.com/blog/latour_litanizer/. This marks Bogost's attempts to automate the list-making process, circumventing the need for human construction. Of course, the technology and code used to produce the 'automated' lists are human-made, as are the Wikipedia webpages available for inclusion. As is often the case in the field of OOO/SR, the role of human praxis – no matter how disparaged – cannot be fully eradicated after all.

18 Jane Bennett, *Vibrant Matter: A Political Ecology of Things* (Durham, NC: Duke University Press, 2010), 3.

19 Timothy Morton, 'Here Comes Everything: The Promise of Object-Oriented Ontology', *Qui Parle* 19/2 (Spring/Summer 2011): 184. 'Uncanny' is Morton's preferred term. Yet it seems a particularly odd choice given that the very idea of the uncanny surely presupposes a relation of sorts. How can any thing be, in and of itself, 'uncanny'? If all that is simply *is*, what could possibly be strange about it? Under what conditions does something become uncanny, and to whom or to what does an object *appear* uncanny? For more on this, see Timothy Morton, *The Ecological Thought* (Cambridge, MA: Harvard University Press, 2010), 38–50, 59–97.

20 Harman, *Guerrilla Metaphysics*, 255.

21 Harman, *Guerrilla Metaphysics*, 239–40. (There is precious little patient listening 'in silence' evident in Harman's own warp-speed proliferation of output.) Writing further of the need for a philosophical method that fosters vulnerability and openness rather than critical mastery, Harman writes: 'It cannot be allowed to degenerate into a kind of ultra-hip mannerism'; Harman, *Guerrilla Metaphysics*, 239. It must be a matter of some regret for Harman that OOO/SR has become the theoretical fashion of the contemporary art world. On the remarkable take-up of OOO/SR in the arts, see the recent *October* questionnaire dedicated to the new materialisms, in which Harman himself appears; see 'A Questionnaire on Materialisms', *October* 155 (Winter 2016): 3–110. As an aside, a recent art student from Lancaster University made the national news by unveiling to a duped audience a cardboard box with the words 'Jeremy Corbyn' written on the side. She explained her work as being inspired by object-oriented ontology; see: www.theguardian.com/artanddesign/shortcuts/2016/may/23/jeremy-corbyn-cardboard-box-hoax-talk.

22 Bogost, *Alien Phenomenology*, 8.

23 Jordana Rosenberg, 'The Molecularization of Sexuality: On Some Primitivisms of the Present', *Theory & Event* 17/2 (2014).

24 Timothy Morton adopts a version of this position, although he argues against the category of 'nature'. Morton also claims that existing approaches to ecological concerns are too parochial and inadequate to the task of genuinely thinking what he calls 'hyperobjects' (such as epochal climate change) that exceed traditional (humanistic) conceptions of relationality, time, and space; Timothy Morton, *Hyperobjects: Philosophy and Ecology After the End of the World* (Minneapolis: University of Minnesota Press, 2013). See also Leon Niemoczynski, who invokes the notion of 'speculative naturalism' to argue that nature can offer lines of insight into its own infinitely productive 'vibrant' ground, which he identifies as *natura naturans*; Niemoczynski, *Charles Sanders Peirce and a Religious Metaphysics of Nature* (Lanham: Rowman & Littlefield, 2011). In addition, one could also point to the return of various vitalisms, which invoke 'life' itself in different registers (both scientific and mystical) as a force of radical and irreducible potential, diversity, and creativity. Vitalist positions can also be found within certain

elements of the autonomist left; for example, see Michael Hardt and Antonio Negri, *Multitude: War and Democracy in the Age of Empire* (London: Penguin, 2004), 146. For a critical account of the return to vitalist thinking, see Eugene Thacker, *After Life* (Chicago: University of Chicago Press, 2010).

25 Christopher Nealon, 'Infinity for Marxists', *Mediations* 28/2 (Spring 2015): 50. This penchant for the hyperobjective expanse is shown in the enthusiasm surrounding the concept of the 'Anthropocene'. Again, concepts like the Anthropocene excise all social, political, and historical meaning and culpability from the world, instead reinscribing catastrophic environmental changes as being the result of the actions of *Homo sapiens* as a whole, rather than particularly egregious and extractive forms of industrial capitalism (with its identifiable geographical and historical centres, political-economic agents, corporate polluters and interests, colonization of underdeveloped populations, etc.). For a critical history of the concept of the Anthropocene, see Christophe Bonneuil and Jean-Baptiste Fressoz, *The Shock of the Anthropocene: The Earth, History and Us* (London: Verso, 2016). For a thorough critique of the Anthropocene, see Jason W. Moore, *Capitalism in the Web of Life: Ecology and the Accumulation of Capital* (London: Verso, 2015).

26 Morton, *The Ecological Thought*, 29–30. It is perhaps no coincidence that Morton's descriptions of the 'mesh' strike a similar tone to those of Latour's 'network'.

27 Harman, *Guerrilla Metaphysics*, 255. It is ironic that Harman and his fellow-travellers appear to be more than happy to delegate all social, political, and historical matters to other disciplines and departments, as if their brave new philosophy had nothing to do with such things.

28 Andrew Cole provides a useful critique of OOO on the basis of its neo-medievalism; see Andrew Cole, 'The Call of Things: A Critique of Object-Oriented Ontologies', *minnesota review* 80 (2013): 106–18. Elsewhere, he attacks OOO from another angle, showing how Harman's differentiation between the 'real object' and the 'sensual object' can be said to recapitulate Kant's distinction between phenomena and noumena; see Andrew Cole, 'Those Obscure Objects of Desire', *Artforum* (Summer 2015): 318–25.

29 Theodor W. Adorno, *Aesthetic Theory*, trans. Robert Hullot-Kentor (London: Continuum, 2004), 193.

30 Patrice Petro, 'Kracauer's Epistemological Shift', *New German Critique* 54 (Autumn 1991): 127–38.

31 For instance, see the denouncements of cinema in the 'Enlightenment as Mass Deception' essay in *Dialectic of Enlightenment*, and in §5 and §131 of *Minima Moralia*. However, in a short and somewhat underworked piece from 1966 entitled 'Transparencies on Film', Adorno appears to relent on the hyperbole and deigns to allow for the possibility that film could contain critical and aesthetic potential on a par with literature, painting, and music; see Theodor W. Adorno, 'Transparencies on Film', [November 1966], *New German Critique* 24/25 (Winter 1981–2): 199–205.

32 Andrei Tarkovsky's works provide ready examples of this practice. According to the actor Alexsander Kaidanovsky, on the set of *Stalker*, Tarkovsky had said to him: 'I don't need your psychology, your expressiveness … The actor is part of the composition, like the tree, like the water'; cited in Graham Petrie and Vida T. Johnson, *The Films of Andrei Tarkovsky: A Visual Fugue* (Bloomington: Indiana University Press, 1994).

33 Obviously, 'objectification', like reification, is itself a highly loaded and suggestive term. Part of my aim here is to (temporarily) neutralize such terminology so as to create a space in which the status of objects/thinghood may be re-evaluated. As

will be clear from my criticisms of OOO/SR, such a move should not be taken as an outright attack on subjectivity, however; it is more an attempt to recognize the current limitations of a subject that does not allow for material relations to affect its thoughts.

34 Miriam B. Hansen 'Introduction', in Kracauer's *Theory of Film: The Redemption of Physical Reality* (Princeton: Princeton University Press, 1997), xi.

35 Cited in Miriam Hansen, '"With Skin and Hair": Kracauer's Theory of Film, Marseilles 1940', *Critical Inquiry* 19/3 (1993): 437–69.

36 'Any huge close-up reveals new and unsuspected formations of matter; skin textures are reminiscent of aerial photographs, eyes turns into lakes or volcanic craters. Such images blow up our environment in a double sense: they enlarge it literally; and in doing so, they blast the prison of conventional reality, opening up expanses which we have explored at best in dreams before'; Kracauer, *Theory of Film*, 48.

37 Adorno, *Aesthetic Theory*, 154.

38 Theodor W. Adorno, *Negative Dialectics*, trans. E.B. Ashton (New York: Continuum, 1973), 52.

39 Theodor W. Adorno, 'The Curious Realist: On Siegfried Kracauer', *New German Critique* 54 (1991): 159–77.

40 Adorno also complains of Kracauer's 'amateurish thinking on his feet', which combines with a 'certain slackness [that] damped self-criticism in favor of playful pleasure in felicitous insights'; Adorno, 'The Curious Realist', 161–2. But Adorno's suspicions about playfulness – evidenced in his criticisms of Kracauer here and of Benjamin elsewhere – appear overstated when we are told in the Introduction to *Negative Dialectics* that 'philosophy contains a *playful element* which the traditional view of it as a science would like to exorcise'. He even likens the practice of philosophy to a kind of 'clowning'; Adorno, *Negative Dialectics*, 14, my emphasis. All the more bizarre then that he would bemoan: 'With Kracauer there was always some clowning in the stance'; Adorno, 'The Curious Realist', 172. I have argued elsewhere that much of Adorno's writing can be seen as a form of clowning; see my seminar paper for the Modernist Studies Association 15 conference, University of Sussex, Seminar 6, 'Narrating the Everyday: Ethical Risks and Rewards', 31 August 2013.

41 See Adorno's letter to Benjamin dated 29 February 1940; Theodor W. Adorno and Walter Benjamin, *The Complete Correspondence, 1928–1940*, ed. Henri Lonitz, trans. Nicholas Walker (Cambridge, MA: Harvard University Press, 1999), 321.

42 Theodor W. Adorno, *Minima Moralia: Reflections on a Damaged Life*, trans. Edmund Jephcott (London: Verso, 2005), 247, my emphasis.

43 Theodor W. Adorno, *Prisms*, trans. Samuel and Sherry Weber (Cambridge, MA: MIT Press, 1983), 240.

44 Adorno, *Negative Dialectics*, 19.

45 Adorno, *Negative Dialectics*, 43.

46 Adorno, *Negative Dialectics*, 192.

47 '[O]bjects do not go into their concepts without leaving a remainder'; Adorno, *Negative Dialectics*, 5.

48 Cited in Susan Buck-Morss, *The Origins of Negative Dialectics: Theodor W. Adorno, Walter Benjamin and the Frankfurt Institute* (New York: Free Press, 1977), 49.

49 Adorno, *Negative Dialectics*, 14.

50 See Fredric Jameson, *Late Marxism: Adorno, Or, The Persistence of the Dialectic* (London: Verso, 2006), 104.

51 Adorno and Horkheimer, *Dialectic of Enlightenment*, 180.

52 This, of course, pertains to the 'death drive', which for Freud represents the irrepressible yet not total desire for calm, stability, and as such a return to an inorganic state (i.e. death). See Sigmund Freud, *Beyond the Pleasure Principle*, trans. James Strachey (New York: W.W. Norton, 1961), 30.

53 Given the 'flat ontology' championed by many speculative realists, as noted previously, one wonders how they might act in such a situation.

54 Adorno and Horkheimer, *Dialectic of Enlightenment*, 180–1.

55 Adorno and Horkheimer, *Dialectic of Enlightenment*, 57.

56 Adorno, *Negative Dialectics*, 40.

57 In defence of this turn, Joel Whitebook classifies Habermas's project as one of 'radical reformism'; see Whitebook, 'The Marriage of Marx and Freud: Critical Theory and Psychoanalysis', in *The Cambridge Companion to Critical Theory*, ed. F. Rush (Cambridge: Cambridge University Press, 2004), 89. But this seems unconvincing, to say the least, since the history of reformism is so closely bound up with the dilution of radical claims and an insistence on political realism all along the line. On the limitations of such political realism, see Chapter 4.

58 Jürgen Habermas, *The Theory of Communicative Action*, Vol. 1, trans. Thomas McCarthy (Boston: Beacon Press, 1984), 390.

59 Habermas, *The Theory of Communicative Action*, Vol. 1, 390.

60 A similarly dismissive perspective is evident in a somewhat throwaway comment by Esther Leslie, whereby amid an otherwise expert elucidation of Benjamin's 'Work of Art' essay, she pauses to complain of Adorno's 'pessimistic sense of the mimetic capacity as the compulsion exerted on culture consumers to conform to the culture industry's images of themselves'; Leslie, *Walter Benjamin: Overpowering Conformism* (London: Pluto, 2000), 154. Of course, Adorno's scepticism towards inflated claims to (mass) cultural autonomy is undeniable, but he does not reduce mimetic capacities to processes of cultural adaptation or placation. Indeed, that form of mimesis is given comparatively little space in Adorno's oeuvre when compared to the myriad other forms of mimetic comportment, especially in relation to aesthetic experience and philosophical practice.

61 Jürgen Habermas, *The Philosophical Discourse of Modernity: Twelve Lectures*, trans. Frederick G. Lawrence (Cambridge: Polity, 1987), 106.

62 Habermas, *The Philosophical Discourse of Modernity*, 119.

63 Habermas, *The Theory of Communicative Action*, Vol. 1, 389–90.

64 Habermas, *The Theory of Communicative Action*, Vol. 1, 383. Interestingly, in an interview from 1990, Habermas defends the importance of 'moral feelings', and explains how rational, moral concepts alone cannot provide an adequate motivational basis for action. He writes: 'Firstly, moral feelings play an important role in the *constituting* of moral phenomena. We will not perceive certain conflicts of action as being at all morally relevant if we do not *feel* that the integrity of a person is being threatened or violated. Feelings form the basis of our own *perception* that something is moral. Anyone who is blind to moral phenomena has blind feelings. He lacks the sensor, as we would say, for the suffering of a vulnerable creature which has a right to the protection of both its physical self and its identity. And this sensor is clearly closely related to sympathy and empathy. Secondly, and most importantly … moral feelings guide us in our *judgement of particular moral instances* … Thirdly, moral feelings clearly play an important part, not just in the application of moral norms but also in their *justification*. At the very least, empathy, that is, the ability to feel one's way across cultural distances into alien and prima facie incomprehensible ways of living, predispositions to react and interpretive perspectives, is an

emotional prerequisite for ideal role-taking which requires everyone to assume the point of view of all the others'; Jürgen Habermas, 'Morality, Society, and Ethics: An Interview with Torben Hviid Nielsen', *Acta Sociologica* 33/2 (1990): 111.

65 Martin Lüdke has criticized a number of German commentators for inadequately differentiating between mimesis and imitation; see Martin Lüdke, *Anmerkungen zu einer 'Logik des Zerfalls': Adorno-Beckett* (Frankfurt: Suhrkamp, 1981).

66 Habermas, *The Theory of Communicative Action*, Vol. 1, 390.

67 Albrecht Wellmer follows Habermas's critical precedent, arguing that Adorno's attempt at a 'critical redemption of metaphysics' remains 'bound up in the problematic premises of the modern philosophy of subjectivity'; Albrecht Wellmer, 'Adorno, Modernity, and the Sublime', in *The Actuality of Adorno: Critical Essays on Adorno and the Postmodern*, ed. Max Pensky (New York: SUNY, 1997), 127.

68 Jameson highlights Adorno's 'absolute hostility to the assimilation of philosophy to aesthetic writing, to play, to art, to *belles-lettres* generally; this absolute differentiation of philosophical thought from artistic production – most unseasonable in the present intellectual climate – is the price to be paid for the detection of those features of philosophical argument which do have something in common with artistic practice'; Jameson, *Late Marxism*, 66.

69 Adorno, *Aesthetic Theory*, 70.

70 Shierry Weber Nicholsen, 'Aesthetic Theory's Mimesis of Walter Benjamin', in *The Semblance of Subjectivity*, ed. Tom Huhn and Lambert Zuidervaart (Cambridge, MA: MIT Press, 1997), 62.

71 Adorno, *Aesthetic Theory*, 74.

72 Adorno, *Aesthetic Theory*, 74.

73 Adorno, *Aesthetic Theory*, 70.

74 This is Hullot-Kentor's translation of the German noun 'Rätselcharakter'.

75 I have opted for the term 'reception' in this instance over the more obvious counterpart 'consumption' on account of the latter's pejorative connotations – such as intellectual passivity and physiological ingestion.

76 Adorno, *Aesthetic Theory*, 72.

77 Jameson, *Late Marxism*, 256.

78 Adorno, *Aesthetic Theory*, 71.

79 Adorno, *Aesthetic Theory*, 178.

80 Adorno, *Aesthetic Theory*, 220.

81 Adorno, *Aesthetic Theory*, 230.

4

Expectant emotion and the politics of hope

'Hope' is the thing with feathers.
　　　　　　　　　　　　　　– Emily Dickinson

Without feathers.
　　　　　　　　　　　　　　– Woody Allen

On 13 March 1956, Max Horkheimer, in conversation with his friend and collaborator Theodor Adorno, made the following remark: 'I do not believe that things will turn out well, but the idea that they might is of decisive import-ance.' This double movement of thought, an open dialectic that abjures the false choice between optimism and pessimism, registers one of the core motivating affects of critical theory: *hope*. Indeed, there are many moments within the oeuvre of early critical theory, which disclose its refusal of despair, even amid the darkest of historical moments. In *Minima Moralia*, following a meditation on the fragility of memory, Adorno concludes the aphorism with the poignant line: 'But he who dies in despair has lived his whole life in vain.'[1] Then there is Walter Benjamin's oft-cited invocation of Kafka: 'only for the sake of the hopeless ones has hope been given to us'.[2] And, of course, there is the voluminous output of Ernst Bloch, whose *The Principle of Hope* comprises an encyclopaedic account and retrieval of hope as manifested in the surplus desires of past cultures, movements, and wish-images.

Yet despite maintaining an enduring, militant hope at its core, most evalu-ations of critical theory, and of its place within the history of leftist thought, point to a profound and debilitating sense of loss, defeat, pessimism, and hopelessness. The Frankfurt School's gloomiest remarks are often invoked simply to reproduce tired caricatures of 'radicals in despair',[3] an aloof group of cultural mandarins offering precious little support for the practical work necessary for concrete political engagement and social reorganization. In this chapter, my aim is to chart the dominant narrative of decline within leftist thought before going on to excavate the utopian desires of critical theory with a view to reigniting an affective politics centred on *hope*. In doing so, I will try to elucidate what is stake for a contemporary politics of the left that is in stark need of an active, restless form of hope that exceeds the narrow confines of socially prescribed, pragmatic or 'realistic' expectations, and how a re-visioning of critical theory through the lens of affect can contribute to such a task. Moreover, in aiming to revive the spirit of hope that subtends critical theory, we might begin to wrest the Frankfurt School's legacy away from those who would pragmatize, liberalize, linguistify, or otherwise domesticate the most far-reaching and ambitious threads of its social critique.

A brief affective history of the left (I): on hopeless narratives

The horror is that for the first time we live in a world in which we can no longer imagine a better one.[4]

Writing an intellectual history of the left inevitably involves the construction of narratives. In turn, this narrativizing, as an act of form-giving, usually entails the careful organization of many disparate, often conflicting parts into an orderly whole, all seen from a retrospective and settled vantage point. Ancillary to this process is the act of compiling 'balance-sheets' for a given period of time as a way of registering historical gains and losses, insights and oversights, successes and failures, rises and falls. This element of narrative construction is crucial, since it shapes and tracks the trajectory of intellectual and affective responses. It also serves to favour or preclude certain readings, positions, arguments, interpretations, and so forth. As Fredric Jameson notes, often 'what is most revealing is not what is said, but what cannot be said, what does not register on the narrative apparatus'.[5] In this regard, one of the most dominant readings of leftist politics is one built upon the notion of *decline*. The story is a familiar one: initial high hopes and ideals are gradually disenchanted, defeated, and crushed under the weight of world events. One finds such a rise and fall narrative repeated right across the political spectrum. Of course, the political right has successfully peddled its post-1989 triumphalism for some time now, merrily proclaiming the 'end of history' in the consolidation of free market capitalism and liberal democracy. While Margaret Thatcher boasted 'there is no alternative', many commentators (most famously Francis Fukuyama) eagerly joined the symbolic burial of socialism. Given the right's scale of ideological investment in preserving and strengthening neoliberal hegemony, such positions are hardly surprising. Perhaps more surprising though is the *left's* response to historical defeats, for it has to a large extent internalized the disillusionment and hopelessness that followed the collapse of 'actually existing socialism' and the subsequent fortification of capitalism.

Such a depressive and submissive position is precisely what Wendy Brown attacks in her provocative article, 'Resisting Left Melancholy', in which she reactivates and redirects the concept of 'left melancholy' first used by Walter Benjamin in his critique of the left-wing Weimar poet, Erich Kästner. Brown calls for an end to the left's self-defeatism and masochistic overinvestment in loss. She writes:

> [Today's] is a Left that has become more attached to its impossibility than to its potential fruitfulness, a Left that is most at home dwelling not in hopefulness but in its own marginality and failure, a Left that is thus caught in a structure of melancholic attachment to a certain strain of its own dead past, whose spirit is ghostly, whose structure of desire is backward looking and punishing.[6]

A similar criticism of this leftist tendency, albeit with different political and philosophical motivations, can also be found in the later work of the pragmatist philosopher Richard Rorty. In his survey of leftist thought in twentieth-century America, Rorty rehearses a familiar complaint about the supposedly damaging influence of 'postmodern' theorists (and their legions of interpreters) over the terrain of social and political thought and practice. For Rorty, the dominance of 'High Theory' has sapped all belief in the powers of democratic procedure, discursive refinement, social inclusion, institutional reflexivity, political legitimacy, and so on. As a result, he argues, 'hopelessness has become fashionable on the Left – principled, theorized, philosophical hopelessness'.[7]

The contrast between these images of a contemporary left paralysed by its past losses, and those of an older left energized by its future achievements, could hardly be starker. In Marx's work, one finds a reaffirmation of the progressivist tradition of Hegel's philosophy and its concomitant belief in the rational development of world history. There is no anti-modern or pre-lapsarian motive at the root of Marx's analyses of capitalism. Thus, while he aims to scrutinize and theorize the move from feudalism to capitalism, and to demonstrate how this newest mode of production inaugurates new and intensified forms of oppression, exploitation, and misery for the working class, the transformation to capitalism is nevertheless held to be a necessary stage in the course of social development. For the Marx and Engels of *The Communist Manifesto*, the victory of the proletariat and the downfall of the bourgeoisie are seen as 'equally inevitable'. Capitalism will not only exploit the proletariat with growing intensity, but will also create conditions that make possible – indeed, *necessitate* – the abolition of capitalism itself. In this view, as a unique and fundamentally contradictory system of production, capitalism compels its own supersession, first by socialism and eventually by full Communism.[8]

But this tripartite faith – (1) in the inevitability of socialist revolution (2) in the universality of the category of the proletariat as subject-object of history, and (3) in the eventual realization of Communism – became harder to maintain in the aftermath of the major missteps of world events throughout the twentieth century. The optimism underpinning the Second and Third Internationals came to be supplanted by a pessimism in later critical theorists whose influences extended beyond Marx to include the gloomier authors of modernity (such as Max Weber, Friedrich Nietzsche, Georg Simmel, and Sigmund Freud). Turning the tools of modern critique towards the modern world itself, critical theorists interrogated the supposed linearity of progress, as well as the certainty of revolutionary transformation, and showed them to be hubristic, especially in light of increasing totalitarian violence and unprecedented levels of industrialized mass extermination. No longer could appeals to the 'cunning of reason' be upheld in the face of such events. It was in such barbarous and unpropitious socio-historical conditions that the left became disabused of all notions of hope and practical world-making, instead retreating to a position of purist negativism.

The downward trajectory is all too familiar in these narratives of the left. The role of critical theory within such narratives is crucial, since its most widely read representatives (especially those of the so-called 'first generation') are often understood as being responsible for penning some of the most sombre and bracing reflections on the disappointments of revolutionary hopes and desires. The Frankfurt School is seen to posit the impossibility of transformative political action in light of the working class's almost total integration into capitalist forms of reproduction, consumption, and recreation. What is to be gleaned from critical theory, in such readings, is not an engaged theorization of revolution so much as a detached lamentation over the non-existence of revolutionary agency within a 'totally administered' society. The position of critical theorists appears to resemble that of Paul Klee's *Angelus Novus*, at least insofar as one endorses Benjamin's seminal interpretation of the artwork. That is to say, they are propelled ever forward whilst looking backward and despairing at the mounting debris and casualties of historical 'progress'. Retrospective philosophical reflection and academic discussions over aesthetics replace political action and the critique of political economy.[9] Indeed, the opening line to Adorno's *Negative Dialectics* would seem to support this reading: 'Philosophy, which once seemed obsolete, lives on because the moment of its realization was missed.'[10] The sense of belatedness infuses his reflections. The utopian images and productivist dreams of building a better future (evident, for example, in many proponents of Soviet Marxism and its artistic corollary in the form of Constructivism) are supplanted by consumerist nightmares of coercion, conformity, indifference, and subjective deformation. In recognizing that the 'attempt to change the world miscarried', the leftist imaginary turns decidedly grey, while its accompanying discourse becomes circumspect, mournful, hopeless.

A brief affective history of the left (II): the exhaustion of utopian energies

The utopian motif has been suspended.[11]

For many commentators, from both the right and the left, the deflation of political hope and the 'exhaustion of utopian energies', as Jürgen Habermas puts it, is welcomed as a sign of maturity, a proverbial 'coming of age', whereby one accepts (either happily or begrudgingly) the extant parameters of praxis, the supposedly inherent limitations of human being, and finally becomes 'realistic'.[12] Indeed, one could hardly overestimate the extent to which our contemporary socio-political horizon is defined by a hard-nosed realism and wilful disregard for the concept of utopia. The renewed vigour with which sociological and political realisms have been embraced is worth commenting on, since a number of writers have taken it upon themselves to discredit utopian thinking in relation to politics once and for all. William Galston offers a useful (albeit openly biased) summary of the rise of 'realist' theory as part of a backlash against the predominance of American 'high liberalism' and its 'ideal' theories. Galston draws together an unusual assortment of figures (whose works are often only tenuously complementary) in order to defend a doggedly realist position that eschews all residues of the utopian. For him, realism stems from the belief that 'preventing the worst is the first duty of political leaders', which means that 'striving for far-reaching social improvement makes sense only when doing so does not significantly increase the odds that some previous abated evil will reappear'.[13]

While Galston's article usefully draws together a number of diverse threads in this fledgling 'realist turn', there are more direct and unabashed proponents of today's anti-utopianism. One such figure is John Gray. *Black Mass: Apocalyptic Religion and the Death of Utopia* is Gray's contribution to the bid to purge contemporary politics of all utopian impulses. For Gray, identifying a political project as utopian is quite straightforward. A project or ideal can be deemed utopian 'if there are no circumstances under which it can be realized'.[14] This definition grounds his attempt to show that utopian political projects are inherently wrong, false, and dangerous, founded as they are on a naive faith in perfectibility. As evidence for our pressing need of a strong political realism that has no truck with the 'pursuit of a condition of harmony', Gray cites a whole host of examples, from the extreme to the mainstream, which include the Jacobin 'terror', Stalinism, Nazism, the unsuccessful attempt to engineer a market economy in post-Soviet Russia, as well as the neo-conservatism of George W. Bush and the United States's recent foreign policy initiatives in light of the so-called 'war on terror'.[15] According to Gray's account, all these phenomena were utopian in nature on the grounds of their patent impossibility, and as a result they were destined to fail. Conditions were simply not suitable; expectations were out of line with the reality on the ground. As omniscient realist and naysayer, Gray can gleefully condemn any politics that does not cut its sails to the prevailing wind, and it is not long before a familiar Hobbesian vision of naturalized conflict is invoked:

> In each case it was clear from the start that the necessary conditions of success were lacking and could not be created by any programme of action. A little insight into human nature and history was all that was needed to be able to know in advance that these experiments would end in a familiar mix of crime and farce.[16]

Gray is not alone in his fanatical promotion of political realism. Similar views are to be found in the most unlikely of places, for instance, in a recent contribution to a new volume of essays on the work of Ernst Bloch. Included in the collection is a chapter by Henk de Berg entitled 'Unlearning How to Hope'. In an otherwise valuable edition of new essays on Bloch, Berg's chapter is comically misplaced and misjudged (assuming that the author is not deliberately playing devil's advocate, which, although not impossible, seems improbable). Berg proposes that we – by which he means self-identifying 'radical cultural critics' – surrender our utopian wishes and political hope so that we might finally recognize today's liberal-democratic, capitalist societies as the great, unparalleled achievements of civilization that they are. Berg writes: 'no social order has ever produced more freedom, more equality, and more justice than the combination of bourgeois capitalism and liberal democracy'.[17] Like Gray, Berg also rests his arguments on a similar Hobbesian presupposition of fear, demonstrated, for instance, in his defence of modern consumer culture, which, according to Berg, 'allows us to simulate the most exceptional actions, the most heroic deeds' and affords us 'a plethora of opportunities for sublimation and surrogate satisfaction'.[18] As such, consumer culture constitutes an alternative to the 'socially more harmful expressions of man's [sic] pro-pensity for barbarity'.[19] As is so often the case with ultra-realist defences, the self-presentation of the writer in question is that of a mature, grounded, cool-headed master – one who has seen through the ramblings of so-called 'radicals' and 'revolutionaries' to attain a more balanced perspective.[20]

This revised realism and anti-utopian rhetoric calls for a more sustained analysis than can be given here. But its influence calls for an effective (and *affective*) response, since such a view implicitly promotes certain forms of disengagement, disbelief, cynicism, and inaction. Realism is always *political*. As Jameson notes, 'the waning of the utopian idea is a fundamental historical and political symptom, which deserves diagnosis in its own right – if not some new and more effective therapy',[21] reinforcing the point that hopelessness is a *learned disposition*, not an inevitable consequence of 'history' or 'human nature'. Indeed, the feigned neutrality and objectivity of a realist position – basing itself on ostensibly unchangeable foundations such as established 'facts', 'history', 'human nature', and so on – disguises its own engagement in discursive politics and ideological struggle. The (re)production of a realist position smuggles under its cloak of pragmatism a quietist affirmation of non-intervention that diminishes the potential of human activity, imagination, and collective endeavour: in short, the political sphere itself. As Karl Mannheim writes, 'the representatives of a given [social] order will label as utopian all conceptions of existence which *from their point of view* can in principle never be realized'.[22] When an active anti-utopianism combines with a passive hope-lessness, the threat of inertia becomes readily apparent.

But is such a hopeless horizon inevitable? Must the existing narratives of loss be replayed *ad infinitum*? Is not a most vital characteristic of critical theory to be found in its dynamic, protean form, its multiple iterations and irruptions throughout history, its irreducibility to context? Was philosophy's 'missed' moment of realization (the one evoked in the famous opening to *Negative Dialectics*) a singular, fatally irrevocable one, signalling the once-and-for-all end of revolutionary hope? Or is there more to be said about the com-plicated and multi-layered structures of feeling that gather around and inflect certain moments, which might inhibit or reconfigure our perceptions of what is possible both in the present and in the future? With this in mind, then, accompanying any *intellectual* history of leftist thought and activity, we would do well to consider its *affective* history too. The affective register within which critical theory has been situated by leading historians and leftists makes much of the biographical and contextual influences over the Frankfurt School's out-put. As a result, most of the utopian impulse, desire, and hope that motivated early critical theory has been downplayed, if not entirely ignored. When cou-pled with the imposition of renewed sociological and political realisms, at the cultural and institutional levels, the prevailing discourses are ones of prohibitive closures rather than speculative openings. For this reason, I am interested in understanding both what is enabled and what is impeded, socially, culturally, and politically, through the imposition of particular affective structures and emphases.[23] In doing so, I aim to move beyond a mere act of historicizing that routinely reduces texts to their contexts, and instead reconstruct a version of critical theory that reorients its affective modes of address to ones more conducive to a politics of hope. This task is a pressing one, for without revivifying and reconnecting the affective and the political in critical theory, the latter will likely remain little more than an academic niche, a museum piece hermetically encased in the display cabinet of leftist curiosities.

Back to the future: a critical theory of hope

Philosophy will have conscience of tomorrow, commitment to the future, knowledge of hope, or it will have no more knowledge.[24]

Everybody's life is pervaded by daydreams; one part of this is just stale, even enervating escapism, even booty for swindlers, but another part is provocative, is not content just to accept the bad which exists, does not accept renunciation. This other part has hoping at its core, and is teachable.[25]

In contrast to its distinct 'image problem' that accentuates a cultural pessimism and universal gloominess about the state of the modern world, it is arguable that critical theory has at its core an indefatigable sense of *hope*. And yet while the concept of hope enjoys much currency in the contemporary political sphere, its importance for a critical theory of society has been largely overlooked. The rest of this chapter will provide an engagement with the work of Ernst Bloch (1885–1977), since no discussion of the politics of hope can afford to ignore Bloch's major contributions to the topic. His three-volume opus *The Principle of Hope* (written between 1938 and 1947, and first published in 1959) is an imposing, esoteric, unpredictable, often rambling and repetitive text, which spans the fields of anthropology, social and cultural history, philosophy, and theology. It offers a veritable treasure-trove of analyses, speculations, digressions, and fragments about the concept of hope and its myriad expressions in culture, from the most modest forms of idle daydreaming and fairy tales, through to the most abstract of imagined teleological fantasies, all sustained by an insatiable human striving for emancipation.

Bloch's project is animated in part by a profound dissatisfaction with the way in which the principle of hope, or what he calls *docta spes* (educated or comprehended hope), has been 'philosophically excluded for so long'.[26] Traditionally, philosophers have shown little concern for the concept of hope. To the truth-seeking, myth-destroying, logic-loving philosopher, whose job description includes the promotion of reasoned adjudication and the invalidation of all illusion, hope must seem like an atavistic irrationalism, a persistent and unedifying 'meme' within the progressive evolution of human being and knowledge. Indeed, for his prolonged philosophical engagement with the concept of hope, Bloch was derided by a number of other thinkers. Manfred Buhr took Bloch to task for involving Marxism in quasi-religious problems.[27] Siegfried Kracauer complained to Leo Löwenthal of Bloch's 'fornication with God',[28] while Jürgen Habermas labeled Bloch a 'Marxist Schelling'.[29] As noted in this book's introduction, the history of philosophy as a discipline is marked by countless efforts to erect rigid dualisms (mind *versus* body, reason *versus* emotion), which underwrite the proud achievement of disinterested, objective knowledge and rational progress, while at the same time preventing the supposedly dangerous incursions of emotion and subjective avarice.

In further service of this overarching rationalism, philosophy gives minimal attention to 'the future' (save the rather crude calculations involved in moral consequentialism). The future is philosophically cordoned off, as it were, because to engage it conceptually would entail a movement away from 'reality' and towards 'fantasy', that is to say, from contemplation of what exists to speculation as to what could exist. One of the best-known and most influential formulations of this argument appears in the Preface to Hegel's *Philosophy of Right* (1821), in which he claims that philosophy is 'its own time apprehended in thoughts'. 'To comprehend what is, this is the task of philosophy, because what is, is reason.'[30] By appointing Reason as the last court of appeal for all belief and knowledge, philosophy in its dominant mode strives to give rational structure to the actual, or rather to *reveal* the rational within the actual. Of course, in order to fulfil such a role, philosophical insight must arrive – much as an investigator to a crime scene – after the event. Hegel concedes as much when he writes: 'As the thought of the world, it [philosophy] appears only when actuality is already there cut and dried after its process of formation has been completed.'[31] In concluding the Preface, Hegel reinforces the necessity of philosophy's belatedness, by way of the now famous remark about the owl of Minerva, which 'spreads its wings only with the falling of the dusk'.

The young Marx criticizes this passive-reflective aspect of Hegelian philosophy, especially as it is uncritically taken up by the Young Hegelians. In *The

Holy Family (1845), his scathing and gleefully juvenile critique of Bruno Bauer, Marx writes:

> In Hegel the Absolute Spirit of history already treats the mass [of human individuals] as material and finds its true expression only in philosophy. But with Hegel, the philosopher is only the organ through which the creator of history, the Absolute Spirit, arrives at self-consciousness by retrospection after the movement has ended. The participation of the philosopher in history is reduced to this retrospective consciousness, for real movement is accomplished by the Absolute Spirit unconsciously, so that the philosopher appears *post festum*.[32]

The habitual retrospection of traditional philosophy, its blindness to the future, is instrumental in prompting Bloch's engagement with the affective politics of hope. Building from Marx's critique of what we might call a vulgar idealism, most succinctly captured in the celebrated eleventh thesis on Feuerbach, Bloch's project attempts to restore, or if necessary create from scratch, a *constructive* and *productive* role for philosophy. His aim is to move the discipline beyond mere contemplation and *post factum* ratification, and towards a practical, speculative, world-making activity: a theory-praxis in league with the *Novum* (the New). According to Bloch, philosophy's fixation on the 'What Has Become' produces only contemplative knowledge, and in doing so it presupposes a closed world in which '[o]ccurrence becomes history, knowledge re-remembering [i.e. Platonic anamnesis], celebration the observance of something that has been'.[33] What the concepts of utopia and hope have in common is a vision that exceeds the contours of the present moment. To reactivate hope and utopian desire is to break through the appearance of the way things are, so as to highlight the contingency, indeterminacy, and incompleteness that lie at the heart of the extant world, that things could have been and can still be otherwise.

For Bloch, as for his fellow-travellers in the Frankfurt School, thinking means transgressing. It is a form of venturing beyond the given: 'Only thinking directed towards changing the world and informing the desire to change it does not confront the future (the unclosed space for new development in front of us) as embarrassment and the past as spell.'[34] The unholy alliance of forces outlined above – a realist political mainstream, a depressed and defeatist left, and a passive, retrospective philosophy – seems intent on foreclosing the future and suppressing what Bloch terms the 'still living, not yet discharged past'.[35] The latter point is important for understanding Blochian critical theory as informed by a philosophy of *process*. Its vision of the world is characterized by a radical sense of the ontological incompleteness of reality, the hunger born of an awareness (at once visceral and cognitive) that 'something's missing'. This persistent yet under-cognized sense of absence or non-fulfilment speaks to the affective impingement of the 'Not Yet' on the present.

The Not Yet plays a pivotal role in Bloch's rehabilitation of political hope, and it appears in two forms: the *Not-Yet-Become* and the *Not-Yet-Conscious*. In deploying these counterfactual concepts of the Not Yet, Bloch seeks once again to repudiate disciplinary paradigms that encourage naturalization of the social, retrospection, and anamnesis. The Not-Yet-Become is Bloch's term for the as yet unrealized potential within material reality. The concept bespeaks of the world's perpetually unfinished state, and in it is retained the idea of a future or futures that remain indeterminately open to alternative and unforeseeable paths. As Ruth Levitas puts it, 'Once the world is seen as in a constant state of process, but a process whose direction and outcome is not predetermined, there are always many possible futures – futures which are real possibilities, rather than merely formal possibilities'.[36] By virtue of its primarily materialist basis, the Not-Yet-Become can be said to represent the *objective* side of the Not Yet. The latter's *subjective* side is captured in the Not-Yet-Conscious.

Bloch proposes the Not-Yet-Conscious as a rejoinder to the predominant forms of psychoanalytical practice of the early and mid-twentieth century. In *The Principle of Hope*, Bloch offers a critical overview of psychoanalysis – at least in its Freudian and Jungian traditions – and argues that the latter is extremely limited in (therapeutic) scope. First, it is too accommodating of the present state of affairs, especially since it fails to address the unique and material features of social, economic, and political life that predispose people to develop certain forms of neurosis and psychic distress. Bloch recalls a visible disclaimer to this effect: 'even in bourgeois déclassé Vienna, the notice hung on the wall of the psychological advice bureau: "Economic and social questions cannot be treated here" '.[37] Second, psychoanalysis is overly preoccupied with the past. In their quest to reveal the working of primordial drives and archetypes, unacknowledged injuries, misidentifications, repressions, thwarted desires, traumatic experiences, and so forth (all of which are, on Bloch's reading, thoroughly hypostatized and de-historicized), the psychoanalyst is only concerned with bringing to light an unconscious that is wholly structured by the past.

For Freud, neuroses and complexes arise as a result of the repression of libidinal drives. Interrupted, unfulfilled or unacknowledged wishes linger in the individual's psyche, but are hidden or turned away from the consciousness of the ego; in other words, primal drives are censored and made unconscious so that the individual may adhere to the injunctions of life in 'civilized' society. The repression of sexual drives can produce 'sublimation' – the redirecting of sexual energies into other, ostensibly more productive activities (and for

Freud, 'culture' is the crowning achievement of sublimation). But ordinarily such repression creates a range of neurotic behaviours and psychopathologies, such as parapraxes (slips of the tongue), seemingly groundless oversensitivity, fetishes, complexes, and so on. The aim of Freudian psychoanalysis is to delve into the patient's unconscious in order to bring to consciousness the preconditions of one's neurotic symptoms. Once the underlying cause of a neurosis has been illuminated by the analyst, and wilfully acknowledged by the analysand, the patient is said to be cured.

For Carl Jung (whom Bloch refers to as 'the psychoanalytic fascist'[38] and 'the fascistically frothing psychoanalyst'),[39] the libido and its unconscious contents are viewed as expressions of a collective prehistory, a 'primeval unity of all drives'.[40] Bloch credits Freud for at least being a modern liberal and utilizing 'illuminating consciousness' in its capacity to bring repressed material to light, and for treating the unconscious as a repository of individually acquired repressions and neuroses on which the conscious ego can be brought to bear. This is in stark contrast to the anti-modern Jung, who, on Bloch's account, reduces the libido and the unconscious to a general, undivided, primordial ground, invoking *völkisch* irrationalism in the process. For Jung, neurotic conflicts arise once the dominant logic of the civilized intellect destroys the archaic-instinctual basis of the drives and the imagination. He claims that all psychic phenomena are founded on a substratum of primeval 'archetypes', which together constitute the 'collective unconscious' – an innate, universal datum that endows every individual with the same pre-existent forms of experience and imagery. Since there is seen to be no value in pursuing the rational resolution of neuroses, and there is no sublimation of frustrated desires into other pursuits, Jung instead advocates a reconnection to this collective unconscious, plunging further and further into the primitive past, the 'five-thousand-year-old shaft beneath the few thousand years of civilization', to explain psychic behaviour in the present.[41]

Bloch's damning critique of Jung is undoubtedly politically motivated in large part, and it is worth remembering that Jungian psychoanalysis proved highly amenable to Nazi appropriation. But Bloch's more general concerns over the socio-political deficiency of psychoanalysis stem from the latter's attachment to an already established past, by which the present and the future are encumbered. 'The unconscious of psychoanalysis', Bloch concludes, is '*never a Not-Yet-Conscious*, an element of progressions; it consists rather of regressions. Accordingly, even the process of making this unconscious conscious only clarifies What Has Been'.[42] The Not-Yet-Conscious is Bloch's attempt to inject a sense of indeterminacy and futurity into the structuring of the unconscious (at both the individual and the collective level). As Levitas notes, the 'unconscious is also the pre-conscious, is intrinsically creative and the source of the utopian impulse'.[43] The Not-Yet-Conscious consists of the subjective representations, desires, and images of the objectively Not-Yet-Become. Where the psychoanalytical unconscious plays host to an assortment of repressed material from a traumatic past that is viewed solely retrospectively, the Not-Yet-Conscious is home to pre-conscious material that is readable speculatively as expressions of potentiality. The unfolding of this potentiality, as opposed to its renunciation and further repression, 'extend[s], in an anticipating way, existing material into the future possibilities of being different and better'. So, rather than seeking to diminish, deflect, or sublimate unconscious desires in support of a fixed reality, Bloch's concept of the Not-Yet-Conscious calls for the exploration and expansion of unfulfilled and unacknowledged desires in service of an alternative, indeterminate and open future, the Not Yet of our world-in-process. The Not-Yet-Conscious is futural in its condition of prefiguring possibility. Bloch's use of the term *Vorschein* signals this 'forward dawning' and 'shining ahead' that is transmitted via the Not-Yet-Conscious, 'the preconscious of what is to come, the psychological birthplace of the New'.[44]

In championing the elaboration, experimentation, and development of utopian longing born of unmet needs and unfulfilled wishes in the here and now, Bloch concedes that this will unavoidably also include the proliferation of some wholly undesirable desires. For instance, his analysis of the Nazis' rise to power diverges from the most prominent explanations at the time. While most analyses tend towards a crude economic reductionism – viewing fascism as the armed wing of the bourgeoisie – Bloch views fascism as quasi-religious in form and arising out of human desire or striving. Rather than dismiss such desire as simply deluded, basic, primitive, and so on, Bloch takes it seriously as expressive of a genuine human impulse towards freedom and a better life. As Thompson notes, Bloch abhors the *völkisch* romanticism and constructed nostalgia that undergirded the rise of fascism, but he nonetheless acknowledges the legitimacy of the originary impulse.[45] Human desire may take multiple forms, all of which ought to be subject to collective adjudication, but the desire itself should at least be recognized, nurtured even, rather than rejected outright or forcibly repressed. Jameson usefully elaborates on this point when he foregrounds the intertwining of the ideological and the utopian, or rather the utopian kernel *within* the ideological shell, as it were:

> Works of mass culture cannot be ideological without at one and the same time being implicitly or explicitly Utopian as well: they cannot manipulate unless they offer some genuine shred of content as a fantasy bribe to the public about to be so manipulated. Even the 'false consciousness' of so monstrous a phenomenon of Nazism was nourished by collective fantasies of a Utopian type, in 'socialist' as well as in

nationalist guises ... [T]he works of mass culture, even if their function lies in the legitimation of the existing order – or some worse one – cannot do their job without deflecting in the latter's service the deepest and most fundamental hopes and fantasies of the collectivity, to which they can therefore, no matter in how distorted a fashion, be found to have given voice.[46]

The material inheritance represented by cultural beliefs, archetypes, images, artifacts, and so forth, marks the intersection of affect and ideology. It forms the locus of desire and knowledge, which is not merely an accumulation of things past, but also extends the material of the past into the Not Yet of the future. Where a reactionary politics marshals *fear* to facilitate either a retreat to an imagined past or resignation to a bad present, a utopian politics mobilizes *hope* in the service of an indeterminate future of irreducible potentiality. Indeed, Bloch's affective politics of hope is bound up with potentiality and temporality. The very terminology of the Not Yet registers both future expectation and present lack, since the German '*noch nicht*' can mean both 'not yet' and 'still not'.[47] Likewise, Bloch characterizes hope (like fear) as an *expectant emotion*. This is so because hope is primarily (although by no means straightforwardly, as will be shown presently) oriented towards the future: 'The intention in all expectant emotions is one that points ahead, the temporal environment of its content is future.'[48] The form of this future often remains open, unspecifiable and abstract, to the extent that hope need not be directed towards a specific object or aim. Of course, hope can also be aimed at or attached to more concrete goals, changes, objects, relations, actions, and so on. But in both its forms – abstract and concrete – hope remains thoroughly *anticipatory*. It is a processive affective state, an emotion in motion, as it were. Hope is born of but leads out of the present.

And yet despite this general invariance of direction, hope is not simplistically future-oriented. Contrary to its pejorative associations with unjustified belief, naivety and wishful thinking, Blochian hope is neither ignorant of the past nor blind to the present. Rather, hope is temporally Janus-faced in its relation to the miscarried potential of previous times (the unfulfilled, defiled, or suppressed dreams of the dead and vanquished), and to the as yet undetermined and even unconscious possibility that constitutes the future. As Bloch puts it, 'true action in the present itself occurs solely in the totality of this process which is unclosed both backwards and forwards'.[49] The 'rigid divisions between future and past thus themselves collapse, unbecome future becomes visible in the past, avenged and inherited, mediated and fulfilled past in the future'.[50] As such, substantive social and political critique cannot simply proceed by way of describing and revealing the covert strategies and ideologies at work in the contemporary moment (important though such work remains). Critique must also be a creative act of (re)discovery, excavation, and mobilization of the forgotten dreams, missed opportunities, and lost potential of betrayed ancestors. We must take cognizance of the fact that today is but a mangled version of a tomorrow that was promised yesterday. Which is not to say that all that exists *now* is an irrevocable failure in need of wholesale destruction, but rather that the present carries within it an inherited surplus of desire and knowledge from past generations, which can provide counterfactual drivers for non-conformist, transgressive thought and practice in the here and now.

To this end, another crucial feature of Bloch's critical theory of hope lies in its attempt to retrieve and analyse a variety of materials from the pre-bourgeois epoch that fail to fully register in the onward march of world-historical progress, but which nonetheless convey the utopian longing that exceeds the confines of epistemological protocol. Bloch writes:

> [T]his Ratio [of the bourgeois epoch] is not the sole inheritance, on the contrary, preceding societies and even many myths in them ... may also provide a philosophy which has surmounted the bourgeois barrier of knowledge with possibly progressive inherited material, even though, as is obvious, this material particularly requires elucidation, critical acquisition, functional change.[51]

The task of the social critic, then, is to recall and scrutinize ideas from the past, to recirculate and revivify cultural artefacts that have yet to be fully realized or illuminated, and to discern the hidden utopian potential within these forgotten, outmoded, or simply reified forms. The call for 'functional change' in the above passage can be seen as being in line with a broadly modernist imperative to wrest cultural heritage from its paid and vested gatekeepers, wrenching objects and ideas out of their original contexts and thrusting them into provocative new formations and formulations. This act of reworking or working through cultural traditions is not simply a matter of cataloguing the varied wishes, desires, images, myths, archetypes, and beliefs of days gone by. Rather, it is a creative and critical endeavour that establishes new (or reestablishes old or lost) connections to a society's past. Bloch's theory and practice can be seen to converge in this regard, insofar as his writing style – like that of many of his peers and fellow theorists – is markedly esoteric, formalist, expressionistic, and dialectical. Bloch's work draws upon anachronistic concepts, religions, artworks, and traditions, and organizes them in a form that resolutely resists easy or quick comprehension and, by extension, simple commodification. Again, this is a thoroughly modernist strategy to uphold a cultural distinction that will safeguard Bloch's work from the threat of becoming merely another item of *kitsch* or commodified culture. However, it is notable that unlike most writers associated with the Frankfurt School, whose cultural interests rarely extend beyond the realm of 'high' modern art, Bloch turns his attention to a far wider range of socio-cultural phenomena. Juxtaposing the sacred and the profane, the ideal and the material, the subjective and the objective, the religious and the secular, the past and the present, Bloch seeks a way beyond the strict dictates of crude accumulation (of capital and culture) and towards a more constructive (re)appropriation and curation of things past.

Bloch's notion of the importance of 'inherited material' that necessitates elucidation, critical acquisition, and functional change is one shared by other first-generation critical theorists. Most directly, the redemptive reconstruction of the past in the present follows in the tradition of weak messianism evoked by Walter Benjamin in his 'Theses on the Philosophy of History', in which he famously claims:

> The past carries with it a temporal index by which it is referred to redemption. There is a secret agreement between past generations and the present one. Our coming was expected on earth. Like every generation that preceded us, we have been endowed with a *weak* Messianic power, a power to which the past has a claim.[52]

Bloch too takes seriously the temporal connectedness of successive generations, and the redemptive hope that underpins Benjamin's weak messianism, for the ways in which they give voice to a state of incompleteness, a sense of human striving and an acute awareness of dissatisfaction with the status quo. In this view, suffering and failures from the past are not simply erased or written out of history (despite the best efforts of triumphalist historians' glorification of the victors); rather, past suffering and sorrow persists in that which exists as the underside or 'bad side' of history, as Marx put it. As society hurls itself forward, seemingly at an ever-accelerating pace, the past does not remain static, frozen, merely 'of its time'. As both Bloch's processual Marxism and Benjamin's weak messianism propose, the past might even erupt in and explode the Now in an unexpected and untimely fashion.

Bloch uses the somewhat cumbersome term *Ungleichzeitigkeit* (non-contemporaneity, or non-synchronism) as a way of conceptualizing the (often untimely) expression and attempted instantiation of a genuine utopian impulse. To illustrate the concept, Bloch takes the example of the peasant uprising of 1525 led by Thomas Müntzer. For Bloch, Müntzer's movement stands out as an important early attempt to actualize communized property relations and a more egalitarian social order, but it occurred at a time when the conditions for its realization were unpropitious. In other words, the emancipatory impulse, while both right and justified, could not find full expression in its own time. The impulse itself should not be dismissed simply on account of its failure to be realized, since at another, more developed socio-historical juncture, it might well achieve actualization. The content of the past seeps into and continues to affect the present. Bloch takes Müntzer's experience as exemplary of non-contemporaneity, arguing that 'not all people exist in the same Now. They do so only externally, by virtue of the fact that they may all be seen today. But that does not mean that they are living at the same time with others'.[53]

For both Benjamin and Bloch, the principle of hope is a real (or at least latent) productive force in the world, not only the world of the individual, but also that of the collective. That is to say, the ways in which hope is valued and experienced – whether it is extinguished or sparked, denied or affirmed, educated or fraudulent – can be decisive in the creation of affective structures that have a profound impact upon subjective desire and objective possibility. This is why it is crucial to appreciate the sociality of affect, since it disrupts the insularity so characteristic of individualistic readings of emotion and feeling. Instead of supporting the latter's overly simplistic accounts of agency, which too readily presume a sovereign, self-contained individual to whom emotions and affects belong, the affective model informing Bloch's critical theory opens out the subjective into the objective, the private into the public, and vice versa, so as to foreground the instability and not-yet-ness of the extant world. Both the individual and the social are always in process, ever unsettled and incomplete. Thus, the diffusion and contagion of particular forms of affect play a crucial role in producing or precluding certain future developments and possibilities.

Bloch makes much of this affective-productive ground of hope, placing it within a dialectical framework that repudiates any straightforward dichotomy that would posit determinism on one side and contingency on the other. So while the *principle* of hope can exceed concrete historical conditions and indefinitely expand the possibilities of an open future, it is also the case that, at a given moment in time, the likelihood of actualizing some possible futures will inevitably outstrip that of others. There is no necessary development from potentiality to actuality. Indeed, much concerted praxis is needed to procure a better future for all. Nonetheless, the very *expectancy* of hope as a processual, affective mode of engagement with the world provides the motivational and imaginary ground for a critical theory guided towards social transformation. Without such *affective* force underpinning it, critical theory would risk duplicating and reinforcing the debilitating structure of feeling that it seeks to abolish. In that regard, we have already seen how the reproduction and internalization of hopelessness can correspond to the decreased capacity of a body or group to affect and be affected (an example of which was given in the countless narratives of decline that circulate on the left, and which reduce the latter's horizons both theoretically and practically). The diminishing of such a capacity results in a sorrowful, passive, and depressive state. As a counter to this, Bloch argues, the more active and joyful affect of hope should be cultivated, learned, and mobilized.

We might note here that Bloch's enlisting of hope as a productive and joyful affect ultimately derives from the work of Spinoza. In his *Ethics*, Spinoza conceives of *affectus* as the power to affect and to be affected. 'By affect I understand affections of the body by which the body's power of acting is increased or diminished, aided or restrained, and at the same time, the ideas of these affections.'[54] The initial clause here, focused as it is on the 'body' and its power to act, suggests the strongly materialist side of Spinoza's thought. But the addition of 'the ideas of these affections' to the equation is indicative of his unique treatment of the mind and the body in tandem. Spinoza's analyses of reason and emotion, mind and body, differ from that of most of his contemporaries. Where Descartes, Hobbes and Locke commence their philosophies from the foundational notion of the isolated individual in a hypothetical state of nature, Spinoza's philosophy of affect is social through and through. For Spinoza, neither reason nor emotion can be said to substantively generate out of the individual. Instead, they derive from collective experience, that is, the endless interaction and circulation of bodies and affects. The mind's capacity to think corresponds to the body's power to act, without either the body determining the mind, or the mind determining the body. For Spinoza, while the mind and the body remain relatively distinct and autonomous, they develop and proceed in parallel. As Michael Hardt notes, 'the mind's power to think corresponds to its receptivity to external ideas; and the body's power to act corresponds to its sensitivity to other bodies'.[55] Affect, then, in its original Spinozist form, serves as a foundational concept that combines the corporeal and the cognitive in a way that registers the inescapable flow of energies and contact between complex bodies within any system.

The primacy of affect in Spinoza's philosophy leads him to posit strict demarcations and categorizations between different forms and manifestations of affect, most notably between active/passive and joyful/sorrowful. These distinctions signal the role of reason within Spinoza's philosophy of affect. Affects can be active (arising from *internal* causes) or passive (determined by *external* causes). Correspondingly, the passive affects are inherently sorrowful, since they diminish the body's power to act and the mind's power to think, while the active affects are necessarily joyful on account of them being determined solely by internal causes. That is to say, the active affects are stronger, positive emotions shaped by reasoning and the intellect. Reason's task within this schema is not to transcend or subdue the affects; rather, reason ought to be employed to activate, enliven, and strengthen the affects. For Spinoza, the only way to effectively move beyond the passivity of an enervating affect is by displacing it with a stronger, more active and joyful affect: 'An affect cannot be restrained or taken away except by an affect opposite to, and stronger than, the affect to be restrained'.[56] Importantly, this preference for internally given (i.e. reasoned) actions over externally determined passions does not promote isolation, for the increased power to affect always also corresponds to an increase in the power to be affected by others. As such, on Spinoza's account of action, one cannot simply retreat to a fortified interiority of being, since any enhanced autonomy necessarily implies an augmented receptivity.[57]

This last point is further illustrated by Spinoza's use of *affection* to refer to the ways in which affect is mediated and transmitted, that is to say, how one body both affects and is affected by other bodies. So, rather than positing affect as a kind of raw, immediate modality of experience, the Spinozist-Blochian view is one premised upon constant, open-ended relationality and mediation. This perspective expands rather than contracts the territories of the individual and the social. It marks the *transmission* of affect between bodies. As Teresa Brennan argues, the 'transmission of affect means that we are not self-contained in terms of our energies. There is no secure distinction between the "individual" and the "environment" '.[58] The latter seeps into the former, and vice versa, until the idea of there being any clear or rigid division between the two is rendered insignificant. The transmission of affect, then, does not imply that one person's feelings simply become those of another. Rather, the notion of affect's transmissibility suggests the co-production and communality of affective intensities, some of which may diminish our capacities to act and be acted upon, while others may augment them. Indeed, the (quantitative) intensity of (qualitative) affect primes a body or group for certain forms of action; an affective intensity can structure how we engage (rationally and emotionally, theoretically and practically) with the world. It can make visible tendencies and latencies that lie within the contingency of the present, participating in the actualizing of real but obscured potential.

One finds this ontology of incompleteness, affect, and potentiality replicated in Bloch's work. He follows in Spinoza's footsteps by claiming that hope, as an *active* affect, can productively reconfigure our relations in the world and increase our capacity to act. Building from the quasi-anthropological claim that hopelessness is 'in a temporal and factual sense, the most insupportable thing, downright intolerable to human needs',[59] Bloch avows a form of critical pedagogy that aims at cultivating the principle of hope in order to counter the negative affects that so pervade and diminish social experience. For Bloch, then, it is 'a question of learning hope. Its work does not renounce, it is in love with success rather than failure. Hope, superior to fear, is neither passive like the latter, nor locked into nothingness'.[60] Of course, the 'success' of which Bloch writes is more ambiguous than it might appear. For the concretization of hope is only really possible through the utopian impulse and the endless human striving that is born of the recognition of a void, the continual sense that *'something's missing'* (the phrase repeated by Paul Ackermann in Brecht's *Mahagonny*, and one that reverberates in Bloch's figuring of utopian thought). Hope is most provocative and productive on account of its dual character, which is comprised of expectancy on the one hand and 'disappointability' [*Enttäuschbarkeit*] on the other; that is to say, hope is both anticipatory and yet is bound to be disappointed precisely because of its future orientation that refuses to be sated by the offerings of the Now.

Hope's positive longing indexes the negativity (the not) of the Not Yet; it is a registering of a hunger and a negativity born of lack. This wilful striving, or *conatus* (to use Spinoza's terminology), is animated not simply by the presence of desire, but also by the absence of its reconciliation. Since the manifold daydreams, wish-images, desires, and longings, so diligently chronicled in Bloch's work, arise out of the very conditions that they seek to overcome, to attain a complete realization of them would be to simultaneously negate their essential utopian core, making peace with the world as it is, rather than opening out the field of potentiality beyond the existent. For this reason, then, hope and utopian striving are wilfully 'unrealistic' when considered within the framework of ongoing capitalist catastrophe.[61] Perpetually exceeding whatever is given, spilling over the topographical outlines of the pre-mapped territories and the experiential limitations of the present, the utopian impulse, on Bloch's account, is decidedly anti-programmatic. It will be taken up and will manifest itself in wildly diverse, unpredictable, and as yet unimaginable ways, and in a variety of different concrete situations.

In acknowledgement of such an unavoidable element of contingency and surplus, Bloch's theory of hope – despite undertaking creative excavations of historical and cultural material as *Vorscheine* (pre-illuminations) – is purposely devoid of blueprints and reassurances. We must proceed without guarantees. In both its affective structure and its methodology, hope 'dwells in the region of the not-yet, a place where entrance and, above all, final content are marked by an enduring indeterminacy'.[62] As such, contrary to familiar derisions of it as mere Micawberism, hope is in fact suffused with risk and uncertainty. Indeed, as Bloch remarks, 'hope is the opposite of security. It is the opposite of naïve optimism. The category of danger is always within it'.[63] By virtue of its restlessness, openness, untimeliness, activeness, and the impossibility of it ever achieving complete fulfilment, hope – at once 'the most important expectant emotion'[64] and a *'directing act of a cognitive kind'*[65] – stands at the centre of Bloch's critical theory of process or becoming [*werden*]. Such a marked shift in the left's affective dispositions, orientations, and structures of feeling will likely prove invaluable for any active intervention in today's socio-political sphere, even or especially when the demands born of hope's utopic desire explode the ostensible horizons of the possible, creating new ones in the process.

One of the central motivations behind this chapter was a sense of dissatisfaction with overly deterministic analyses of capitalism, particularly those Marxist analyses that provide expert accounts of the structural development of social forms within capitalism, but at the cost of totally expunging the labouring subjects whose practice reproduces those very forms and social relations. As if the formal architectonics of capital were entirely autonomous and capable of functioning *ad infinitum*. Of course, systemic critiques of political economy remain invaluable, particularly at a time when new, post-critical modes of theorizing appear to be shifting focus away from the social and the human as areas of concern. But what do such accounts have to say about the outbreak of riots (as in England in 2011, or Athens, or Paris, or Ferguson, or Charlotte),[66] or large-scale strike actions in China and India, or movements like Black Lives Matter and Occupy? Myriad protests from the unusable or displaced surplus populations make visible the violence – both symbolic and material – inherent to the functioning and maintenance of capitalism. But despite the underlying oppression and exploitation at the core of our economic system, protest and disorder are still exceptional. They remain fleeting outbursts rather than sustained counteractions. This calls forth new sets of questions that supplement the political-economic sphere. For instance, what sort of affective economies accompany the formal and informal money economies? How are the affects of hope and fear produced and experienced in relation to socio-economic conditions, state forces, and mass culture? In what ways are political utopias and realisms alike used to support or undermine certain ideas and praxes?

On the one hand, we might note, after Jameson, that affect and utopian impulses have steadily waned, as positivist forms of quantification and probability become the dominant methods by which all practical activity and theoretical systems are judged. But on the other hand, it seems more likely that utopian thinking and affect have simply mutated and migrated, resurfacing in the far-fetched visions of the most excitable free-market ideologues, for whom the dream of variable capital flowing freely across national borders (a kind of Kantian cosmopolitanism in a monstrous, parodic form) represents the ultimate *telos* of financial capital. Indeed, Karl Polanyi once described the idea of a completely self-regulating free market as a 'liberal utopia'. What is more, despite the apparent depletion of future-oriented energies in the socio-political sphere, we should not forget that the future figures prominently within the financial markets in the form of 'speculation'. On closer inspection, then, it would seem that the ostensibly wholesale eradication of utopian thought and action, and of hopes anchored in the idea of a better future, might be better understood as having undergone a marked shift in focus. On this view, it is not that the contemporary social world is bereft of hope, or that utopian energies have been exhausted, but rather that they have been significantly redefined and redirected so as to serve what Bourdieu calls the 'utopia of endless exploitation'. The point, then, must be to reclaim and refunction our utopian imaginary, galvanizing an affective politics of hope in the process. By revisiting early critical theory, in this chapter I have tried to counter the common understanding of hope as merely a compensatory ideology (a hangover of religious thought) that promotes retreat and placation. While the cynical shell of liberal-democratic ideology can be seen to transform 'hope' into just another instrument of political capital, the kernel of truth at its heart remains intact. As critical theory reminds us, ideology is never simply the production and circulation of falsity or deception; rather, in order to be effective and have social traction, ideology must incorporate or carry within it a truth-content. Bloch's work remains vital today for it revivifies hope as a politically and affectively charged basis for struggle and engagement.

Notes

1 Theodor Adorno, *Minima Moralia: Reflections on a Damaged Life*, trans. Edmund Jephcott (London: Verso, 2005), 167.
2 The phrase resonates with Franz Kafka's statement to Max Brod: 'plenty of hope, an infinite amount of hope – but not for us'. Benjamin frequently cites this remark in his notes; Werner Hamacher, 'The Gesture in the Name: On Benjamin and Kafka', in *Premises: Essays on Philosophy and Literature from Kant to Celan*, trans. Peter Fenves (Stanford: Stanford University Press, 1996), 303.
3 The phrase 'radicals in despair' is used by Tom Bottomore; see Bottomore, *The Frankfurt School and Its Critics* (London: Routledge, 2002), 37. Erich Fromm uses similar language in criticizing (or better, *diagnosing*) his former colleague Herbert Marcuse: 'Marcuse is essentially an example of an alienated intellectual, who presents his personal despair as a theory of radicalism'; Fromm, *The Revolution of Hope: Toward a Humanized Technology* (Riverdale: American Mental Health Foundation Inc., 2010), 21.
4 Adorno, in Theodor Adorno and Max Horkheimer, 'Towards a New Manifesto?', *New Left Review* 65 (2010): 61. Of course, this remark by Adorno in conversation with Max Horkheimer is somewhat complicated by the *Bilderverbot* (ban on graven images), which is usually seen as the Judaic principle underlying critical theory's apparent aversion to imagining concrete futures. In this regard, even if it were possible to imagine

a better world, Adorno and Horkheimer would not do so, since it would contravene the prohibitions of the *Bilderverbot*. This view, which makes much (perhaps too much) of the Jewish character of critical theory, is well established. However, it is seldom noted that there are numerous suggestive traces of utopian imagery scattered among Adorno's writings, which surely serve to question the strength with which he actually enforces the *Bilderverbot* in his own thinking. See, for example, the famous aphorism entitled 'Sur l'eau', in which he writes: '*Rien faire comme une bête*, lying on water and looking peacefully at the sky, "being, nothing else, without any further definition and fulfilment," might take the place of process, act, satisfaction, and so truly keep the promise of dialectical logic that it would culminate in its origin. None of the abstract concepts come closer to the fulfilled utopia than that of eternal peace'; Adorno, *Minima Moralia*, 157.

5 Fredric Jameson, *Archaeologies of the Future: The Desire Called Utopia and Other Science Fictions* (London: Verso, 2005), xiii.

6 Wendy Brown, 'Resisting Left Melancholy', *boundary 2* 26/3 (1999): 26. For a critique of Brown's argument from a queer perspective, see Heather Love, *Feeling Backward: Loss and the Politics of Queer History* (Cambridge, MA: Harvard University Press, 2007), 146ff. I also provide an alternative account of melancholy in Chapter 2.

7 Richard Rorty, *Achieving Our Country: Leftist Thought in Twentieth-Century America* (Cambridge, MA: Harvard University Press, 1999), 37.

8 One should recall here that despite the lasting influence of the notion of 'inevitable' capitalist collapse and socialist revolution, Marx did not actually propose any iron laws of history, and instead confined his analyses to the development of capitalism in Western Europe. In a letter of 1877 addressed to Nikolai Danielson, prominent spokesperson for the *Narodniki* (Russian Populists), Marx responds directly to some comments made by N.M. Mikhailovsky, a leading theorist of the Populists. Mikhailovsky had suggested that Marx keep his theories grounded firmly in Europe and out of Russia, since the latter was striving for a national development that would bypass the capitalist stage. In his letter to Danielson, Marx complains of how Mikhailovsky 'feels he absolutely must metamorphose my historical sketch of the genesis of capitalism in Western Europe into a historico-philosophic theory of the general path every people is fated to tread, whatever the historical circumstances in which it finds itself, in order that it may ultimately arrive at the form of economy which ensures, together with the greatest expansion of the productive powers of social labour, the most complete development of man. But I beg his pardon. (He is both honouring and shaming me too much)'; Karl Marx, 'Letter to Mikhailovsky', in *Karl Marx: Selected Writings*, ed. David McLellan (Oxford: Oxford University Press, 2000), 618.

9 One of the best-known formulations of this view of Western Marxism as a discourse of defeat and pessimism is Perry Anderson's *Considerations on Western Marxism* (London: New Left Books, 1976).

10 Theodor W. Adorno, *Negative Dialectics,* trans. E.B. Ashton (New York: Continuum, 1973), 3, translation modified.

11 Leo Löwenthal, cited in Martin Lüdke, 'The Utopian Motif Is Suspended: Conversation with Leo Löwenthal', *New German Critique* 38 (Spring–Summer 1986): 105.

12 This developmental model could easily be read along Freudian lines, inasmuch as the pattern replicates the way in which an originary, untutored 'pleasure principle' eventually gives way to a mature 'reality principle'. Of course, rather than the latter entirely superseding the former, the process is more like a dialectical *Aufhebung*

(cancelling and preserving), although Freud would not use such terminology; see Sigmund Freud, 'Formulations on the Two Principles of Mental Functioning', in *The Standard Edition of the Complete Psychological Works of Sigmund Freud*, Vol. 12, ed. James Strachey (London: The Hogarth Press, 1958), 223.

13 William A. Galston, 'Realism in Political Theory', *European Journal of Political Theory* 9/4 (2010): 394. For an engaging critique of the unacknowledged analytical realism of contemporary political philosophy, see Lorna Finlayson, *The Political is Political: Conformity and the Illusion of Dissent in Contemporary Political Philosophy* (London: Rowman & Littlefield International, 2015).

14 John Gray, *Black Mass: Apocalyptic Religion and the Death of Utopia* (London: Penguin, 2007), 20.

15 In common with many anti-utopian strands of political theory, Gray's account deploys an excessively broad understanding of 'utopia' all the more to (unwittingly?) fortify the existing social and power structures. In doing so, Gray and his fellow-travellers confirm Karl Mannheim's apt remark: 'It is no accident that an observer who consciously or unconsciously has taken a stand in favour of the existing and prevailing order should have such a broad and undifferentiated conception of the utopian'; Mannheim, *Ideology and Utopia* (Abingdon: Routledge, 1997), 177. As an aside, it is interesting to note that Gray's previous work, *Straw Dogs*, betrays the sort of utopian imagination that he so fervently disdains elsewhere. For instance, when he envisions the extinction of the human species and the 'play of life' on Earth continuing unabated in our absence, Gray's prose takes on a certain utopian bent, albeit in the service of his stringent anti-humanism; see Vincent Geoghegan, 'An Anti-humanist Utopia?', in *The Privatization of Hope: Ernst Bloch and the Future of Utopia*, ed. Peter Thompson and Slavoj Žižek (Durham, NC: Duke University Press, 2013), 47.

16 Gray, *Black Mass*, 20.

17 Henk de Berg, 'Unlearning How to Hope: Eleven Theses in Defence of Liberal Democracy and Consumer Culture', in *The Privatization of Hope: Ernst Bloch and the Future of Utopia*, ed. Peter Thompson and Slavoj Žižek (Durham, NC: Duke University Press, 2013), 275. It is easy enough to subvert this claim by inserting one of Marx's favoured terms of abuse, namely, *bourgeois*. Thus, the passage should read: 'no social order has ever produced more [bourgeois] freedom, more [bourgeois] equality, and more [bourgeois] justice than the combination of bourgeois capitalism and liberal democracy'.

18 Berg, 'Unlearning How to Hope', 282.

19 Berg, 'Unlearning How to Hope', 282. In this stance, Berg repeats a refrain that has been recently popularized by the likes of Steven Pinker, namely, that our present moment marks the most civilized and least violent point in the history of humanity; Steven Pinker, *The Better Angels of Our Nature: A History of Violence and Humanity* (London: Penguin, 2011).

20 One need only note Berg's (ironic) lack of self-awareness to glean the glorification of the existent that underpins his theses. Ostensibly 'neutral' and objective examples he uses include: the role of 'policeman' as an opportunity for 'genuine heroism'; 'work, hobbies, even bourgeois family life' as offering ways of surpassing other people and going beyond ourselves at any given time. The latter is also apparently evidenced by 'the lawyer who wins a court case, the associate professor who is appointed full professor, the secretary who explains the new computer system to her [sic!] boss'.

21 Fredric Jameson, 'The Politics of Utopia', *New Left Review* 25 (2004): 36.

22 Mannheim, *Ideology and Utopia*, 176–7.
23 Such work is ongoing in recent queer theory, from which contemporary critical theory could learn a lot. On the relevance of notions of (anti-)utopia and (anti-)futurity for a queer politics, compare the works of Lee Edelman and José Esteban Muñoz, respectively: Edelman, *No Future: Queer Theory and the Death Drive* (Durham, NC: Duke University Press, 2004); Muñoz, *Cruising Utopia: The Then and There of Queer Futurity* (New York: New York University Press, 2009).
24 Ernst Bloch, *The Principle of Hope*, Vol. 1, trans. Neville Plaice, Stephen Plaice, and Paul Knight (Cambridge, MA: MIT Press, 1986), 7.
25 Bloch, *The Principle of Hope*, 3.
26 Bloch, *The Principle of Hope*, 7.
27 See Manfred Buhr, 'A Critique of Ernst Bloch's Philosophy of Hope', *Philosophy Today* 14 (Winter 1970): 259–71.
28 Rolf Wiggershaus, *The Frankfurt School: Its History, Theories, and Political Significance*, trans. Michael Robertson (Cambridge, MA: MIT Press, 1995), 69.
29 Jürgen Habermas, *Philosophical-Political Profiles*, trans. Frederick G. Lawrence (Cambridge, MA: MIT Press, 1983), 61.
30 G.W.F. Hegel, 'Preface', *Hegel's Philosophy of Right*, trans. Tom Knox (Oxford: Oxford University Press, 1978), 11.
31 Hegel, 'Preface', 12–13.
32 Karl Marx, 'The Holy Family', in *Karl Marx: Selected Writings*, ed. David McLellan (Oxford: Oxford University Press, 2000), 158. Similarly, albeit with less theoretical engagement and considerably more bombast, Friedrich Nietzsche denounces Hegel for his apparent 'naked admiration for success' and 'idolatry of the factual'; cited by Georg L. Kline, 'The Use and Abuse of Hegel by Nietzsche and Marx', in *Hegel and His Critics: Philosophy in the Aftermath of Hegel*, ed. William Desmond (Albany: SUNY Press, 1989), 5.
33 Bloch, *The Principle of Hope*, 6.
34 Bloch, *The Principle of Hope*, 8.
35 Bloch, *The Principle of Hope*, 9.
36 Ruth Levitas, *The Concept of Utopia* (Bern: Peter Lang, 2010), 102.
37 Bloch, *The Principle of Hope*, 66.
38 Bloch, *The Principle of Hope*, 56.
39 Bloch, *The Principle of Hope*, 59.
40 Bloch, *The Principle of Hope*, 59.
41 Jung, cited in Bloch, *The Principle of Hope*, 60.
42 Bloch, *The Principle of Hope*, 56.
43 Levitas, *The Concept of Utopia*, 101.
44 Bloch, *The Principle of Hope*, 116.
45 Peter Thompson, 'Introduction', in *The Privatization of Hope: Ernst Bloch and the Future of Utopia*, ed. Peter Thompson and Slavoj Žižek (Durham, NC: Duke University Press, 2013), 16. Bloch laments the left's inability to effectively mobilize desire and affect towards progressive ends, at least to the same extent that the far right was able to do so as a prelude to reactionary violence.
46 Fredric Jameson, 'Reification and Utopia in Mass Culture', *Social Text* 1 (Winter 1979): 130–48.
47 Levitas, *The Concept of Utopia*, 102.
48 Bloch, *The Principle of Hope*, 108.
49 Bloch, *The Principle of Hope*, 9.
50 Bloch, *The Principle of Hope*, 8–9.

51 Bloch, *The Principle of Hope*, 9.
52 Walter Benjamin, 'Theses on the Philosophy of History', in *Illuminations,* ed. Hannah Arendt, trans. Harry Zohn (Suffolk: Fontana, 1973), 256.
53 Ernst Bloch, 'Nonsynchronism and the Obligation to Its Dialectics', *New German Critique* 11 (Spring 1977): 22–38.
54 Benedict de Spinoza, *Ethics* (London: Penguin, 1996), 70.
55 Michael Hardt, 'Foreword: What Affects Are Good For', in *The Affective Turn: Theorizing the Social,* ed. Patricia Ticineto Clough, with Jean Halley (Durham, NC: Duke University Press, 2007), x.
56 Spinoza, *Ethics*, 120, original emphasis.
57 Hardt, 'Foreword', x.
58 Teresa Brennan, *The Transmission of Affect* (Ithaca, NY: Cornell University Press, 2004), 6.
59 Bloch, *The Principle of Hope*, 4–5.
60 Bloch, *The Principle of Hope*, 3. The psychoanalyst Erich Fromm, also an affiliate of the Frankfurt School, deploys a similar (albeit more 'realist') distinction between 'activeness' and 'passiveness' in his discussion of hope; see Fromm, *The Revolution of Hope*, 24–5.
61 Henri Lefebvre defends the transgressive potential of the utopian in precisely these terms in the following passage: 'reflection necessarily involves a form of utopia if it is not content to reflect and ratify compulsions, blindly accept authority and acknowledge circumstances; it implies an attempt to interfere with existing conditions and an awareness of other policies than those in force. Utopia? Yes indeed; *we are all utopians*, so soon as we wish for something different and stop playing the part of the faithful performer or watch-dog'; Henri Lefebvre, *Everyday Life in the Modern World* (London: Continuum, 2002), 74–5.
62 Ernst Bloch, 'Can Hope Be Disappointed?', in *Literary Essays*, trans. Andrew Joron (Stanford: Stanford University Press, 1998), 341.
63 Ernst Bloch, 'Something's Missing: A Discussion between Ernst Bloch and Theodor W. Adorno on the Contradictions of Utopian Longing', in *The Utopian Function of Art and Literature: Selected Essays*, trans. Jack Zipes and Frank Mecklenburg (Cambridge, MA: MIT Press, 1988), 16.
64 Bloch, *The Principle of Hope*, 11.
65 Bloch, *The Principle of Hope*, 12, original emphasis.
66 Joshua Clover makes a timely intervention in this regard by attempting to theorize the return of the riot from a political-economic (Arrighian) perspective. At the same time, his work remains cognizant of the particular characteristics that differentiate contemporary riots from their historical precedents; Joshua Clover, *Riot. Strike. Riot: The New Era of Uprisings* (London: Verso, 2016).

Coda

In lieu of a summary restatement of the preceding chapters, it seems more appropriate to finish by considering the role of affective politics in our contemporary moment. Much has already been written about 2016 marking a uniquely turbulent year of political upheaval, expressive of widespread discontent with the 'establishment', elites, and experts. What might a critical theory of affect have to say in response to the ostensibly seismic political events encompassed in Brexit, Donald Trump, and our supposedly new 'post-truth' age? Let us take the last feature as a starting point, because in unpacking the covert presuppositions of the very notion of a 'post-truth' politics, one can begin to better understand not only why the votes for Brexit and Trump actually came to pass, but also why they were unforeseen by so many commentators and pollsters.

Oxford Dictionaries announced that their 'word of the year' for 2016 was 'post-truth'. They define it as 'relating to or denoting circumstances in which objective facts are less influential in shaping public opinion than appeals to emotion and personal belief'. The OED notes the spike in the term's usage in the coverage of both the UK referendum on membership of the European Union, and the US presidential campaigns.[1] While much has been made of this 'post-truth' turn, it seems wholly disingenuous, for it can only have any purchase within the most naive or arrogant of insulated liberal mindsets. If the post-ness of 'post-truth' is meant to convey a temporal break, after which the political realm has become denuded of 'facts' and 'truth' (or simply that the latter have become irrelevant), then this begs the question: was politics prior to 2016 defined by its factual, evidence-based, truthful nature? Is it not the case that, for better or for worse, the political has always been suffused with affect, persuasion, rhetoric, and sentiment? If one need resort to the confection of a new 'post-truth' era in order to explain recent events – events whose implications and effects are genuinely perturbing – this indicates a rather limited understanding of political history. It betokens the dominant form of centrist liberalism that has accompanied most post-war capitalist economies – at least for as long as it proved economically viable to do so (say, from 1947 until 1973, with a brief bump in the late 1990s). Economically, such liberalism follows classical accounts of human nature undergirded by notions of utility-maximization, rational choice theory, and methodological individual-ism. Philosophically and politically, it can be seen as an outgrowth of the same rationalist legacy set out in this book's Introduction. It stems from the same school of liberal thinking that celebrates the virtue of the better argument, while disavowing all viscerality and affectivity from thought, as if the reasoned or accurate argument alone will suffice to move people to act.[2] In light of these underlying beliefs, liberal hegemony views facts as merely scientifically (and neutrally) discovered truths, simple and disinterested units to be ordered and managed by the appropriate users, managers, and technicians.[3] In the electoral realm, this managerial liberalism culminated in the phenomenon of 'triangulation' – a strategy of appearing bi-partisan in the hope of appealing to a broader range of the electorate. Bill Clinton was the first to successfully adopt this tactic ahead of his re-election in 1996; Tony Blair would follow the same approach a year later in the United Kingdom.

Again, it is worth recalling the specific political-economic conditions that enabled self-appointed 'centrists' to become the leading political forces at that time. On the back of the modest financial bump afforded by the 'dot-com bubble' in the mid- to late 1990s, figures like Clinton and Blair were able to speak across traditional political divisions, invoking the dual language of social welfare and responsibility on the one hand, and upward social mobility and acquisitiveness on the other. They could still conjure up the image of a socially progressive form of capitalism in which economic growth went hand in hand with the liberalization of values. If there is one thing that must be acknowl-edged of our present moment, it is that those times are over. What is more, they will not be returning. Anyone who speaks wistfully of bygone 'Third Way' schemes without referring to the political and economic conditions that ena-bled them has corpses in their mouth (to paraphrase Raoul Veneigem).

The intrusion of the 'post-truth' storm into this liberal idyll is really just the return of the repressed. The affective underpinning to political theory and praxis has always been there; it has just been overlooked or suppressed for the sake of securing certain ends. Political economy too has always been augmented by affect: hope and fear, pleasure and pain, love and hatred, happiness and dis-content. It is perhaps the case that the lamentable Brexit and Trump campaigns succeeded precisely where their opponents failed, namely, in seizing and shaping the affective terrain of political contestation. The inconsistency of their claims and positions proved to be less important than the manner in which they appealed to and actively amplified existing affective connections to certain ideas, visions, and narratives. Some of these were positively charged – sover-eignty ('taking back control'), the nation, the people, etc. – while others carried negative connotations – unelected bureaucrats, migrants, elites, experts, etc.

In response to the advent of Brexit and Trump, many will appeal to the supposedly liberal institutions of the capitalist state for support, or to the legal, parliamentary, or constitutional structures intended to forestall populist disturbances to the routine functioning of representative democracy. But in light of what has been explored throughout this book, I think it would be a grave mistake to return to the same liberal, exclusively rationalist discourse that has proven so woefully incapable of understanding recent politics and its affective supplement. Recognizing the shortcomings of a political discourse that has proven itself both ineffective and in-affective does not mean jettisoning all argumentation and pandering to the whims of individual agents or imagined grievances. Rather, it means re-establishing the connection – a potentially revolutionary one to boot – between thought and feeling. It will require imagination and passion to foster persuasive and binding narratives about how the existing social order is systematically failing the vast majority of people in the world, and how a future one could be arranged to the mutual benefit of all.

When I say I am a Communist, it is not because I have studied a sufficient amount of political economy to realize that capitalism is an irredeemably flawed economic system containing insurmountable contradictions; it is because as a result of these systemic flaws and contradictions, *capital destroys lives*. No matter how diligent we might be in our research and fact-checking, no matter how well we might chart the (inevitable) falling trajectory of profit rates, if we do not feel viscerally connected to the lives and interests of other people (as well as to the fragile ecology that supports our very existence as a species), it is unlikely that such knowledge will ever translate into effective action. And it is up to those on the left to positively engage anew with an affective politics to counter that of the most vocal and reactionary forces that are resurgent today, to reinvigorate the physical and emotional bonds of solidarity that depend upon unconditional support and mutual recognition, to be proudly and unequivocally internationalist in vision, and to passionately fight against the oppressive and exploitative relations of capital that continues to hold a gun to the head of everyone living under its rule.

Notes

1 See: https://en.oxforddictionaries.com/word-of-the-year/word-of-the-year-2016. Of course, the spike in the term's popularity is largely a result of cumulative use, as political journalists and commentators respond not only to certain events, but also to one another's *responses* to the responses, and so on. As such, once a term is introduced into a sector, it will tend to accumulate much interest and comment, often outstripping whatever merits the term itself might actually have.

2 As Spinoza notes in the first proposition of Part IV of his *Ethics*: 'Nothing positive which a false idea has is removed by the presence of the true insofar as it is true.'

3 Frédéric Lordon has convincingly argued that the uproar surrounding the notion of 'post-truth politics' enters the scene arm-in-arm with that of 'post-political truth', that is, an assertion of a neutral terrain of truth freed from all political interpretation. As Lordon writes: 'Correctly established facts will never be the be-all and end-all of politics, but barely its beginning, because facts *have never said anything by themselves*. Nothing! Facts are only ordered by way of a labour of mediations, which is not internal to these facts themselves. They only make sense when they are grasped from the outside by beliefs, ideas, interpretative schemas – in short, when there is politics, *ideology*'; see Lordon, 'Post-Truth Politics or Post-Political Journalism?', 11 January 2017, available at: www.versobooks.com/blogs/3043-post-truth-politics-or-post-political-journalism.

Bibliography

Adorno, Theodor W. *Aesthetic Theory*. Translated by Robert Hullot-Kentor. London: Continuum, 2004.

— 'The Curious Realist: On Siegfried Kracauer'. *New German Critique* 54 (1991): 159–77.

— 'Education After Auschwitz'. In *Critical Models: Interventions and Catchwords*, edited and translated by Henry W. Pickford, 191–204. New York: Columbia University Press, 1998.

— 'Introduction to Benjamin's *Schriften*'. In *On Walter Benjamin: Critical Essays and Recollections*, edited by Gary Smith, 2–17. Cambridge, MA: MIT Press, 1988.

— *Kant's Critique of Pure Reason*, edited by Rolf Tiedemann. Translated by Rodney Livingstone. Stanford: Stanford University Press, 2001.

— *Kierkegaard: Construction of the Aesthetic*. Translated by Robert Hullot-Kentor. Minnesota: University of Minnesota Press, 1989.

— 'Marginalia to Theory and Praxis'. In *Critical Models: Interventions and Catchwords*, edited and translated by Henry Pickford, 259–78. New York: Columbia University Press, 1998.

— *Minima Moralia: Reflections on a Damaged Life*. Translated by Edmund Jephcott. London: Verso, 2005.

— *Negative Dialectics*. Translated by E.B. Ashton. New York: Continuum, 1973.

— *Prisms*. Translated by Samuel and Sherry Weber. Cambridge, MA: MIT Press, 1983.

— 'The Schema of Mass Culture'. In *The Culture Industry: Selected Essays on Mass Culture*, edited by J.M. Bernstein, 61–98. Translated by Nicholas Walker. London: Routledge, 2001.

— 'Sociology and Psychology' (Part 1). *New Left Review* 1/46 (1967): 67–80.

— 'Sociology and Psychology' (Part 2). *New Left Review* 1/47 (1968): 79–97.

— 'Transparencies on Film' [November 1966]. *New German Critique* 24/25 (Winter 1981–2): 199–205.

Adorno, Theodor W. and Walter Benjamin. *The Complete Correspondence, 1928–1940*, edited by Henri Lonitz. Translated by Nicholas Walker. Cambridge, MA: Harvard University Press, 1999.

Adorno, Theodor W. and Max Horkheimer. *Dialectic of Enlightenment*. Translated by John Cumming. London: Verso, 1997.

— 'Towards a New Manifesto?' *New Left Review* 65 (2010): 33–61.

Agger, Ben. *The Discourse of Domination: From the Frankfurt School to Postmodernism*. Evanston: Northwestern University Press, 1992.

Ahmed, Sara. *The Cultural Politics of Emotion*. Edinburgh: Edinburgh University Press, 2004.

— 'Imaginary Prohibitions: Some Preliminary Remarks on the Founding Gestures of the "New Materialism"'. *European Journal of Women's Studies* 15/1 (2008): 23–39.

— *The Promise of Happiness*. Durham, NC: Duke University Press, 2010.

Althusser, Louis. 'Philosophy and Marxism'. In *Philosophy of the Encounter: Later Writings 1978–1987*, 251–89. London: Verso, 2006.

Anderson, Amanda. *The Way We Argue Now: A Study in the Cultures of Theory.* Princeton: Princeton University Press, 2005.

Anderson, Ben. 'Becoming and Being Hopeful: Towards a Theory of Affect'. *Environment and Planning D: Society and Space* 24 (2006): 733–52.

Anderson, Perry. *Considerations on Western Marxism.* London: New Left Books, 1976.

Babb, Lawrence. *The Elizabethan Malady: A Study of Melancholia in English Literature from 1580 to 1642.* East Lansing: Michigan State University Press, 1965.

Barrett, Estelle and Barbara Bolt (eds). *Carnal Knowledge: Towards a 'New Materialism' Through the Arts.* London: I.B. Tauris, 2012.

Benjamin, Walter. 'Central Park'. *New German Critique* 34 (Winter 1985): 32–58.

— 'The Destructive Character'. In *Reflections*, edited by Peter Demetz, 301–3. Translated by Edmund Jephcott. New York: Schocken Books, 2007.

— *Illuminations*, edited by Hannah Arendt. Translated by Harry Zohn. Suffolk: Fontana, 1973.

— 'Left-Wing Melancholy'. In *Walter Benjamin: Selected Writings, 1931–1934*, Volume 2, Part 2, edited by Howard Eiland, Michael W. Jennings, and Gary Smith, 423–7. Cambridge, MA: Belknap Press, 2005.

— *One-Way Street and Other Writings.* Translated by Edmund Jephcott and Kingsley Shorter. London: New Left Books, 1979.

— *The Origin of German Tragic Drama.* Translated by John Osborne. London: Verso, 2003.

— 'Surrealism: The Last Snapshot of the European Intelligentsia'. In *Reflections*, edited by Peter Demetz, 177–92. Translated by Edmund Jephcott. New York: Schocken Books, 2007.

— 'Theses on the Philosophy of History'. In *Illuminations*, edited by Hannah Arendt, 255–66. Translated by Harry Zohn. Suffolk: Fontana, 1973.

Bennett, Jane. *Vibrant Matter: A Political Ecology of Things.* Durham, NC: Duke University Press, 2010.

Bennett, Oliver. *Cultural Pessimism: Narratives of Decline in the Postmodern World.* Edinburgh: Edinburgh University Press, 2001.

Berg, Henk de. 'Unlearning How to Hope: Eleven Theses in Defence of Liberal Democracy and Consumer Culture'. In *The Privatization of Hope: Ernst Bloch and the Future of Utopia*, edited by Peter Thompson and Slavoj Žižek, 269–87. Durham, NC: Duke University Press, 2013.

Berlant, Lauren. *Cruel Optimism.* Durham, NC: Duke University Press, 2011.

Bersani, Leo. *Homos.* Cambridge, MA: Harvard University Press, 1995.

Best, Stephen and Sharon Marcus. 'Surface Reading: An Introduction'. *Representations* 108/1 (2009): 1–21.

Bewes, Timothy. 'Reading with the Grain: A New World in Literary Criticism'. *Differences: A Journal of Feminist Cultural Studies* 21/3 (2010): 1–33.

Bloch, Ernst. 'Alienation, Estrangement'. In *Literary Essays*. Translated by Andrew Joron, 239–45. Stanford: Stanford University Press, 1998.

— 'Can Hope Be Disappointed?'. In *Literary Essays*, 339–44. Translated by Andrew Joron. Stanford, CA: Stanford University Press, 1998.

— 'Nonsynchronism and the Obligation to Its Dialectics'. *New German Critique* 11 (Spring 1977): 22–38.

— *The Principle of Hope*, Volume 1. Translated by Neville Plaice, Stephen Plaice, and Paul Knight. Cambridge, MA: MIT Press, 1986.

— 'Something's Missing: A Discussion between Ernst Bloch and Theodor W. Adorno on the Contradictions of Utopian Longing'. In *The Utopian Function of Art and Literature: Selected Essays*, 1–17. Translated by Jack Zipes and Frank Mecklenburg. Cambridge, MA: MIT Press, 1988.

Blühdorn, Ingolfur. *Post-Ecologist Politics: Social Theory and the Abdication of the Ecologist Paradigm*. London: Routledge, 2000.

Bogost, Ian. *Alien Phenomenology, or What It's Like to Be a Thing*. Minneapolis: University of Minnesota Press, 2012.

Bonneuil, Christophe and Jean-Baptiste Fressoz. *The Shock of the Anthropocene: The Earth, History and Us*. London: Verso, 2016.

Bottomore, Tom. *The Frankfurt School and Its Critics*. London: Routledge, 2002.

Bourdieu, Pierre. *Distinction: A Social Critique of the Judgement of Taste*. Translated by Richard Nice. Abingdon: Routledge, 2010.

— *Outline of a Theory of Practice*. Translated by Richard Nice. Cambridge: Cambridge University Press, 1977.

Braidotti, Rosi. *Nomadic Subjects: Embodiment and Sexual Difference in Contemporary Feminist Thought*. New York: Columbia University Press, 1994.

Brassier, Ray. 'Ray Brassier interviewed by Marcin Rychter: I am a nihilist because I still believe in truth'. *Kronos* (2011). Retrieved from: www.kronos.org.pl/index. php?23151,896.

Braver, Lee. *A Thing of This World: A History of Continental Anti-Realism*. Evanston: Northwestern University Press, 2007.

Brennan, Teresa. *The Transmission of Affect*. Ithaca, NY: Cornell University Press, 2004.

Brodersen, Momme. *Walter Benjamin: A Biography*. London: Verso, 1996.

Brown, Wendy. 'Resisting Left Melancholy'. *boundary 2* 26/3 (1999): 19–27.

Bryant, Levi R., Nick Srnicek, and Graham Harman (eds). *The Speculative Turn: Continental Materialism and Realism*. Melbourne: re.press, 2011.

Buck-Morss, Susan. *The Origins of Negative Dialectics: Theodor W. Adorno, Walter Benjamin and the Frankfurt Institute*. New York: The Free Press, 1977.

Buhr, Manfred. 'A Critique of Ernst Bloch's Philosophy of Hope'. *Philosophy Today* 14 (Winter 1970): 259–71.

Caserio, Robert L., Lee Edelman, Judith Halberstam, José Esteban Muñoz, and Tim Dean. 'The Anti-Social Thesis in Queer Theory'. *PMLA* 121/3 (May 2006): 819–28.

Clough, Patricia Ticineto (ed.). *The Affective Turn: Theorizing the Social*. Durham, NC: Duke University Press, 2007.

Clover, Joshua. *Riot. Strike. Riot: The New Era of Uprisings*. London: Verso, 2016.

Cole, Andrew. 'The Call of Things: A Critique of Object-Oriented Ontologies'. *minnesota review* 80 (2013): 106–18.

— 'Those Obscure Objects of Desire'. *Artforum* (Summer 2015): 318–25.

Comay, Rebecca. 'Materialist Mutations of the *Bilderverbot*'. In *Sites of Vision: The Discursive Construction of Sight in the History of Philosophy*, edited by David Michael Levin, 337–78. Cambridge, MA: MIT Press, 1997.

Connerton, Paul. *The Tragedy of Enlightenment: An Essay on the Frankfurt School*. Cambridge: Cambridge University Press, 1980.

Connolly, William E. *Neuropolitics: Thinking, Culture, Speed*. Minneapolis: University of Minnesota Press, 2002.

Coole, Diana and Samantha Frost (eds). *New Materialisms: Ontology, Agency, and Politics*. Durham, NC: Duke University Press, 2010.

Damasio, Antonio. *Looking for Spinoza: Joy, Sorrow, and the Feeling Brain*. London: Vintage, 2004.

Davies, William. *The Happiness Industry: How the Government and Big Business Sold Us Well-Being*. London: Verso, 2015.

De Sousa, Ronald. *The Rationality of Emotion*. Cambridge, MA: MIT Press, 1987.

Deleuze, Gilles and Félix Guattari. *A Thousand Plateaus*. Translated by Brian Massumi. London: Continuum, 2004.

Derrida, Jacques. *Who's Afraid of Philosophy? Right to Philosophy 1.* Translated by Jan Plug. Stanford: Stanford University Press, 2002.

Dolphijn, Rick and Iris van der Tuin (eds). *New Materialism: Interviews & Cartographies.* Ann Arbor: Open Humanities Press, 2012.

Edelman, Lee. *No Future: Queer Theory and the Death Drive.* Durham, NC: Duke University Press, 2004.

Eiland, Howard and Michael W. Jennings. *Walter Benjamin: A Critical Life.* Cambridge, MA: Belknap Press, 2014.

Federici, Silvia. *Caliban and the Witch: Women, the Body and Primitive Accumulation.* New York: Autonomedia, 2004.

Felski, Rita. 'After Suspicion'. *Profession* 8 (2009): 28–35.

— 'Critique and the Hermeneutics of Suspicion'. *M/C Journal* 15/1 (2012). Retrieved from: http://journal.media-culture.org.au/index.php/mcjournal/article/viewArticle/431.

— *The Limits of Critique.* Chicago: University of Chicago Press, 2015.

— 'Object Relations'. *Contemporary Women's Writing* 1/1–2 (2007): 185–91.

— 'Suspicious Minds'. *Poetics Today* 32/2 (2011): 215–34.

Ferber, Ilit. *Philosophy and Melancholy: Benjamin's Early Reflections on Theater and Language.* Stanford: Stanford University Press, 2013.

Finlayson, Lorna. *The Political is Political: Conformity and the Illusion of Dissent in Contemporary Political Philosophy.* London: Rowman & Littlefield International, 2015.

Flatley, Jonathan. *Affective Mapping: Melancholia and the Politics of Modernism.* Cambridge, MA: Harvard University Press, 2008.

Frank, Adam. *Transferential Poetics: From Poe to Warhol.* New York: Fordham University Press, 2014.

Frank, Adam and Elizabeth A. Wilson. 'Like-Minded: A Response to Ruth Leys'. *Critical Inquiry* 38/4 (Summer 2012): 870–7.

Freud, Sigmund. *Beyond the Pleasure Principle.* Translated by James Strachey. New York: W.W. Norton, 1961.

— 'Formulations on the Two Principles of Mental Functioning'. In *The Standard Edition of the Complete Psychological Works of Sigmund Freud,* Volume 12, edited by James Strachey, 218–26. London: The Hogarth Press, 1958.

— 'Mourning and Melancholia'. In *The Standard Edition of the Complete Psychological Works of Sigmund Freud,* Volume 14, edited by James Strachey, 237–60. London: The Hogarth Press, 1963.

Fromm, Erich. *The Revolution of Hope: Toward a Humanized Technology.* Riverdale: American Mental Health Foundation Inc., 2010.

Galston, William A. 'Realism in Political Theory'. *European Journal of Political Theory* 9/4 (2010): 385–411.

Geoghegan, Vincent. 'An Anti-humanist Utopia?'. In *The Privatization of Hope: Ernst Bloch and the Future of Utopia,* edited by Peter Thompson and Slavoj Žižek, 37–60. Durham, NC: Duke University Press, 2013.

Goleman, Daniel. *Emotional Intelligence.* New York: Bantam Books, 1995.

Gray, John. *Black Mass: Apocalyptic Religion and the Death of Utopia.* London: Penguin, 2007.

Greenspan, Patricia. *Emotions and Reasons: An Inquiry into Emotional Justification.* New York: Routledge, 1988.

Grosz, Elizabeth. *Volatile Bodies: Towards a Corporeal Feminism.* Bloomington: Indiana University Press, 1994.

Habermas, Jürgen. 'Morality, Society, and Ethics: An Interview with Torben Hviid Nielsen', *Acta Sociologica* 33/2 (1990): 93–114.

— 'The New Obscurity: The Crisis of the Welfare State and the Exhaustion of Utopian Energies'. In *The New Conservatism: Cultural Criticism and the Historians' Debate,* edited by Shierry Weber-Nicholsen, 48–70. Cambridge, MA: MIT Press, 1989.

— *The Philosophical Discourse of Modernity: Twelve Lectures.* Translated by Frederick G. Lawrence. Cambridge: Polity, 1987.

— *Philosophical-Political Profiles.* Translated by Frederick G. Lawrence. Cambridge, MA: MIT Press, 1983.

— *The Theory of Communicative Action,* Volume 1. Translated by Thomas McCarthy. Boston: Beacon Press, 1984.

Hamacher, Werner. 'The Gesture in the Name: On Benjamin and Kafka'. In *Premises: Essays on Philosophy and Literature from Kant to Celan,* 294–336. Translated by Peter Fenves. Stanford: Stanford University Press, 1996.

Hansen, Miriam. 'Introduction'. In *Theory of Film: The Redemption of Physical Reality,* by Siegfried Kracauer, vii–xlvi. Princeton: Princeton University Press, 1997.

— '"With Skin and Hair": Kracauer's Theory of Film, Marseilles 1940'. *Critical Inquiry* 19/3 (1993): 437–69.

Hanssen, Beatrice. 'Portrait of Melancholy (Benjamin, Warburg, Panofsky)'. *MLN* 114 (1999): 991–1013.

Hardt, Michael. 'Foreword: What Affects Are Good For'. In *The Affective Turn: Theorizing the Social,* edited by Patricia Ticineto Clough, with Jean Halley, ix–xiii. Durham, NC: Duke University Press, 2007.

Hardt, Michael and Antonio Negri. *Multitude: War and Democracy in the Age of Empire.* London: Penguin, 2004.

Harman, Graham. *Guerrilla Metaphysics: Phenomenology and the Carpentry of Things.* Chicago: Open Court, 2005.

— 'The Well-Wrought Broken Hammer: Object-Oriented Literary Criticism'. *New Literary History* 43/2 (2012): 183–203.

Hegel, Georg Wilhelm Friedrich. *Lectures on the Philosophy of World History.* Translated by H.B. Nisbet. Cambridge: Cambridge University Press, 1975.

— 'Preface'. In *Phenomenology of Spirit.* Translated by A.V. Miller, 1–45. Oxford: Oxford University Press, 1977.

— 'Preface'. In *Hegel's Philosophy of Right.* Translated by Tom Knox, 1–13. Oxford: Oxford University Press, 1978.

Heinrich, Michael. *An Introduction to the Three Volumes of Karl Marx's Capital.* Translated by Alexander Locascio. New York: Monthly Review Press, 2012.

Horkheimer, Max. *Eclipse of Reason.* London: Continuum, 1974.

— 'The Present Situation of Social Philosophy and the Tasks of an Institute for Social Research'. In *Between Philosophy and Social Science: Selected Early Writings,* 1–14. Translated by John Torpey. Cambridge, MA: MIT Press, 1993.

— 'Traditional and Critical Theory'. In *Critical Theory: Selected Essays,* 188–243. Translated by Matthew J. O'Connell. New York: Continuum, 2002.

Hudson, Wayne. 'Bloch and a Philosophy of the Proterior'. In *The Privatization of Hope: Ernst Bloch and the Future of Utopia,* edited by Peter Thompson and Slavoj Žižek, 21–36. Durham, NC: Duke University Press, 2013.

Hullot-Kentor, Robert. 'Right Listening and a New Type of Human Being'. In *The Cambridge Companion to Adorno,* edited by Tom Huhn, 181–98. Cambridge: Cambridge University Press, 2004.

Jameson, Fredric. *Archaeologies of the Future: The Desire Called Utopia and Other Science Fictions.* London: Verso, 2005.

— *Late Marxism: Adorno, Or, The Persistence of the Dialectic.* London: Verso, 2006.

— 'The Politics of Utopia'. *New Left Review* 25 (2004): 35–54.

— 'Reification and Utopia in Mass Culture'. *Social Text* 1 (Winter 1979): 130–48.

Jay, Martin. *The Dialectical Imagination: A History of the Frankfurt School and the Institute of Social Research, 1923–1950*. London: Heinemann, 1973.

Kant, Immanuel. *Anthropology from a Pragmatic Point of View*, edited by Robert B. Lauden. Cambridge: Cambridge University Press, 2006.

Kline, Georg L. 'The Use and Abuse of Hegel by Nietzsche and Marx'. In *Hegel and His Critics: Philosophy in the Aftermath of Hegel*, edited by William Desmond, 1–34. Albany: SUNY Press, 1989.

Kracauer, Siegfried. *Theory of Film: The Redemption of Physical Reality*. Princeton: Princeton University Press, 1997.

Latour, Bruno. 'An Attempt at a "Compositionist Manifesto"'. *New Literary History* 41 (2010): 471–90.

— *The Pasteurization of France*. Translated by Alan Sheridan and John Law. Cambridge, MA: Harvard University Press, 1993.

— 'Why Has Critique Run Out of Steam? From Matters of Fact to Matters of Concern'. *Critical Inquiry* 30 (Winter 2004): 225–48.

Laval, Christian and Pierre Dardot. *The New Way of the World: On Neoliberal Society*. London: Verso, 2014.

Lawlor, Clark. *From Melancholia to Prozac: A History of Depression*. Oxford: Oxford University Press, 2012.

Layard, Richard. *Happiness: Lessons from a New Science*. London: Penguin, 2006.

Lefebvre, Henri. *Everyday Life in the Modern World*. Translated by Sacha Rabinovitch. London: Continuum, 2002.

Lepenies, Wolf. *Melancholy and Society*. Translated by Jeremy Gaines and Doris Jones. Cambridge, MA: Harvard University Press, 1992.

Leslie, Esther. *Walter Benjamin: Critical Lives*. London: Reaktion Books, 2007.

— *Walter Benjamin: Overpowering Conformism*. London: Pluto, 2000.

Levitas, Ruth. *The Concept of Utopia*. Bern: Peter Lang, 2010.

Leys, Ruth. 'The Turn to Affect: A Critique'. *Critical Inquiry* 37/3 (Spring 2011): 434–72.

Libet, Benjamin. 'Unconscious Cerebral Initiative and the Role of Conscious Will in Voluntary Action'. *Behavioral and Brain Sciences* 8 (December 1985): 529–39.

Love, Heather. 'Close but not Deep: Literary Ethics and the Descriptive Turn'. *New Literary History* 41 (2010): 371–91.

— *Feeling Backward: Loss and the Politics of Queer History*. Cambridge, MA: Harvard University Press, 2007.

Löwy, Michael. 'Naphta or Settembrini? Lukács and Romantic Anticapitalism'. In *George Lukács: Theory, Culture, and Politics*, edited by Judith Marcus and Zoltán Tarr, 189–206. New Brunswick: Transaction, 1989.

Lüdke, Martin. *Anmerkungen zu einer 'Logik des Zerfalls': Adorno-Beckett*. Frankfurt: Suhrkamp, 1981.

— 'The Utopian Motif Is Suspended: Conversation with Leo Löwenthal'. *New German Critique* 38 (Spring–Summer 1986): 105–11.

Mannheim, Karl. *Ideology and Utopia*, Volume 1. Abingdon: Routledge, 1997.

Marasco, Robyn. *The Highway of Despair: Critical Theory After Hegel*. New York: Columbia University Press, 2015.

Marcus, Sharon, Heather Love, and Stephen Best. 'Building a Better Description'. *Representations* 135/1 (2016): 1–21.

Marx, Karl. *Capital: A Critique of Political Economy*, Volume 1. Translated by Ben Fowkes. Harmondsworth: Penguin, 1976.

— 'The Eighteenth Brumaire of Louis Bonaparte'. In *Karl Marx: Selected Writings,* edited by David McLellan, 329–55. Oxford: Oxford University Press, 2000.

— *Grundrisse: Foundations of Political Economy.* Translated by Martin Nicolaus. New York: Vintage, 1973.

— 'The Holy Family'. In *Karl Marx: Selected Writings,* edited by David McLellan, 145–70. Oxford: Oxford University Press, 2000.

— 'Letter to Mikhailovsky'. In *Karl Marx: Selected Writings,* edited by David McLellan, 617–19. Oxford: Oxford University Press, 2000.

— 'The Poverty of Philosophy'. In *Karl Marx: Selected Writings,* edited by David McLellan, 212–33. Oxford: Oxford University Press, 2000.

Marx, Karl and Frederick Engels. *The Communist Manifesto.* London: Verso, 2012.

— 'The Holy Family, or Critique of Critical Criticism'. In *Collected Works, Vol. 4: 1844–1845,* 5–211. London: Lawrence & Wishart.

Massumi, Brian. *Parables for the Virtual: Movement, Affect, Sensation.* Durham, NC: Duke University Press, 2002.

Meillassoux, Quentin. *After Finitude: An Essay on the Necessity of Contingency.* Translated by Ray Brassier. New York: Continuum, 2008.

Mirowski, Philip. *Never Let a Serious Crisis Go to Waste: How Neoliberalism Survived the Financial Meltdown.* London: Verso, 2013.

Moore, Jason W. *Capitalism in the Web of Life: Ecology and the Accumulation of Capital.* London: Verso, 2015.

Moretti, Franco. *Distant Reading.* London: Verso, 2013.

Morton, Timothy. *The Ecological Thought.* Cambridge, MA: Harvard University Press, 2010.

— 'Here Comes Everything: The Promise of Object-Oriented Ontology'. *Qui Parle* 19/2 (Spring/Summer 2011): 163–90.

— *Hyperobjects: Philosophy and Ecology After the End of the World.* Minneapolis: University of Minnesota Press, 2013.

Muñoz, José Esteban. *Cruising Utopia: The Then and There of Queer Futurity.* New York: New York University Press, 2009.

Nadeau, Maurice. *Histoire du surrealism.* Paris: Editions du Seuil, 1964.

Nealon, Christopher. 'Infinity for Marxists'. *Mediations* 28/2 (Spring 2015): 47–63.

Niemoczynski, Leon. *Charles Sanders Peirce and a Religious Metaphysics of Nature.* Lanham: Rowman & Littlefield, 2011.

Nørretranders, Tor. *The User Illusion: Cutting Consciousness Down to Size.* London: Penguin, 1999.

Nussbaum, Martha C. *Political Emotions: Why Love Matters for Justice.* Cambridge, MA: Harvard University Press, 2014.

— *Upheavals of Thought: The Intelligence of Emotions.* Cambridge: Cambridge University Press, 2003.

Outhwaite, William. *Critical Theory and Contemporary Europe.* London: Continuum, 2012.

Papoulias, Constantina and Felicity Callard. 'Biology's Gift: Interrogating the Turn to Affect'. *Body and Society* 16/1 (2010): 29–56.

Pensky, Max. *Melancholy Dialectics: Walter Benjamin and the Play of Mourning.* Amherst: University of Massachusetts Press, 1993.

Petrie, Graham and Vida T. Johnson. *The Films of Andrei Tarkovsky: A Visual Fugue.* Bloomington: Indiana University Press, 1994.

Petro, Patrice. 'Kracauer's Epistemological Shift'. *New German Critique* 54 (Autumn 1991): 127–38.

Pinker, Steven. *The Better Angels of Our Nature: A History of Violence and Humanity.* London: Penguin, 2011.

Pockett, Susan, William Banks, and Shaun Gallagher (eds). *Does Consciousness Cause Behavior?* Cambridge, MA: MIT Press, 2006.

Radden, Jennifer. *Moody Minds Distempered: Essays on Melancholy and Depression.* Oxford: Oxford University Press, 2009.

— *The Nature of Melancholy: From Aristotle to Freud.* Oxford: Oxford University Press, 2000.

Rorty, Richard. *Achieving Our Country: Leftist Thought in Twentieth-Century America.* Cambridge, MA: Harvard University Press, 1999.

Rose, Gillian. *Hegel Contra Sociology.* London: Athlone Press, 1985.

— *The Melancholy Science: An Introduction to the Thought of Theodor W. Adorno.* New York: Columbia University Press, 1978.

Rosenberg, Jordana. 'The Molecularization of Sexuality: On Some Primitivisms of the Present'. *Theory & Event* 17/2 (2014): 15–30.

Schnädelbach, Herbert. 'Dialektik als Vernunftkritik. Zur Konstruktion des Rationalen bei Adorno'. In *Adorno-Konferenz*, 66–94. Frankfurt: Suhrkamp, 1983.

Scholem, Gershom. 'Walter Benjamin and His Angel'. In *On Jews and Judaism in Crisis*, edited by Werner J. Dannhauser, 198–236. New York: Schocken Books, 1976.

— *Walter Benjamin: The Story of a Friendship.* New York: Review Books, 1981.

Sedgwick, Eve Kosofsky. *Touching Feeling: Affect, Pedagogy, Performativity.* Durham, NC: Duke University Press, 2002.

Sedgwick, Eve Kosofsky and Adam Frank (eds). *Shame and Its Sisters: A Silvan Tomkins Reader.* Durham, NC: Duke University Press, 1995.

Seligman, Martin. *Helplessness: On Depression, Development, and Death.* San Francisco: W.H. Freeman, 1975.

Sherman, Nancy. *Making a Necessity of Virtue: Aristotle and Kant on Virtue.* Cambridge: Cambridge University Press, 1997.

— 'The Place of Emotions in Kantian Morality'. In *Identity, Character, and Morality: Essays in Moral Psychology,* edited by Owen Flanagan and Amélie Oksenberg Rorty, 149–70. Cambridge, MA: MIT Press, 1990.

Sohn-Rethel, Alfred. *Intellectual and Manual Labour: A Critique of Epistemology.* Basingstoke: Macmillan, 1978.

Solomon, Robert C. *True to Our Feelings: What Our Emotions Are Really Telling Us.* Oxford: Oxford University Press, 2007.

Sontag, Susan. 'Introduction'. In *One-Way Street and Other Writings*, by Walter Benjamin, 7–28. London: New Left Books, 1979.

— *Under the Sign of Saturn: Essays.* London: Penguin, 2009.

Spinoza, Benedict de. *Ethics.* Translated by Edwin Curley. London: Penguin, 1996.

— 'Political Treatise'. In *Spinoza: Complete Works,* edited by Michael L. Morgan, 676–754. Translated by Samuel Shirley. Indianapolis: Hackett, 2002.

Stallybrass, Peter. 'Marx's Coat'. In *Border Fetishisms: Material Objects in Unstable Spaces,* edited by Patricia Spyer, 183–207. New York: Routledge, 1998.

Thacker, Eugene. *After Life.* Chicago: University of Chicago Press, 2010.

Theunissen, Michael. 'Negativität bei Adorno'. In *Adorno-Konferenz,* 41–65. Frankfurt: Suhrkamp, 1983.

Thompson, Peter. 'Introduction'. In *The Privatization of Hope: Ernst Bloch and the Future of Utopia,* edited by Peter Thompson and Slavoj Žižek, 1–20. Durham, NC: Duke University Press, 2013.

Thrift, Nigel. *Non-Representational Theory: Space, Politics, Affect.* Abingdon: Routledge, 2008.

Tomkins, Silvan S. *Affect, Imagery, Consciousness.* 4 Vols. New York: Springer, 1962–92.

Toscano, Alberto. *Fanaticism: On the Uses of an Idea.* London: Verso, 2010.

Vogel, Steven. *Against Nature: The Concept of Nature in Critical Theory.* New York: SUNY, 1996.

Weber Nicholsen, Shierry. 'Aesthetic Theory's Mimesis of Walter Benjamin'. In *The Semblance of Subjectivity*, edited by Tom Huhn and Lambert Zuidervaart, 55–91. Cambridge, MA: MIT Press, 1997.

Wellmer, Albrecht. 'Adorno, Modernity, and the Sublime'. In *The Actuality of Adorno: Critical Essays on Adorno and the Postmodern*, edited by Max Pensky, 112–34. New York: SUNY, 1997.

Whitebook, Joel. 'The Marriage of Marx and Freud: Critical Theory and Psychoanalysis'. In *The Cambridge Companion to Critical Theory*, edited by Fred Rush, 74–102. Cambridge: Cambridge University Press, 2004.

Wiggershaus, Rolf. *The Frankfurt School: Its History, Theories, and Political Significance.* Translated by Michael Robertson. Cambridge, MA: MIT Press, 1995.

Witte, Bernd. *Walter Benjamin: An Intellectual Biography.* Translated by James Rolleston. Detroit: Wayne State University Press, 1991.

Wizisla, Erdmut. *Walter Benjamin and Bertolt Brecht: The Story of a Friendship.* London: Libris, 2009.

Wohlfarth, Irving. 'No Man's Land: On Walter Benjamin's "The Destructive Character"'. *Diacritics* 8/2 (Summer 1978): 47–65.

Wolin, Richard. 'Benjamin, Adorno, Surrealism'. In *The Semblance of Subjectivity*, edited by Tom Huhn and Lambert Zuidervaart, 93–122. Cambridge, MA: MIT Press, 1997.

Index

EU authorised representative for GPSR:
Easy Access System Europe, Mustamäe tee 50,
10621 Tallinn, Estonia
gpsr.requests@easproject.com